The Six Topics That All Buddhists Learn

A Text by Khenpo Zhan-ga
Of Dzogchen Shri
Singha College

By Tony Duff
Padma Karpo Translation Committee

First edition, March, 2014
ISBN: paper book 978-9937-572-13-2
ISBN: e-book 978-9937-572-12-5

Janson typeface with diacritical marks and
Tibetan Chogyal typefaces
Designed and created by Tony Duff

Produced, Printed, and Published by
Padma Karpo Translation Committee
P.O. Box 4957
Kathmandu
NEPAL

Committee members for this book: translation and composition, Lama Tony Duff; editorial, Tom Anderson, Jason Watkins; cover design, George Romvari

Web-site and e-mail contact through:
http://www.pktc.org/pktc
or search Padma Karpo Translation Committee on the web.

Contents

Introduction v
About the Author vi
About the Six Topics xii
About the Text xiv
About Key Terms xxii
Other Issues xxviii

❁ ❁ ❁

"A Mirror Revealing Knowables", A Teaching on the Six Topics in Which One is to Become Expert by Zhanphen Chokyi Nangwa 1
Prologue 3
Chapter One: the six topics in which one is to become expert 9
Chapter Two: an explanation of the four dharma summaries of the Great Vehicle 61
Chapter Three: the way to engage in the path of the Middle Way 89

Chapter Four: the way to meditate on Luminosity Great Completion 93
Epilogue 95

❁ ❁ ❁

List of Texts Cited 97
Glossary of Terms 101
Supports for Study 123
Tibetan Text 129
Index 179

Introduction

This book contains a translation of the treatise *"A Mirror Revealing Knowables" A Teaching on the Six Topics in which One is to Become Expert* by Zhan-ga Rinpoche, the most famous of the abbots of the Śhrī Singha College of Dzogchen Monastery, Tibet.

This treatise is similar to Mipham's famous *Treatise Called Doorway to That in which One is to Become Expert*[1]. Both say that they are intended for those who are learning the basics of Buddhist theory. However, this treatise is less complicated and easier to understand than Mipham's treatise. Moreover, this treatise puts the topics to be learned into the context of practice of the Great Vehicle, where Mipham's does not. Finally, this one explains six topics which must be learned by every Buddhist practitioner whereas Mipham's explains eight topics, two of which are not very important to a person practising the Great Vehicle. In short, this treatise is more practical where Mipham's text is more scholarly.

[1] Tib. mkhas 'jug. The text was published under the name "Gateway to Knowledge" some years ago and the name has stuck, even though the meaning of the title is quite different from that name.

About the Author

This text is a sample of the work of a body of truly great teachers who appeared at Dzogchen Monastery and in the districts surrounding it following Jigmey Lingpa's revelations of Quintessence Great Completion in the middle of the 18th century. As mentioned above, this text shows six topics that all Buddhists must learn and shows them as part of the path of a person who will practice the Great Vehicle, including Great Completion or Dzogchen.

Three people of that time are part of the story of this text. Briefly, the story begins with Zhanphen Thaye Ozer [1800–1869] who was also known as Gyalsay Zhanphen Thaye Ozer or "Conquerors' Son Zhanphen Thaye Ozer". He lived when the heart sons of Jigmey Lingpa—Jigmey Trinley Ozer [1745–1841] and Jigmey Gyalway Nyugu [1765–1843]—were alive, at the time of the initial flowering of the Quintessence Great Completion which came through Longchenpa to Jigmey Lingpa, and was very much part of the transmission of that teaching. He was regarded as an extraordinary being whose learning was like that of the great early Tibetan translator Vairochana and whose accomplishment through practice was equally remarkable. He moved at one point in his life to Dzogchen Monastery where he stayed and imparted his tremendous knowledge to the many people studying there.

One of Zhanphen Thaye Ozer's students was Orgyan Tenzin Norbu [1827–1888], who also became both highly learned and accomplished. One of Tenzin Norbu's heart sons was the immediate re-incarnation of Zhanphen Thaye. Named Zhanphen Chokyi Nangwa [1871–1927] and most commonly known as Zhan-ga, he was probably the most learned of all masters who held the throne at Śhrī Singha College, and was also the next official lineage holder of the Great Completion teachings at Dzogchen Monastery.

It is important to understand that Zhanphen Thaye, Orgyan Tenzin Norbu, and Zhan-ga were the greatest of scholars and were highly accomplished, too, with all of them being viewed as primary lineage holders of the Great Completion teachings at Dzogchen Monastery. It is said that their explanations of scholarly matters always went beyond that of a scholar and were marked with an unusual clarity of mind. You will see that Zhan-ga's presentations in the text in this book have a quality which makes them more than just scholarly dissertations.

To fully appreciate these three masters, their connections, and hence this text, it would be best to read their biographies (excellent biographies of all of them can be found in *A Marvellous Garland of Rare Gems*[2], whose extended biographies were used as a basis for the following, short biographies).

Gyalsay Zhanphen Thaye Ozer

Zhanphen Thaye consciously took rebirth as the magical display of both the great Indian abbot Śhāntarakṣhita and the great Tibetan translator Vairochana. At an early age, his character as a member of the Great Vehicle family awoke. He attained the pinnacle of learning, having received teachings on the sūtras, tantras, and other fields of knowledge from many gurus of various schools of Tibetan Buddhism, for example, from Jigmey Gyalway Nyugu who was Avalokiteśhvara in person. In particular, Zhanphen Thaye served Dodrupchen Jigmey Trinley Ozer and so received general teachings of the Kama, Terma, and Dagnang traditions, and the foremost instructions of Great Completion, like one vase being filled to the brim from another. Thus he became a crown jewel over hundreds of learned and accomplished masters. After that he engaged for some time in yogic practice in various places which led to extreme realization. He became a truly great holy being with whom all contact was meaningful.

---

[2] See the List of Cited texts for publication information.

Later, fulfilling a prophecy of Dodrupchen, he went to Dzogchen Monastery where the fourth Dzogchen Rinpoche, Mingyur Namkhay Dorje expressed singular delight in and affection for this kindred spirit, and, praising his great qualities, insisted that he remain at Dzogchen Monastery. Thus, the two of them came to work together.

When they went to view the site for a proposed monastic college, they beheld the Indian master Śhrī Singha at the site, blessing it. The college was built and became a second Nālandā, a wellspring of learned and accomplished masters whose influence, to this day, has extended to the far corners of the earth. All of this resulted from the motivation of the noble one, Zhanphen Thaye and the studies and practices to which he had devoted his entire life.

Having passed away, his immediate rebirth was Zhanphen Chokyi Nangwa, who became a master of explanations of dharma and an abbot of Śhrī Singha college.

Orgyan Tenzin Norbu

Orgyan Tenzin Norbu [1827–1888] was cared for by Zhanphen Thaye from an early age. He devoted his life to studying with Zhanphen Thaye and many other masters at or in the areas surrounding Dzogchen Monastery. He even held discussions with the extraordinary scholar Mipham Namgyal in which each resolved his own doubts. Mipham was thoroughly delighted with Tenzin Norbu and showered him with praise. After hearing enormous amounts of dharma on all levels from the greatest masters of his time and area, he pursued his spiritual practice, undertaking intensive retreats. His intelligence grew like a blazing fire. He reached the end of the path of innermost, unsurpassed Great Completion, having mastered both Thorough Cut and Direct Crossing.

After that he spent his life teaching. He served those whose desire to meditate led them to seek foremost oral instructions. He taught at least five times daily on the mainstream sources of the sūtras, tantras, and other fields of knowledge, sometimes not even stopping for a cup of tea. In that way and for the remainder of his life, he taught an amazing variety of texts, and so forth to others. When he died, he gazed into space and said his last words, which were recorded as his last testament:

> I am Guru Padmakara of Orgyan, a buddha free of birth and death.
> Enlightenment mind is unbiased and free of the concepts of the four or eight extremes.

Of his many students, one of his most extraordinary inner heart sons was Zhanphen Chokyi Nangwa, who received his personal transmission of the explanatory teachings.

Zhanphen Chokyi Nangwa

Zhanphen Chokyi Nangwa [1871–1927] or Zhan-ga developed a very strong renunciation and left his life as a householder. He went to a hermitage to meet his guru of past lifetimes, Orgyan Tenzin Norbu. He underwent great hardships in order to pursue his studies but persevered without complaint.

One day, an older student said to Orgyan Tenzin Norbu, "Precious guru, I thought you were above prejudice but you're not. You always treat this new, talented student Zhan-ga with some deference. It seems inappropriate for a guru to show favouritism towards a student. Can you explain this?" Orgyan Tenzin replied, "Well, it's not that I favour Zhan-ga; it's that all of you are so dense and have such impure perceptions! Zhan-ga is what the sūtras refer to as a bodhisatva[3] who has only one lifetime left before attaining enlightenment. Treating him with disrespect will harm the activities of other important teachers here and interfere with their ability to benefit beings as teachers of the dharma. So, really, I am showing

---

[3] For the spelling of bodhisatva, see satva and sattva in the glossary.

favouritism towards you, my older students." From then on, all the residents of the encampment treated the lord Zhan-ga as they did their guru.

Orgyan Tenzin Norbu gradually conferred teachings from the oral traditions of Zhanphen Thaye and other masters on Zhan-ga, who went on to study the sūtras, tantras, and other fields of knowledge.

Unhindered in explaining, debating, and writing about the teachings, and having taken full monastic ordination, Zhan-ga took as his inspiration the lives of great elders of the Indian Buddhist tradition. His guru came to consider him his single heart son on an inner level. He gave Zhan-ga his own copies of commentaries on the sūtras and tantras, especially the so-called thirteen great texts written by Indian Buddhist scholars[4]. He told Zhan-ga, "Base your teachings primarily on these. The students who uphold your tradition will be like the constellations of stars in the sky, so that the precious teachings of the conqueror will shine like the sun." With such prophecies, Orgyan Tenzin Norbu entrusted Zhan-ga with the teachings, investing him as a lineage holder with permission to explain them.

After Orgyan Tenzin Norbu passed away, Zhan-ga stayed at Orgyan Tenzin Norbu's seat to fulfill his guru's intentions. He taught an enormous number of students who came from many places to hear his teachings. In addition, he continued to receive teachings from many of the gurus and tulkus from Zhechen, Dzogchen, and other monasteries in the area.

Then, at the directive of the fifth Dzogchen Rinpoche, Zhan-ga was invited to Śhrī Singha college where he was appointed an abbot in

---

[4] The Tibetan texts of Zhan-ga's edition are available in electronic edition free from the Padma Karpo Translation Committee web-site under the title *Nineteen Main Indian Texts.*

the line of abbot of the college. He wrote many works there, including the text in this book and his famous annotated commentaries on the thirteen great texts of the Indian tradition. Students from Dzogchen Monastery and its affiliates flocked to the college like geese to a lake in the summer.

When he taught, he did not confine himself merely to the literal sense of the words but would, for instance, present the profound view of the Middle Way Consequence school in keeping with the enlightened understanding of glorious Chandrakīrti. His students thus experienced all phenomena as the eight analogies of illusion. Scholars unanimously praised Zhan-ga because of his definitive conclusions concerning the enlightened understanding of the Consequence school, saying, "A second Chandrakīrti has come." He was regarded as an emanation not only of Zhanphen Thaye but also of Chandrakīrti; he is praised in the Dzogchen Monastery lineage verses as an emanation of both. In the third chapter of the text in this book, he states that Chandrakīrti is the master above all others when it comes to the Middle Way Consequence school:

> ... the Middle Way itself has come to have various levels, higher and lower, within it. However, here we rely on and involve ourselves with the explanations of the one who is like the crowning jewel of all the masters of the Consequence school, glorious Chandrakīrti, who made unsurpassedly good explanations greater in value for those wanting emancipation than even the gems of this world.

Zhan-ga went on to found monastic colleges in many places of East Tibet; the extent of his activity in this regard is amazing and so vast that even an abbreviated version of it would be too much to tell here. He had an enormous number of students, including Palpung Tai Situ, Zurmang Khenchen Padma Namgyal, Zurmang Tenga, and many other truly great beings.

About the Six Topics

Anyone who wants to know Buddhism well must study certain topics and become well-versed if not expert in them. As the Buddha himself said in a Lesser Vehicle sūtra:

> Son of the family! You are to become expert in the skandhas. You are to become expert in the āyatanas. You are to become expert in the dhātus. You are to become expert in pratītyasamutpāda. You are to become expert in topics. You are to become expert in non-topics.

Based on that, it is generally accepted that there are six topics which must be learned by all Buddhist followers. The first four will probably be known to the reader as the aggregates or heaps, sources or igniters, bases or elements, and interdependent origination. The fifth and six are less likely to be known; they are mentioned in the Buddha's discourses concerning karmic causes and effect, where they are used to indicate valid and invalid aspects respectively of the operation of karmic cause and effect.

The six topics are foundation teachings that are important to all Buddhist followers. Some might think that these topics which are the lifeblood of the Lesser Vehicle teachings would not be useful to practitioners of the higher vehicles, but that is not the case. For example, the first three topics form a significant portion of the core teaching of the Abhidharma in both the Lesser and Great Vehicles and are an integral part of the teachings of development stage and completion stage with signs in the Vajra Vehicle. An inspection of the *Heart Prajñāpāramitā Sūtra* will show that the long listing of items following the opening statement that form is emptiness is an exact listing of the six topics; thus, they are fundamental to understanding the emptiness of all phenomena as taught in the Great Vehicle. Then, this issue of whether these six topics are needed for all levels of practice or not is taken up in the prologue to Zhan-ga's text; in it, he recounts what his former incarnation, Zhanphen Thaye, said about it:

> Through not knowing the six topics in which one is to
> become expert
> The divisions of dharma are not known ...
> Through appearances not being known as mind,
> The fundament[5] consciousness is not known ...
> Through the secret key point of fundament not being
> known ...
> The Middle Way's view is not known.
> Through the Middle Way's view not being known ...
> The unification of appearance and emptiness is not
> known.
> Through the unification of appearance and emptiness
> not being known ...
> Great Completion is not known ...

Knowing the divisions of dharma will be the Lesser Vehicle level of understanding; knowing the fundament consciousness (see the glossary) will be the Mind Only Great Vehicle understanding; knowing the secret key point of the fundament consciousness will be the Middle Way Great Vehicle understanding; and knowing the unification of appearance and emptiness will be the Great Completion level of understanding. Thus, his words very clearly show how the six topics are a basis for every level of Buddhist understanding.

---

[5] Fundament is the translation used throughout this book for the all-important Sanskrit term "ālaya", translated into Tibetan with "kun gzhi". The term is most often translated with the literal translation of the Tibetan term "all-base". However, the original Sanskrit term means "a layer which underlies and is the base for everything above it". It is like a floor which sits under carpeting and all the other things placed above that, supporting all of it. Fundament has that meaning exactly, so is used. See also "alaya" in the glossary. Moreover, the term alaya is extensively explained in the second chapter of the text.

About the Text

A Teaching on the Six Topics in which One is to Become Expert starts with a chapter of prefatory material, continues with four chapters of actual teaching, and ends with a concluding chapter. The first chapter of actual teaching explains the six topics discussed above. A second chapter explains the fundaments of the Great Vehicle using the Mind Only definitions found in Asaṅga's texts. The third and fourth chapters explain the Middle Way and Great Completion approaches respectively; these chapters are short and primarily indicate which sources should be relied on when studying and practising the Middle Way and Great Completion teachings.

Buddhism in Tibet followed the literary habits of Indian Buddhism in which texts were written with a preliminary, main, and concluding section. For this text, the preliminary section has been called the prologue, the main section consists of the four chapters of the text, and the concluding section has been designated the epilogue, in accordance with English literary style. The preliminary section in Indian Buddhist literature would further consist of four parts called "title, homage, expression of worship, and declaration of composition". These are present in this text and have been indicated for the reader in footnotes.

That the text includes teachings on how to study and practise the highest of all teachings, Great Completion, is not surprising. The author of the text was the most famous of all masters who have held the abbot's seat at the Śhrī Singha monastic college of Dzogchen monastery in East Tibet. Continuing the last quotation, his principal guru said:

> Therefore, those who wish to obtain
> Complete buddhahood in this very human life
> First must train in the six topics in which one is to
> become expert!

After that, they must train in fourfold summary of the
Great Vehicle!
Then they must enter the Middle Way
And meditate on Luminosity Great Completion!

This remark shows the need to train in the six topics as part of the Great Completion level of practice, and especially the Quintessence Great Completion level of practice in which the focus is on final attainment in this very life. I know through years of having lived at Dzogchen Monastery in Tibet, that the emphasis, even within the study environment of the Śhrī Singha college, is on Great Completion practice, with the result that the explanations of vehicles below that of Ati are always put within the framework of the Great Completion teaching of the Ati vehicle.

The Style of Presentation of the Six Topics

There are four major schools of Buddhist philosophy at the sūtra level: Particularist, Followers of Sūtra, Mind Only, and Middle Way[6]. The first two are Lesser Vehicle schools and the latter two are Great Vehicle schools.

The six topics are initially explained from the Particularist point of view. Within the Tibetan tradition, the text called *Treasury of Abhidharma* by Vasubandhu, the younger brother of Asaṅga, is the accepted statement of the Particularist point of view. In fact, Vasubandhu wrote the text to negate what he saw as many wrong views of the Particularist school which were being strongly presented at the time by the Kashmiri master Chandabhadra. The *Treasury of Abhidharma* was Vasubandhu's answer to Chandabhadra and his views. The text here mentions a point over which the two masters disagreed. The reader who wants to know more about Vasubandhu and his works will want to investigate the history of the rivalry between these two masters.

---

[6] In Sanskrit, these are Vaibhaśhika, Sautrāntika, Chittamātra, and Madhyamaka respectively.

Note is occasionally made in the text of differences between the views of the Particularist and those of the next higher school, the Followers of Sūtra school.

The Great Vehicle approach to the six topics is often different from the Particularist approach. Within the Tibetan tradition, the text called *Compendium of Abhidharma* by Asaṅga, the elder brother of Vasubandhu, is the accepted statement of the Mind Only point of view of the Great Vehicle, so the text quotes it frequently to show the differences between the Particularist and Mind Only (which more or less comes down to the differences between the Lesser Vehicle and Great Vehicle) approaches.

A Little About the First Three Topics

There is a set of three epithets of the Buddha found in the very important *Sūtra of the Recollection of the Noble Three Jewels* which says:

> He is utterly completely-liberated from the skandhas.
> He does not possess dhātus. His āyatanas are restrained.

The explanation of those three epithets in my own major commentary to that sūtra[7] explains a little about the first three topics of skandhas, āyatanas, and dhātus and gives a sense of why a practitioner needs to understand them:

> *Completely-liberated* is a standard phrase in Buddhist philosophy with a specific meaning. Thus, it is possible that he could be partially completely-liberated, but he is not, he is utterly completely liberated.
>
> Clear descriptions of the psycho-physical makeup and the perceptual process of beings living in saṃsāra were an important part of the Buddha's early teaching. The skandhas, dhātus, and āyatanas are the fundaments of those descriptions. The skandhas or aggregates are the

---

[7] See the List of Cited Texts for publication information.

basic building blocks that make up a samsaric being. That makeup houses a samsaric perceptual process that consists of three main elements: sense objects, sense faculties, and the sense consciousnesses produced by them. Those three sets of elements were taught as a group; they were called the dhātus, meaning elements. By knowing the dhātus, a practitioner has a ready-reference to all the elements of samsaric perception. Samsaric consciousness is something that Buddhists want to stop, therefore, the question has to be asked, "What is the source of samsaric consciousness? What gets it started?" The answer is that the sense objects and sense faculties are the sources or igniters of samsaric consciousness. Therefore, those two sets of the elements of samsaric perception were highlighted by teaching them as a separate group; they were called the āyatanas or igniters of samsaric consciousness. By knowing the āyatanas, a practitioner knows precisely what the source of samsaric consciousness is and can do something to transcend it.

The first epithet above points out that the Buddha has completely and utterly gone beyond the psycho-physical makeup of a samsaric being. The second and third epithets point out that he does not have the perceptual process of a samsaric being: firstly, he does not have the dhātus, the elements of samsaric perception; and secondly, he does have the āyatanas, the igniters of samsaric perceptions because, having completely abandoned dualistic mind, he has constrained the igniters into a wisdom context.

"Dhātu" is a Sanskrit word with many meanings. Here it refers to those parts of samsaric being which act as the elements or constituents of the process of samsaric perception. The Buddha taught them in order to expose the basic constituents or elements of samsaric perception and hence the root causes of samsaric existence. There are eighteen dhātus in three sets of six: the objects of the eye, ear, nose, tongue, body, and mind sense faculties; the faculties that sense them; and the consciousnesses generated by those twelve. Thus, to say that the Buddha *does not possess dhātus* means that his buddha type of existence does not contain any of the elements of samsaric perception.

There are twelve āyatanas or igniters. They are the six sense objects and the six sense faculties. When they connect, samsaric consciousness is ignited and, as the Buddha described it, the burning house of saṃsāra appears. The twelve are the same as the first twelve dhātus but the Buddha put them into a group separately to identify them as a crucial part of the evolution of samsaric existence. The subject of āyatanas is very profound and was taught in both the sūtras and tantras. In the sūtra approach, the āyatanas are explained as part of the problem; in the tantric approach they are explained as part of the solution. Simply eliminating them would result in a kind of non-existence that would be useless to others. Therefore, the possibility is taught of not eliminating them but restraining them from a samsaric style of being into a non-samsaric one. Thus, *his āyatanas are restrained* means that he is not like samsaric beings whose āyatanas run rampant within ignorance, resulting in suffering now and later, but that he has attained wisdom and, having constrained his āyatanas into a wisdom context has freed himself from suffering.

In short, the Buddha has liberated himself from a samsaric style of being with its heaps, elements, and igniters.

A Little About Topics and Non-Topics

As mentioned above, talk of topics and non-topics primarily appears within the Buddha's discourses on karmic cause and effect. Khenchen Zhan-ga's text says:

> Expertise in the topics and non-topics of the śhrāvaka's level is classed as being expert in certain details of interdependent origination. Specifically, expertise in topics and non-topics of the "this exists" type brings knowledge of different causes, and with that, the results of the full-ripening of virtuous and non-virtuous karmas.

Therefore, topics and non-topics as two of the six topics that all Buddhists must learn are those things which either become a topic for further discussion when the causes and effects connected with interdependent origination—the details of karma and its workings—are considered or which do not require any further discussion. For example, when a person creates a negative karma, there is a topic for discussion—what the karma was, what strength it has, what its results will be, and how to purify it so that its effects are either not experienced or mitigated. On the other hand, when a person does something but there is no negative karma produced because of the motivation involved or an absence of self at the time of the action, the Buddha identified it as a "non-topic" meaning that there was "nothing about it needing further discussion".

The following extract from the Great Vehicle *Noble One, Sutra of the Store of the Tathāgata* shows exactly how the Buddha used the terms "topic" and "non-topic" within the teachings on the workings of karmic cause and effect. You will see at the end of the extract how he defines topic and non-topic as the presence or absence of karmic production that necessitates, or which has become a topic for, discussion. The Buddha is speaking here of someone who has made very strong non-virtuous karmas and who therefore has a "topic" for discussion. What has to be discussed includes the fact that the person could try to remove the karmic seeds in order to avoid their undesirable results but that a more effective approach would be for the person to dedicate himself to realizing that all phenomena are without a self.

> Kāśhyapa! In regard to what else it is, it is also that acting to remove the life of a pratyekabuddha is, within the acts of killing, a heavy one. It is like this: stealing the goods of the Three Jewels is, within the acts of taking what has not been given, a heavy one. It is like this: having sexual relations with one who is both mother and an arhati, is, within the acts of having wrong sexual relations due to desire, a heavy one. It is like this: denigrating the tathāgata is, within the acts of lying, a heavy one. It is like this: making a schism in the saṅgha is, within the acts of divisive speech, a heavy one. It is like this: criticising the noble ones is, within the acts of rough speech, a heavy one. It is like this: distracting those wanting dharma is, within the acts of gossip, a heavy one. It is like this: having a mind to steal the acquisitions of those who have gone into the authentic and those who are engaged in the authentic is, within the acts of covetous mind, a heavy one. It is like this: getting ready to do one of the immediates is, within the acts of a harmful mind, a heavy one. It is like this: development of a dense thicket of views is, within the acts of wrong views, a heavy one. All of these ten paths of non-virtuous action are wrongdoings.
>
> Kāśhyapa! Suppose one or more sentient beings were to become possessed of these great wrongdoings, the karmas of the paths of the ten non-virtuous actions, and, moreover, were to enter into the tathāgata's dharma teaching that has with it information about causes and conditions and think "There is not at all a self or sentient being or life-force or person[8] who has done this

---

[8] These things were enumerated by the Tīrthikas of the Buddha's time as the various attributes that truly existed, therefore here the Buddha

(continued...)

> or will experience something because of it", and were like that to engage all phenomena as being a contrivance and not compounded and without total affliction and illusory dharmatā and by nature luminosity and to develop true faith in and strong belief in all phenomena being primally complete purity. If they developed this strong belief, I would not say that such sentient beings would be going to the bad migrations.
>
> Why is that? For the afflicted things there is no existence as an assemblage; because of the birth and perishing of all afflicted things, they degrade. They are born due to the assemblage of causes and conditions and immediately they are born, they also cease; whatever is that perishing connected with birth is also what is called the perishing also of all afflicted things. Whenever there is belief in what I have said, for that person there is no downfall and no topic of downfall. In the absence of obscuration, what would become a topic of downfall is a non-topic, is without status.[9]

In general, that sort of discussion of "topics" and "non-topics" is found in the śhrāvaka teachings because that is where the Buddha gave the most extensive explanations of karmic cause and effect. However, it is also seen in the Great Vehicle teachings as shown in the sutra just quoted and in the Vajra Vehicle teachings. The terms

---

[8](...continued)
is using their wrongly stated ideas of a self to present the idea of non-self.

[9] Topics are that which can validly be discussed and non-topics are that which have no basis for discussion. Thus, for a person who has overcome karmic obscurations by realizing non-self, the issue of downfalls which would otherwise be a topic for those who have created them becomes a non-topic, meaning that there is nothing to be discussed, no basis for any further discussion.

topic and non-topic are also found in the discussions of vows at all levels of Buddhism—the vows of personal emancipation, the bodhisatva vows, and the samayas of the Vajra Vehicle—because breakage and corruption of the vows entails the production of negative karma which then becomes a topic for discussion. For example, the Great Completion text *Oceanic Single Understanding Prayer of the Bardo* by Jigmey Lingpa says:

> The topics of my breakages and corruptions of
> samaya …

where "topics" means "the breakages and corruptions of tantric vows that have created negative karmas and which need to be discussed in terms of the effects they will have and how they should be purified so that those effects will be mitigated".

About Key Terms

A Teaching on the Six Topics in which One is to Become Expert is essentially a catalogue of items to be understood, accompanied by definitions and explanations. The names of these items have been translated into English previously. However, some names are difficult to translate into English because the original Sanskrit terms refer to things for which there is no equivalent in English, some of the mental events, for example. Nevertheless, I have translated terms into English whenever possible. To assist the reader with understanding the meaning of the original terms and their translations, copious notes and a glossary have been added.

In doing this work, it is very obvious that some terms whose translations have been more or less accepted in English are not satisfactory. The skandhas or heaps and the names for their five components provide a number of examples of terms whose current translations are insufficient. These are the first terms encountered in the book and they form the framework for the rest of the definitions in the text, therefore they are discussed here, before the text.

1. The Aggregates

The original Sanskrit term is "skandha" and the Tibetan is "phung po". The original Sanskrit term has several meanings, most of them referring to a grouping of things which function together. For example, "a skandha" is the name of: a specific grouping of soldiers in an army; a "troop" of soldiers in general; and a "grouping of several or many things" in general. For example, the Buddha divided the psycho-physical makeup of sentient beings into five major groupings, each consisting of several items, and referred to them as the "skandhas" of psycho-physical existence.

The Tibetans translated "skandha" with their term "phung po", meaning a heap of things constituting one body or group. Thus, Khenpo Zhan-ga himself explains in the text translated in this book:

> The etymological definition of skandha is that many things are heaped (or piled up) together. Therefore "skandha" is an aggregate.

In Buddhism, "skandha" is used specifically to refer to the five groupings identified by the Buddha of the components of a sentient being. This usage of the term has been translated into English with both "aggregate" and "heap". "Aggregate" is a better translation because it gives a better sense of a grouping of several items and because, like the original Sanskrit term, it is a distinctive term whose meaning is easily identified. The term "heap" is not wrong but is a very general term that does not so readily convey the specific meaning of "skandha".

1.1. The aggregate of form

The first aggregate is called "rūpa" in Sanskrit and "gzugs" in Tibetan. A minor point is that this one word has two meanings: form in general, and visual form in particular. Normally, one has to distinguish the two based on context, though to help the reader, when visual form is being referenced, it has often been written as "visual form".

1.2. *The aggregate of feeling*

The second aggregate is called "vedana" in Sanskrit and "tshor ba" in Tibetan, meaning a sensation that is known to mind. The term is used as the name for this aggregate and also to indicate sensations in general which occur to the body or mind. When it is used as the name of the aggregate, there is a strong implication of the tone of the sensation—it is either good, unsatisfactory, or neutral—so it has been called "feeling" in this context even though it has to be translated as "sensation" in all other contexts, and this translation as "feeling" has become entrenched. In fact, I believe that "feeling" is wrong here, that the translation should be changed to "aggregate of sensation".

1.3. *The aggregate of perception*

The third aggregate is called "saṃjña" in Sanskrit and " 'du shes" in Tibetan. There have been a number of English translations used over the last forty years, with "perception" being the most commonly used at the time of writing. However, perception is a highly inadequate translation. The Sanskrit term means "that which produces knowledge", though a key point is that it only refers to the process which produces conceptual knowledge. Thus this aggregate consists of the things involved in the conceptual process of knowing. The main thing involved is the words or labels used in the language of concept. They are called "concept tokens" because they are the tokens used when the process of concept is operating.

Therefore, there is a major problem here. "Perception" in English does not at all have the meaning just indicated; to begin with, there are many types of perception and not all of them are concept-based. An older translation is cognition, but that too does not have the specific meaning required. An even earlier translation is "re-cognition" used to convey the sense of cognition done through concepts tokens rather than direct perception. Again, it does not immediately convey the required meaning.

Interestingly, a second meaning of the original Sanskrit term, and one that does apply exactly in this context, is "the use of signals to produce knowledge or convey information". This aggregate is about the concept tokens which themselves are the signals used to produce the conceptual knowledge of conceptual process, which are the very concepts themselves used to convey knowledge within the operation of conceptual mind. A much better translation of the name of this aggregate, and one very close to the original Sanskrit would then be "concept knowing" or even "signalled knowing".

1.4. The aggregate of formatives

The fourth aggregate is called "saṃskāra" in Sanskrit and " 'du byed" in Tibetan. The first chapter of the text gives the standard definition of formative simply and clearly. This term has been badly misunderstood in Western circles. For example, it has been called "formations". A formation is the product of that which caused its formation; the meaning here is not the result of the process but the formative or agent which will cause a formation. In particular, the formatives of this aggregate cause the production of a future set of aggregates for the mindstream involved. Another popular but wildly mistaken translation is "compounded aggregate" or the like. This mistranslation comes from looking at the content of the aggregate and thinking that it is an aggregate consisting of many things. The aggregate indeed consists of many things but it does not get its name from that. Again, this is the aggregate of those aspects of being which specifically function *to form*—that is, to bring together and cause to be manifest—a future set of aggregates.

There are two types of formative in the aggregate, ones which have equivalence and ones which do not. "Having equivalence" essentially means that this class of formatives are "mind-type things". This type of formative is the afflictions, virtuous, non-virtuous, and otherwise which, as events of mind, have the power to cause future instances of the aggregates. The ones that "do not have equivalence" are events that can occur in life and, because of their occurrence, can have the effect of producing future sets of skandhas. For example, you might acquire, or gain as it is called, the Buddha's teachings and the mere doing of that could affect your future existences in a positive way, and that would be how this type of formative could result in a future set of aggregates, even though it is a "not mind-type thing".

1.5. *The aggregate of consciousness*

The fifth aggregate is called "vijñāna" in Sanskrit and "rnam par shes pa" in Tibetan. The term means "awareness of superficies[10]". A consciousness is a dualistic (*jñā*) awareness which simply registers a certain type of (*vi*) superfice; for example, an eye consciousness by definition[11] registers only the superficies of visual form. A very important point is that the addition of the "*vi*" to the basic term "*jñā*" for awareness conveys the sense of a less than perfect way of being aware. This is not a wisdom awareness which knows every superfice in an utterly uncomplicated way but a limited type of awareness which is restricted to knowing one kind of superfice or another and which is part of the complicated—and highly unsatisfactory process—called (dualistic) mind. Note that this definition, which is a crucial part of understanding the role of consciousness in samsaric being, is fully conveyed by the Sanskrit and Tibetan terms but not at all by the English term "consciousness".

2. *The Igniters*

The second of the six topics is what is called "āyatana" in Sanskrit. The Sanskrit term has several meanings. The main one operative here is "that special place which is the home of something" and that is modified by its being the name of the fire-pit in which the fire for

---

[10] For superficies, see the glossary.

[11] This point is mentioned several times in the text.

fire offerings is ignited so that fire offerings can be made. In short, it is the place from which something else gets started. Thus, it has been translated into English with "source", but this is not sufficient as can be seen from the translation made by the early Tibetan translators who translated it with "skye mched", with "skye" meaning "to be produced" and "mched" meaning "to flare up". In other words, the āyatanas in a Buddhist context are "igniters".

3. *The Dhatus*

The third of the six topics is what is called "dhātu" in Sanskrit. This word has twenty-two classically accepted meanings. Faced with this, Tibetan translators did not translate this one term with one term of their own but used a number of terms to capture the various main meanings.

In the case of the dhātus of skandhas, āyatanas, and dhātus, it was translated with the Tibetan word "khams" meaning an element or constituent of a larger whole, because "dhātu" in that context has that meaning. Those dhātus are the various elements of the process of samsaric perception as a whole. One of those elements is the object of mind, the entirety of phenomena (dharmas) known by the mind. The word for that dhātu in Sanskrit is "dharma dhātu", meaning dharmas or phenomena as an element of the samsaric process of perception.

The same term "dharma dhātu" has another, quite different meaning in Sanskrit. In this other case, it refers to the zone or space or expanse in which all dharmas or phenomena are produced and exist.

In Sanskrit, one would hear this word dharmadhātu and understand which of the two meanings was intended according to context. That was not satisfactory to the early Tibetan translators, so they used a different Tibetan word to translate each of these meanings of "dhātu". They translated the dhātu of skandhas, āyatanas, and dhātus with "khams" for the dhātu portion, again meaning an element or constituent of a larger whole. They translated the dhātu of "dharmadhātu", meaning the zone of dharmas, with "dbyings", meaning an expanse which is a basis for the existence of something. This leaves us with the question of how we should translate this term dhātu?

It is not sufficient to say, as many might, that "Tibetan was a perfect translation from Sanskrit, therefore it should be used as a basis for translations into European and other languages". A detailed examination of this issue can be read in the book *Unending Auspiciousness*, so it will not be repeated here. The issue comes down to whether the two distinct meanings contained in "dhātu" can be represented in one word or phrase (given that dhātu itself is a noun phrase) of another language or not. That seems unlikely in English. In this book, the word "dhātu" has been left untranslated and dharmadhātu has had its meaning noted whenever it appears, so that the reader will not be confused over which of the two possible meanings is intended.

Other Issues

Sanskrit and diacriticals

Sanskrit terminology is properly transliterated into English with the use of diacritical marks. These marks often cause discomfort to less scholarly readers and can distance them from the work. However, the text here deals with technical issues, therefore diacritical marks have been used throughout.

Annotations

The Tibetan text contains annotations. They are always shown in place in the text, marked off in parentheses. Annotations by the translator have always been made as footnotes so that the two types of annotation cannot be confused. Note that the annotations in the text itself are often very terse; if some of them seem hard to understand, that is because that is how they are in the original text.

Study aids

The Tibetan text was obtained from the Tibetan Buddhist Resource Centre as a scanned image of a Tibetan reprint of the original. The reprint had a number of errors which were corrected during the work of digitizing and translating the text. The corrected text has been included in this book for those wanting to study the Tibetan more closely. A digital version of the text in our TibetD software format is available from the PKTC web-site.

To aid study of the text, page numbers of the Tibetan text have been inserted into both the Tibetan text and the English translation. Page numbers in the Tibetan text are marked between Tibetan housings, as they are called, like this ༼༢༣༽, and page numbers in the English text are marked like this {23}.

Further study

Generally speaking, Padma Karpo Translation Committee has amassed a range of materials to help those who are studying this and related topics. Please see the Supports for Study chapter at the end of the book for the details.

Normally, I feel inspired to write a little verse at this point, wishing the reader well. In this case, I feel moved simply to say: please study assiduously then practise!

Lama Tony Duff,
Swayambhunath,
Nepal,
March 2014

Plate 1. Śhrī Singha Institute at Dzogchen Monastery, Tibet
Photograph by the author, 2007

"A Mirror Revealing Knowables"

A Teaching on the Six Topics in Which One is to Become Expert

Prologue

{2} I prostrate to the guru and the special deity[12].[13]

> I bow down to he who, having gained the utter knowledge that pervades the space of the limitless knowables, in essence like the sun[14],
> Illuminates the ways of dharma for migrators using the four individual right cognitions[15],
> To the chief editor translator expert in the topics needed to make annotations, Vairochana himself who,

---

[12] "The special deity" is the yidam deity one has chosen from amongst all yidam deities as the one for one's own practice.

[13] This line is the homage of the preliminary section.

[14] The text says "the sun's essence", though it means "having the same quality as the sun". Wisdom, like the sun, has the quality of being an un-obscured brilliance which illuminates everything. This metaphor is commonly seen in Great Completion teachings, which is fitting here given the author and his lineage. This image of a brilliance which illuminates everything will now be joined with Zhanphen Thaye.

[15] These are possessed by bodhisatvas high on the levels, giving them the knowledge needed to impart dharma to individual sentient beings in the most helpful way. They are listed in the second chapter.

Having gained the ordinary and supreme siddhis,
vanished into the sky like a rainbow.[16] [17]

He appeared once again as a moon of utter knowledge
That dispels the darkness of our degenerate time,
As The One Who Benefits Others Infinitely with his
illumination of the dharma[18]
A glory for the nine types of beings.

I have heard only a portion of what
That holy one so well explained,
But if I have discovered a personal path of
knowledgeability unafraid of others,
Why would I not be extremely joyful at having this?[19]

---

[16] Vairochana was one of the chief editors during the great translation of Buddhist works into Tibetan. He had the knowledge, including that of the topics set out in this text, needed to make editorial notes on the draft translations of the translators.

[17] This first verse has been fifteen units to the line. The remainder of the verse is in seven units to the line. The ability to switch from one length of line to another in the middle of a piece of verse is regarded as a mark of an author of the highest literary capacity.

[18] Zhanphen Thaye Ozer, whose name means The One Who Benefits Others Infinitely, benefited others by illuminating the dharma. There is a great play on words here because "with his illumination of dharma" is both his activity and the name of his immediate re-incarnation, Zhanphen Chokyi Nangwa, the author of the text. The "nine types of beings" are three types each of beings in the desire, form, and formless realms.

[19] Tib. spob pa. This term is used a few times in the text. It is fully explained in *Unending Auspiciousness*. With knowledgeability, there is an absence of fear due to certainty of knowledge. Zhanphen Chokyi Nangwa was famous for finding his own path of being a supreme scholar yet having ultimate accomplishment. Note another play on

(continued...)

So then, for the good path which is travelled by all
The conquerors and {3} conquerors' sons,
It is appropriate to start by engaging in this,
The jewel of hearing, the eye of the nine beings.[20 21]

Now in regard to that, I heard my refuge guardian, son of the conquerors, The One Who Benefits Others Infinitely With Light Rays[22] say this:

You, fortunate ones, who want liberation in this life
Must train in the six topics in which one is to become expert!
Through not knowing the six topics in which one is to become expert
The divisions of dharma are not known.
Through not knowing the divisions of dharma,
Outer and inner, true and false are not known.
Through not knowing outer and inner, true and false,
Truly established external facts[23] do not cease.

---

[19](...continued)
words: he was also known as Zhan-ga or Taking Joy in Others, which is the meaning cleverly woven into the fourth line of the verse.

[20] Paraphrase: "So, having explained the lineage through which I have received the teachings of wisdom, others who would like to tread the path to wisdom will start with learning, beginning with texts like this one, in which the basic topics are taught. The knowledge that comes from learning is very precious because it becomes an eye through which all types of beings in saṃsāra gain sight of the teaching".

[21] The preceding section of verse was the expression of worship.

[22] Zhanphen Thaye Ozer.

[23] Tib. don. In the Mind Only presentation of the Great Vehicle and in the higher tantras such as Dzogchen, the objects of consciousness are not external, physical objects, but are mind appearing to be external
(continued...)

Through truly established external facts not ceasing,
Entry into the internal is not known.
Through not knowing entry to the internal,
Appearances are not known as mind.
Through appearances not being known as mind,{4}
The fundament consciousness[24] is not known.
Through the fundament consciousness not being
known,
The secret key point of fundament is not known[25].
Through the secret key point of fundament not being
known,
Freedom from elaboration beyond rational mind is not
known[26].
Freedom from elaboration beyond rational mind not
being known,
The Middle Way's view is not known.
Through the Middle Way's view not being known,
Emptiness's luminosity is not known.
Through emptiness's luminosity not being known,
Appearance's luminosity is not known.
Through appearance's luminosity not being known,

---

[23](...continued)
objects. These are then given a special name to indicate this type of object: they are called facts, where a fact is the knowledge of something on the surface of mind. A dualistic mind sees such facts as truly established. See also fact in the glossary.

[24] For fundament, see the footnote in the introduction and see the glossary. There are extensive explanations of the fundament consciousness in the second chapter of this text.

[25] There is samsaric fundament consciousness within which the enlightened mind is hidden; that hidden enlightened mind is described here as the secret (meaning hidden) key point (because through it one can become enlightened) of the fundament consciousness.

[26] For elaboration and rational mind see the glossary.

The unification of appearance and emptiness is not
known.
Through the unification of appearance and emptiness
not being known,
Unification luminosity is not known.
Through unification luminosity not being known,
Great Completion is not known.
Through Great Completion not being known,
Buddhahood in this life is not attained.
Therefore, those who wish to obtain
Complete buddhahood in this very human life
First must train in the six topics in which one is to
become expert!
After that, they must train in fourfold summary of the
Great Vehicle!
Then they must enter the Middle Way
And meditate on Luminosity Great Completion![27]

Thus, there are four parts to determining the meaning of what he said, consisting of explanations of[28]:

1. the six topics in which one is to become expert;
2. the Great Vehicle fourfold summation of dharma;
3. the way to engage in the path of freedom from extremes, the Middle Way;
4. the way to meditate on Luminosity Great Completion.

---

[27] This section of verse has been the declaration of composition.

[28] This paragraph introduces the subject matter of the text, showing the four main topics in it.

Chapter I

The Six Topics in which One is to Become Expert

A sūtra says:

> Son of the family! You are to become expert in the aggregates. You are to become expert in the igniters. You are to become expert in the dhātus.{5} You are to become expert in interdependent origination. You are to become expert in topics. You are to become expert in non-topics.

Thus, there are six.

1. The Aggregates

The etymological definition of skandha is "many things in an aggregate", therefore it is "aggregate".[29]

---

[29] Note that the Tibetan term "phung po" for the Sanskrit "skandha" can have the meaning simply of "a heap" and can also have the meaning of "many things forming one grouping which is then part of a larger whole". The latter meaning is the one here, so it would be a mistake to translate it as heap. This point has been explained in the introduction.

It has five divisions: the aggregate of form; aggregate of feeling; the aggregate of perception; the aggregate of formatives; and the aggregate of consciousness[30].

1.1. The Aggregate of Form

This has two parts: characteristic and divisions.

1.1.1. Characteristic

It has the characteristic of form which can be form.

1.1.2. Divisions

It has two divisions: causal form and resultant form.

1.1.2.1. Causal form

There are four causal forms: earth, water, fire, and wind.

1.1.2.2. Resultant form

This has eleven divisions: the forms of the five faculties, the forms of the five objects, and the non-revelatory form[31].

---

[30] See *About Key Terms* in the introduction for important notes on aggregate, form, feeling, perception, and formative, consciousness, igniters, and dhatus.

[31] Skt. vijñāpti. There are two types of form: one which makes itself known (revelatory) and one which does not make itself known (non-revelatory). The first ten divisions just listed are revelatory and the eleventh is non-revelatory. The term has been translated as "perceptible" but this is on the side of the viewer where the actual term is on the side of the object. Full translations of the original Sanskrit terms are "that which reveals itself in superfice" and "that which does not reveal itself in superfice". The addition of "superfice", meaning what any object actually presents itself to consciousness as, makes an unwieldy

(continued...)

For the five faculties, the Particularist asserts that they have form. That school goes on to say:

> The eye faculty is like a flax flower. The ear faculty is like the spiralling bark of a birch tree. The nose faculty is like two copper tubes side by side[32]. The tongue faculty is like a half circle. The body faculty, when functioning as touch, is like the smooth skin[33].

The Followers of Sūtra school asserts that "faculty" refers to the special ability which exists in those faculty supports of being able to apprehend an object[34].

The five objects are: visual form, sound, smell, taste, and touch. *The Treasury*[35] says:

> There are two types of visual form, twenty types in all.
> Sounds are of eight types.
> Smells are of four types, tastes of six types.{6}
> Touches are eleven altogether.

---

[31](...continued)
translation but it has to be understood to be there, otherwise the explanations of the term cannot be understood. Note this for when you read explanations involving revelatory and non-revelatory form.

[32] The Tibetan says "paired copper conches" but this is the Tibetan translation of the Sanskrit which says "two copper tubes side by side".

[33] The words are further explained to mean that the touch faculty is spread over the whole body, like the skin is stretched out over the whole body. Some texts additionally say that the body faculty is just under the skin, covering the whole body.

[34] ... which differs from the Particularist who, as in the quote just given, take the literal approach of the subtle forms of shape just described as the actual faculties.

[35] All texts are listed and explained in the chapter List of Cited Texts on page 97.

1.1.2.2.1 Visual forms

If visual form is divided, there are eight visual form shapes and twelve visual form colours, totalling twenty.

The eight visual form shapes are: long and short, raised and lowered, spherical and cubic, even and uneven. The twelve colours of visual form consist of four primary colours and eight secondary colours. The primary colours are: blue, yellow, white and red. Green is a combination of colours so it is not listed there. The secondary colours are: cloudiness and smokiness, dustiness and haziness, illuminated and darkened[36], sunlight and shade.

The Compendium says that there are twenty-five by adding five items to those: for shape both subtle and coarse atoms and for colour the visible case (meaning that it is without obstruction to its being known) and the revelatory case (meaning that it is showing itself as a superfice[37])[38] and the sky (meaning that space comes to have a blue colour) making eleven colours.

1.1.2.2.2 Sounds

Sound consists of four sounds coming from elements connected with knowing and four coming from elements not connected with knowing, making eight.

---

[36] ... meaning un-illuminated and hence "dark".

[37] For superfice here, see the earlier discussion of the etymology of the Sanskrit words for revelatory and non-revelatory form. For superfice in general, see the glossary.

[38] The text has its own annotations which are shown in the text enclosed in parentheses.

The first consists of the two of being articulated and not articulated to sentient beings[39] and then each of those being nice and not nice, making four. To give examples for those in sequence: dharma teaching, harsh words, striking small cymbals together, and banging fists.{7}

The last consists of the two of being articulated and not articulated to sentient beings and then each of those being nice and not nice, making four. To give examples for those in sequence: dharma taught by persons who are manifestations, harsh words spoken by them, sounds of musical instruments, and sounds of rocks falling away from mountain sides.

In regard to this, *The Compendium* teaches an enumeration of eleven:

> Pleasing, not pleasing, and both, arisen from the cause of the great elements with knowing, not with knowing, and both (such as hand and clay drum[40]), the audibles made by the world (that which is included in ordinary persons' language), what is taught by the accomplished ones (taught by the noble ones[41]), and that which is nothing but designation by thought[42] (that which is taught in the

---

[39] "Articulated to sentient beings" means that one sentient being has vocally articulated something to another sentient being. This major division based on articulation comes from the Indian science of sound, in which all sounds are divided into two types, articulated and non-articulated, meaning sounds which are vocalized by sentient beings and those which are not, for example, the sound of a waterfall.

[40] The name of a medium to large size drum from ancient India, whose body is made of terra cotta. The drum is beaten with the hand or a striker.

[41] For noble one, see the glossary.

[42] "Nothing but designation by thought" has the sense of "totally
(continued...)

> Tīrthika[43] teachings), the designation of conventions by the noble ones (this is done from the stance of the conventions seen in the latter two, and so on), and designation by those who are not noble ones.

1.1.2.2.3 Smells

Smells consists of the two, unified and mixtures[44], each of which has nice and not nice, making a division into four. To give examples for those in sequence: agaru smell[45], garlic smell, solid incense[46] smell, and smells which are a number of bad smells combined.

The Compendium teaches six:

> Good smells, bad smells, equal smells[47] (like agaru), unified, coming as a mixture, and coming from change{8} (like ripened fruit).

---

[42](...continued)
imaginary, having no relation to the actual things of the world". It is the same as the first character of the Mind Only school, which is explained at length in the second chapter.

[43] For Tīrthika, see the glossary.

[44] The Tibetan for "unified" is literally "simultaneous"; the meaning is a type of smell which might or might not have several components but which is experienced as a single smell. The other type of smell is one which is several smells experienced as a mixture, for example, the smell of a stinking outdoor toilet wafting together with fragrant smells of the outdoors.

[45] "Agaru" is the Indian name for a wood which has a pleasant aroma and which is therefore commonly used in the manufacture of incense.

[46] The Tibetan term for solid incense means a compound of pastes of various substances dried into solid form, such as incense sticks.

[47] ... where equal means equal parts of good and bad ...

1.1.2.2.4 Tastes

Taste when divided consists of six types: sweet, sour, bitter, astringent, hot[48], and salty. To give examples for those in sequence: sugar-cane juice, Emblic Myrobalan, tigta, Yellow Myrobalan, citraka, and salt[49]. *The Compendium* teaches an enumeration of twelve by adding to those: pleasing, not pleasing, and neither, unified, coming as a mixture, and coming from change (these can be understood through smell[50]).

1.1.2.2.5 Touches

Touches[51] consists of the four contacts with the elements and seven contacts with physical substance arising from the elements, making eleven. The first four are: the hardness of earth, wetness of water, heat of fire, and lightness of wind. The later seven are: the two of smooth (a touch which is of the class of combined fire and water) and coarseness (combined earth and wind), the two of heaviness (combined earth and water) and lightness (combined fire and wind), the two of hunger (combined earth and fire) and thirst (combined fire and wind), and cold (combined water and wind).

The Compendium teaches as many as twenty-two enumerations:

---

[48] In this case "hot" specifically means heat due to spice, such as from chilli, not heat due to cooking.

[49] Emblic and Yellow Myrobalan are two of the several varieties of the Myrobalan fruit. "Tigta" is the exact word used in Sanskrit for "bitter" as one of the six tastes generally accepted in ancient India; it is also used to name several plants, all of which are presumably bitter. "Citraka" is the Sanskrit name for *Plumbago zeylanica*, which ayurvedic medicine says has a pungent (meaning hot) quality.

[50] You can understand this for yourself by looking into smells.

[51] The Tibetan and Sanskrit literally means contact, with the specific meaning here being bodily contact.

> It is like this: smoothness, roughness, lightness, heaviness, suppleness, relaxed and not relaxed, cold, hunger, thirst, contentment, with strength{9} and with little strength, fainting, itchiness, slipping, sickness, aging, death, fatigue, rest, and courage (not being afraid).

For non-revelatory form, *The Treasury* says:

> Distracted or mindless even (particulars of circumstance)
> Virtue and non-virtue's (particulars of entity[52]) follow on (the reference is to time) which
> Will become a cause of the great elements (the particular of cause)
> Is referred to as non-revelatory form[53] (according to what the early translators said, one's own doing of motivated occurrence[54] does not make itself known to another, therefore its is called "form which does not make itself known").

And in terms of divisions, the same text says:

> "The three kinds of non-revelatory forms" refers to:
> Vowed, not vowed, and other.
> Vow refers to "personal emancipation[55]" and

---

[52] For entity, see the glossary.

[53] Non-revelatory form is a form which "does not make itself known (to observers) by way of a superfice of form that can be known with the five senses".

[54] Tib. kun nas slong ba. "Motivated occurrence" is a motivation such as virtue or non-virtue in the mind which will, not immediately but at a later time, cause a verbal or physical manifestation, in the same being connected with the mindstream of the motivation.

[55] Skt. prātimokṣha. These are the various vows of the Lesser Vehicle (continued...)

> Similarly, to a dhyāna without outflows[56] having been born.

These (the characteristics[57]) are written according to what master Vasubandhu accepted (master Chandabhadra[58] gave an explanation of them that was different from that). When they are summarized, all of them are contained within the three: showable, obstructing forms which are within the eye's domain; non-showable, obstructing forms which are in the domains of the other four, the ear, and so on;{10} and non-showable, non-obstructing forms, such as the non-revelatory one.

1.2. *The Aggregate of Feeling*

This has two parts: characteristic and divisions.

1.2.1. Characteristic

It has the characteristic of feeling what is experienced[59].

1.2.2. Divisions

If it is summed up into one, then as a sūtra says:

---

[55](...continued)
given by the Buddha as a means to obtain emancipation for oneself.

[56] For un-outflowed and dhyāna, see the glossary.

[57] ... mentioned above in the presentation of form which has just been concluded ...

[58] Tib. slob dpon 'dun bzang.

[59] "To experience" in this context has the specific meaning "to have contact arise due to the assemblage of object, faculty, and consciousness", a process which immediately precedes feeling. In other words, feeling provides the detail of the reaction to the experience of contact.

> All feelings, whatever they might be, are unsatisfactory[60]. If you ask why that is, good feelings have the nature of unsatisfactoriness of change, unsatisfactory feelings have the nature of unsatisfactoriness of unsatisfactoriness; and in-between feelings have the nature of pervasive unsatisfactoriness of the formatives[61].

Thus it teaches that all the feelings in the mind-streams of individualized beings[62] are, either directly or indirectly, unsatisfactory in nature.

If it is divided into two, it consists of body feelings and mind feelings. Or, if it is divided into three, it consists of good, unsatisfactory, and in-between feelings. If divided into four, it consists of the two of body feelings and mind feelings, with each of those also being divided into the two sides of total affliction and complete purification[63]. If it is divided into five, it consists of: good, unsatis

---

[60] For unsatisfactoriness, see the glossary.

[61] The three kinds of unsatisfactoriness which the Buddha taught to sum up all kinds of samsaric unsatisfactoriness are used to make the point. The third one, the pervasive unsatisfactoriness of the formatives refers to the self-perpetuating aspect of samsaric existence—formatives make future existences and those very existences made by formatives are again subject to them, with formatives arising again in those existences and immediately creating more causes of future samsaric existence. This kind of unsatisfactoriness pervades every moment of samsaric existence.

[62] Skt. pudgala, Tib. so so skye bo. Individualized beings are ones who have restricted themselves into a discrete being within saṃsāra. Noble beings, are the ones who have removed themselves from that enmeshment in individualized being by having exited saṃsāra. The former are regarded as "ordinary" and the latter as "spiritually superior".

[63] For affliction and for total affliction and complete purification, see

(continued...)

factory, mentally good, mentally not good, and neutral. If it is divided into six, it consists of feelings known through the condition of contact included within eye, ear, nose, tongue, body, and mental mind. By dividing those according to threefold good, unsatisfactory, and in-between, there are eighteen altogether. By further dividing each of those{11} according to the sides of total affliction and complete purification, there are thirty-six altogether. By further dividing each of those according to the three times, it comes to a total of one hundred and eight.

The Compendium says[64]:

> The feelings which arise from contacts included within the eye can either be good, unsatisfactory, or neither unsatisfactory nor good. And the feelings which arise from contacts included with the ear, nose, tongue, body and mental mind can either be good, unsatisfactory, or neither unsatisfactory nor good. Good ones can be of the body (has equivalency with the five consciousnesses[65]), unsatisfactory ones can also be of the body, and neither unsatisfactory nor good ones can also be of the body. Good ones can be of the mind, unsatisfactory ones can also be of the mind, and neither unsatisfactory nor good ones (has equivalency with the mental consciousness) can also be of the mind. Good ones together with this and that (has equivalency with

---

[63](...continued)
the glossary.

[64] The text from *The Compendium* is mistakenly quoted in the Zhan-ga's text; there are spelling and punctuation errors which lead to an incorrect presentation of the original meaning. The text has been corrected in the edition in this book. The notes within the quotation are not part of *The Compendium* but were provided by Zhan-ga so that his audience could better understand the meaning.

[65] "Having equivalency" is explained in the fourth aggregate.

> craving[66] for the body) can be unsatisfactory and neither unsatisfactory nor good together with this and that. Good without this and that (the case without craving) can also be unsatisfactory and neither unsatisfactory nor good without this and that. Good ones dependent on clinging[67] (this has equivalence with craving for desirable objects){12} also can be unsatisfactory and neither unsatisfactory nor good ones dependent on clinging. Good ones dependent on manifest occurrence (this does not have craving for desirables) also can be unsatisfactory and neither unsatisfactory nor good ones dependent on manifest occurrence.

In that, the six feelings have been divided according to good, unsatisfactory, and in-between, making eighteen. Moreover, with fifteen included in the body and three included in the mind, the former have been divided according to there being this and that or not and the latter according to dependence on clinging and manifest occurrence, making thirty six altogether.

1.3. *The Aggregate of Perception*

This has two parts: characteristic and divisions.

1.3.1. Characteristic

It has the characteristic of perception done through apprehending concept tokens[68].

---

[66] "Craving" is one of the twelve links of interdependency, and is explained in the fourth of the six topics.

[67] For clinging, see the glossary.

[68] For concept tokens, see the glossary.

1.3.2. Divisions

It has two divisions: perception with apprehension[69] of concept tokens and perception without concept tokens. The first is divided into three: less extensive, more extensive, and limitless. The second one is apprehension without concept tokens.

The Compendium teaches the divisions of perception as twelve:

> There are perceptions which arise from contacts included within the eye and perceptions which arise from contact included within the ear, nose, tongue, body, and mental mind. They are either the ones which with concept tokens (excluding the equilibria[70] of purification of the path of conventions and absence of concept tokens and the equilibrium of the peak of becoming[71] are not included) correctly know or the ones which without concept tokens (excluding the ones with concept tokens) or with lesser ones (the perceptions of desire) or vaster ones (the perceptions of the form realm) or limitless ones (the two of space and consciousness) or the igniters of nothing whatsoever due to thinking "there is nothing whatsoever" (the perceptions of nothing whatsoever, and so on) correctly know.

1.4. The Aggregate of Formatives

This has two parts: characteristic and divisions.

---

[69] Apprehension is dualistic "knowing".

[70] Skt. samāhita, Tib. snyom 'jug. Equilibrium is used to indicate complete and undisturbed absorption in some state of mind. It mainly refers to the absorptions of the formless realm and the arhats.

[71] Tib. srid rtse. The peak of becoming is the highest possible birth in the formless realm and therefore also in samsaric existence as a whole.

1.4.1. Characteristic

It has the characteristic of a formative, that which causes the manifest formation of sets of four aggregates other than the current ones.

1.4.2. Divisions

It has two divisions: formatives which have equivalence and formatives which do not have it.

1.4.2.1. Formatives which have equivalence

It has the equivalence of the five mutual equivalences of minds and mental events[72], therefore it is named accordingly. They are the equivalences of reference, superfice, basis, substance, bases, and time. Those five are as follows. 1) Equivalence of reference using the eye consciousness to illustrate it is that, at the point when eye consciousness has been produced due to referencing visual form, its retinue of mental events also will have been produced through referencing visual form; similarly with the ear consciousness referencing sound, and so on. 2) Equivalence of superfice is that, at the point when eye consciousness has been produced in the superfice of a pillar, its retinue of mental events also will have been produced having a superfice of a pillar. 3) Equivalence of support{14} is that, at the point when the eye consciousness has been produced in dependence on the eye faculty, its retinue of mental events also will have been produced in dependence on the eye faculty. 4) Equivalence of substance is that in this case all minds and mental events are equivalent in there being nothing else other than each of them. 5) Equivalence of time is that mind and mental events having been produced at the one same time also cease together.

---

[72] Tib. sems dang sems byung. In mind and mental events, mind is a consciousness, whatever it might be, and mental events are the various events which occur in a moment of that consciousness.

The mental events which arise from mind are, according to *The Treasury*, as follows. When it says,

> (1) Feeling, (2) minding, (3) perception,
> (4) Intention, (5) contact, (6) intelligence, (7) memory
> (8) Mentation, (9) interest, and
> (10) Samādhi are in every mind.

it is referring to the ten in the category of mind. And when it says

> Faith, heedfulness, thoroughly processed,
> Equanimity, shame, propriety,
> The two types of root, non-harmfulness, and
> Perseverance always occur as virtue.

it is referring to the ten in the category of virtue. And when it says,

> Stupidity[73], carelessness, laziness,
> Non-faith, dullness, and agitation
> Always occur as an afflicted state.

it is referring to the six which are in the category of great affliction. And when it says,

> Non-virtue is lack of propriety and
> lack of shame ...

it is referring to the two which are in the category of non-virtue. And when it says,

> ... belligerence,
> Grudge-holding, dishonesty,
> Jealousy, spite, concealment, avarice,
> Pretence, conceit, and harmfulness
> Are the ones at the level of lesser affliction.

---

[73] Stupidity specifically means the dullness of a mind which does not know about or which misunderstands something. For example, in English, one refers to a "dullard" which is a person having this particular quality. We also call someone "stupid" when they do not know about something.

it is referring to the ten in the category of lesser affliction. Those, together with the eight indefinite ones taught by Venerable Vasumitra[74] when he said,

> The eight called examination, analysis, regret,{15}
> Sleep, anger, attachment,
> Pride, and doubt,
> Are explained to be indefinite.

means that forty-six mental events are asserted. *The Compendium* adds the five of non-delusion, view, forgetfulness, un-alertness, and complete distractedness to those, accepting fifty-one mental events altogether.

Of those mental events, **feeling** and **perception** have already been explained above. Now the others will be explained a little in the sequence found in *The Compendium*. **Minding** causes mind to be formed and brought into manifestation. Its function is that it causes mind to enter the object. **Mentation** is the engagement of mind, that is, putting mind onto an object. Its function is that it causes mind to be held on its reference. **Contact** is the meeting of the three of object, faculty, and consciousness. Its function is that it creates the basis for feeling. Those are the five omnipresent ones; they are given their name because "they *go* as the retinue of *every* mind"[75].

---

[74] Venerable Vasumitra was one of the group of arhats who compiled the seven Abhidharma sūtras from recollection of the Buddha's talks. The sūtra mentioned here is one of the seven.

[75] Tib. kun 'gro. A main mind is a moment of consciousness. A mental event is a mind event that occurs within a moment of consciousness. There are five mental events that *go* with or are present with *every* main mind. In English, this has been accepted as "omnipresent".

Intention[76] is desire for a particular thing that has been thought about. Its function is that it creates the basis for perseverance[77]. **Interest**[78] is to hold with certainty to a particular thing which has been ascertained. Its function is to not be stolen away from something. **Mindfulness** is to be without forgetfulness in relation to the thing with which mind is mixed. Its function is to be completely undistracted. **Samādhi**[79] is one-pointedness of mind.{16} Its func-

---

[76] Skt. cchanda. Tib. 'dun pa. There is no specific term for this mental event in English, which can be problematic because, together with what has been called "interest" above, it is the most commonly mentioned of all the mental events in Buddhist teaching. It has the feature of mind directing or orienting itself towards what it has decided is worthwhile. It implies interest but is primarily concerned with where the mind has oriented itself. The term was used frequently by the Buddha with the meaning of the direction towards which mind was motivated. For example, he famously said "All dharmas arise from conditions; dwell at the vanguard of intention", meaning "stay right at the forefront of mind's intention because the direction in which it is intending to go will be the deciding factor in what occurs for you".

[77] Zhan-ga has defined its function in terms of the practice of dharma, but this is a mental event that goes with all states of mind, both virtuous and non-virtuous ones. In fact, its function is that it causes a person to decide that the current object of mind is worthwhile and hence it becomes the basis for having the energy to pursue that object. This mental event functions to get you "turned on" to something whereas the next one functions to make you stick with that object.

[78] Tib. mos pa. Like "intention", this is one of the most commonly mentioned of all the mental events in Buddhist teaching. It is similar to "intention" but not the same. This mental event is similar to having an idea in mind which one intends to follow; the same word is also used to mean "to visualize".

[79] ... or concentration.

tion is that it creates the basis for awareness. **Prajñā**[80] is the utter dissection of phenomena. Its function is the turning away of doubt. Those are the five object ascertainers, that is, they are what *ascertains an object*, therefore are named accordingly.

Faith belongs to the pure portion of mind; it is to have manifest trust. Its function is that it creates the basis for intention[81]. **Shame**[82] is avoidance of wrongdoing based on concern for oneself. Its function is that it creates the basis for keeping vows nicely. **Propriety** is avoidance of wrongdoing based on concern for what the world will think. The function is the same as for the preceding one. **Non-attachment** is absence of attachment to becoming and the things of becoming. Its function is that it creates the basis for not engaging in bad actions. **Non-anger** is the absence of all types of harmful mind towards others. Its function is the same as the preceding one. **Non-delusion** is trust in the four truths, and so on. Its function is the same as the preceding one. **Perseverance**[83] is for the mind to take overt delight in virtue. Its function is that it causes the virtuous side to be fully completed. **Thoroughly processed**[84]

---

[80] … or correct discernment.

[81] … the mental event mentioned just above.

[82] English does not have an exact pair of words for what have been called here shame and propriety. They are the same basic state of mind—a sense of embarrassment at bad behaviour. They have the one difference that what has been called propriety here means that one is embarrassed because of considering what the world will think if one does a certain action whereas what has been called shame here means that one is embarrassed because of considering what one will think of oneself if one does a certain action.

[83] … or diligence.

[84] This has been called pliancy and also catharsis; the former is incomplete, the latter simply wrong. Thoroughly processed can be used in

(continued...)

is that body and mind are workable. Its function is that it is a dispeller of all obscurations. **Heedfulness** is making a practice of being careful in regard to all places that one might enter. Its function is that it causes the full accomplishment of all perfections. **Equanimity** is mind which has been taken to the balance point between sinking and agitation. Its function{17} is that it causes total affliction to not start. **Non-harmfulness** is the antidote to harmfulness; it is compassion itself. Its function is to not be troublesome towards others. Those are called "the eleven virtuous ones"; all virtuous karmas are included within them.

Desire is hankering after the three realms. Its function is that it causes the production of unsatisfactoriness. **Anger** is mind filled with a harmful attitude. Its function is that it stops one from staying happy and is the creation of the basis for bad action. **Pride** is a mind which in dependence on wrong view has become puffed up. When divided, there are seven types: pride, pride of superiority, pride even more than pride, pride of thinking "I am!", overt pride, pride of thinking "I am lesser", and wrong pride. Its function is that it does not respect others and creates the basis for the occurrence of unsatisfactoriness. **Ignorance** is not knowing the three realms. Its function is that it creates a basis for non-comprehension, wrong thoughts, and doubt, and for the arising of total affliction. **Doubt** is to be in two minds about what is true. Its function is that it creates the basis for not entering the virtuous side. **Views** is fivefold as follows. 1) The view of the perishable, having seen "I" and "mine" in the five aggregates and viewed them as true, has the function of creating the basis of all views. 2) Views holding to extremes{18} view the aggregates as permanent or nihilate, so they

---

[84](...continued)
reference either to body or mind or to both. It is the result of training in śhamatha through to the end, at which point both body and mind are thoroughly processed and with that comes many good qualities such as the physical ability to fly and the mental ability to know with extrasensory perceptions.

have the function of creating an obstacle to becoming renounced[85]. 3) Wrong views make exaggerations in relation to cause and effect, so they have the function of severing roots of virtue and tightly holding to non-virtue. 4) Views holding as supreme are ones which hold those views as supreme; they have the function of overtly clinging to bad views. 5) Holding disciplines and yogic acts as supreme has the view that activities related to those views will definitely bring forth purification and liberation; they have the function of creating a basis for hardships undertaken for no result. Of those, the view in relation to the perishable collection when divided has twenty divisions: the views that form is I, that I possesses form, that form is mine, that I is present within form, and similarly that feeling, perception, formation, and consciousness are I, and so on. Viewing extremes when divided has the four views of the extreme of existence, the extreme of non-existence, the extreme of both, and the extreme of neither or, alternatively, has the eight views of ceasing, and so on. The other views are easy to understand. These are the six root afflictions, because they are the roots of all affliction.

Belligerence is a mind included as part of aggression, so is a mind filled with harm. Its function is that it creates the basis for preparing to harm. **Grudge-holding**[86] is holding to a mind begrudging something from the past. Its function is that it creates the basis for not being patient. **Concealment** is embracement of wrongdoing. Its function is{19} that it creates a basis for not staying happy. **Spite** is a belligerence included within aggression and is a mind which precedes grudge holding, so is a mind filled with harm. Its function is that it creates a basis for harsh words. **Jealousy** is that, being attached to gain and honour, one is unable to bear the perfections

---

[85] Tib. nges par byung ba. The term usually translated as "renunciation" means to have turned towards and committed oneself to a process that is good and reliable. In other words, it refers to the positive step that we take after first being revolted by, and then renouncing, saṃsāra.

[86] … or resentment.

of others. Its function is that it is an unhappy mind. **Avarice** is a mind which is obsessed with possessions. Its function is that it creates a basis for not diminishing one's concern with possessions. **Pretence**[87] is clinging to gain and honour and, although one has no good qualities, feigning that one does. Its function is that it creates a basis for wrong livelihood. **Dishonesty** is that, being attached to gain and honour, although one has faults, one pretends that one does not. Its function is that it creates an obstacle to obtaining true advice. **Conceit**[88] is a puffed up mind; when divided it has five types: of family, of form, of power, of youth, and of learning. Its function is that it creates a basis for all of the afflictions and proximate afflictions. **Harming** is absence of love. Its function is that it causes one to make trouble for others. **Lack of shame** is the non-avoidance of bad out of concern for oneself or the dharma. Its function is that it aids all afflictions and proximate afflictions. **Lack of propriety** is the non-avoidance of bad out of concern for what the world will say. Its function is like that of the preceding one. **Dullness** is mind descending into darkness. Its function is like that of the preceding one.{20} **Agitation** is a mind included as part of desire which is completely unpeaceful. It has the function of creating an obstacle to calm abiding. **No faith** is not having trust in the virtuous dharmas. Its function is that it creates a basis for laziness. **Laziness** is a mind not delighting in virtue. Its function is that it creates an obstacle to perseverance. **Heedlessness** is not having a part of oneself watching out for bad action. Its function is that it creates a basis for the rise of non-virtue and the fall of virtue. **Forgetfulness** is to forget about the object with which a virtuous mind was previously mixed. Its function is that it creates a basis for distraction. **Unalertness** is to enter into being unalert in regard to whatever activity is engaged. Its function is that it creates a basis for the occurrence of downfalls. **Distraction** is a mind included within the three poisons which is full of elaboration. When divided it

---

87 ... or deceit.

88 ... or literally "being full of oneself".

consists of six types of distraction. 1) Essential nature distraction[89] is like the consciousnesses of the five doors. 2) Distraction to the external is, at the time of being engaged in virtue, starting to elaborate about other, desirable things. 3) Internal distraction is, at the time when one is engaged in samādhi, the arising of faults such as following the experiences of sinking and agitation, and so on. 4) Concept distraction is that one has engaged in virtue because of others trusting that oneself is virtuous, so it is degenerate from the outset. 5) Distraction of accepting a bad place is that, at the time of being engaged in virtue, good feelings, and so on which arise are grasped at as being I and mine, causing the virtuous side to be made into non-virtue. 6) Mentation distraction{21} is degeneration of the authentic's fact[90] such as occurs through entering some other equilibrium or abiding in another vehicle. Its function is that it creates an obstacle to separation from desire. These are called "the twenty proximate afflictions" because they are the same type of thing as the root afflictions.

Sleep is not being able to hold onto body and mind. Its function is that it creates a basis for losing activity. **Regret** is that mind, having changed direction from that involved with some earlier activity, is not happy in regard to it. Its function is that it creates an obstacle to mind being settled. **Examination**[91] is the apprehending merely

---

[89] This is the technical term for what we normally would call "distraction itself", what it is in essence.

[90] 'The authentic's fact" is a name for superfact.

[91] Skt. vitarka, Tib. brtags pa. This is a coarse type of conceptual understanding of the object of consciousness because of which it has sometimes been translated into English with "coarse conceptual understanding". In fact, it means that the object is known simply with a thought. It is explained always as one of the pair vitarka and vicāra; see the next mental event for vicāra.

of what a fact is; it is a coarse mind. **Analysis**[92] is analysis of the details of a fact; it is a subtle mind. The function of these two is that they create a basis for remaining and not remaining happy. Also, their function in relation to virtuous dharmas is that they abandon what is not conducive for oneself. Their function in regard to affliction and proximate afflictions is that they hinder them by providing the appropriate antidote. These four are called "the four variable ones" because they can change into being both virtuous and non-virtuous.

Why then, of the fifty-one mental events, do feeling and perception have to be treated separately? It is because of the three reasons{22} given in *The Treasury*:

> Because they become roots of argument,
> Because they are causes of saṃsāra, and because they are
> successive causes,
> Of the mental events, feeling and
> Perception are separated out and defined as aggregates[93].

---

[92] Skt. vicāra, Tib. dpyad pa. This is a fine type of conceptual understanding of the object of consciousness because of which it has sometimes been translated into English with "fine conceptual understanding". It means that the object is investigated carefully with an analytic type of mind. It is explained always as one of the pair vitarka and vicāra; see the previous mental event for the other one of the pair.

Note that "examination" and "analysis" are often mentioned together because they represent the ways in which conceptual mind knows about the object of consciousness. The two are only found as conceptual mental events within dualistic mind, therefore, when speaking of non-dualistic types of awareness, it is common to say "without examination (or thought) and analysis" meaning that the non-dualistic mind knows without the presence of mind and mental events as typified by these two.

[93] Sentient beings enter argument and all afflictions because of these

(continued...)

1.4.2.2. Formatives which do not have equivalence

The Treasury says:

> Gain, not gain, same lot,
> Absence of perception equilibrium,
> Life, characteristics,
> Names' group, and so on ...

According to that there are fourteen: gain, no gain, same lot or concordant level, absence of perception and its equilibrium and cessation equilibrium, the life faculty, birth, staying, old age, impermanence, and the groups of names, phrases, and letters. *The Compendium* teaches an enumeration of twenty-three by adding nine to those: engagement, individual ascertainment, connection, rapidity, sequence, time, place, count, and assemblage.

Gain is the dharma which is obtained, whether virtuous, non-virtuous, or indeterminate. The noble ones' dharma **not gained** is an individualized being. **Absence of perception equilibrium** is the separation from desire of the third dhyāna and the non-separation from desire of the ones above that, the sixfold group[94] having been stopped and abiding in that. **Cessation equilibrium** refers to the noble ones who have obtained the mind of the peak of becoming

---

[93](...continued)
two mental events. Moreover, the first one feeling, leads directly to the second one perception, which in turn leads to the development of saṃsāra. The Buddha said that, for these three reasons, he pulled these two mental events out and highlighted them by making them individual skandhas.

[94] Tib. tshogs drug. The sixfold group is the set of six consciousnesses, eye through mind. It is usually translated as "groups of consciousness" but this is mistaken, with a failure to realize how the word group (Tib. tshogs) is used in the sense of a single set consisting of multiple items. Note that the term "eightfold group" will later be used to refer to the set of eight consciousnesses defined in the Mind Only teachings.

where the sixfold group together with the afflicted mental mind has ceased. **Absence of perception**{23} is the result of the prior equilibrium; it is to have been born as a god without perception. **Life faculty** is what causes remaining in a stream of aggregates, like that of one human life. **Concordant level**[95] is for this and that level of a sentient being to be similar to each other. **Birth** is the new production of a set of aggregates of a sentient being. **Old age** is for its continuum to change to something else[96]. **Abiding** is to abide in a continuity of formatives of concordant level[97]. **Impermanence** is for that continuity to disintegrate. **The name group**[98] is the words which stand for an actual entity, for example, "god" and "man"[99].

---

[95] As mentioned earlier, concordant level is another name for same lot.

[96] Paraphrase: we are changing as we get older.

[97] Concordant level was just defined.

[98] The three groups of names, phrases, and letters are in reference to Sanskrit (and Tibetan following it) grammar. Whereas English has letters and words only as the basis of the meaningful expressions of the language, Sanskrit and Tibetan have what are called letters, names, and phrases. The names and phrases of Sanskrit and Tibetan are not like the names and phrases of English—there is a major difference between the languages at this point but it would take too long to explain this fully here. Instead, the reader is referred to the very clear explanation of these points given in *Standard Tibetan Grammar Volume I, The Thirty Verses of Minister Thumi*. A shorter but clear explanation can be found in the beginner's grammar called *The Great Living Tree Grammars, Beginner's Level Tibetan Grammar Texts by Yangchen Drubpay Dorje and Tony Duff*. Both books by Tony Duff and published by Padma Karpo Translation Committee are available on the PKTC web-site.

[99] The "names" of Sanskrit and Tibetan grammar are similar to but not the same as English nouns because they have a larger function than merely being naming words. Therefore, it would not be correct to call them nouns. This point is clearly explained in the two texts cited in the previous footnote.

The phrase group is the phrases which are their specializations[100] as in "gods are supreme". **The letter group** is the changeless positions in both of them, for example, "a" and "i"[101]. Like the "a" just mentioned, they cannot change to show a meaning other than what they are, therefore they are called "changeless". **Engagement** is an uninterrupted continuum in cause and effect. **Individual ascertainment** is viewing cause and effect as different. **Connection** is effect following on with consistency from cause. Also, although cause and effect are known to be different, an effect which is appropriate, that is, certain, exists and ceases which is the rapid occurrence of cause and effect. **Sequence** means that cause and effect occur as former followed by later. **Time** is cause and effect's three times.{24} **Place** is cause and effect's ten directions. **Count** is two and three, and so on. **Assemblage** is the conditions of cause and effect complete.

1.5. *The Aggregate of Consciousness*

This has two parts: characteristic and divisions.

---

[100] The "phrases" of Sanskrit and Tibetan grammar are defined as a single name with a single phrase linker (Tib. tshig phrad) attached. The attachment of the phrase linker causes the name, which is like a noun, to be modified in various ways, allowing the noun-like name to be brought into use in the language. Again, this is fully explained in the texts mentioned in the previous footnote.

[101] This example relates to the Tibetan "names" in the example just given of the name group, which are spelt with the vowels "a" and "i". To follow through on the example as translated into English, this would have to be changed to "o" and "a" (in god and man).

1.5.1. Characteristic

It has the characteristic of consciousness[102] of being luminous and knowing[103].

1.5.2. Divisions

There are the six ways of being consciousness that happen through the consciousnesses of eye, ear, nose, tongue, body, and mental mind[104].

Each of those is determined through the five things of: reference, superfice, sequence, function, and entity of the awareness[105]. Their

---

[102] See important notes about consciousness in the glossary.

[103] A book containing an explanation of this definition and many other definitions which will be invaluable as a support for this kind of study is available free from the Padma Karpo Translation Committee web-site: *A Partial Commentary to "The Miraculous Key which Opens a Door to the Treasury Of Knowledge and Sums Up the Reasonings in the Ocean Of Texts on Reasoning" by the Author of the Text Khenpo Tsultrim Gyatso, Compiled by Tony Duff.* Note that the Tibetan term "gsal ba" in the definition is an abbreviation of " 'od gsal ba" which refers to the luminosity aspect of the mind; it does not mean "clear" as is commonly but mistakenly translated.

[104] Skt. manas, Tib. yid. "Mental mind" is a general name for the thinking, dualistic mind of sentient beings. It is not the same as "mind" (Skt. citta, Tib. sems) which is the overall process of dualistic samsaric mind. It is important to distinguish the two, therefore "mental mind" is always used in this book to refer to this particular mind and "mind" to refer to the other. The very important term "mentation" is used to refer to the mental mind when it is functioning, as explained earlier under the mental events, of which it is one.

[105] Skt. jñā, Tib. shes pa. See the glossary for important notes on the term awareness. Note that the word for awareness "shes pa" is some-

(continued...)

references in order are: form, sound, smell, taste, touch, and dharmas. **Superfice** goes from eye consciousness being produced in a superfice of visual form up to mental consciousness being produced in a superfice of dharmas. **Sequence** is that in the first instant the three of object, faculty, and mentation[106] assemble, then, in the second instant, the first instant of eye consciousness is produced, and in the third, the first instant of mental consciousness is produced. Now, in terms of divisions of instants, the instants which are the smallest portion of time are those which are one sixtieth of the period of time in a finger snap, for example, one hundred and twenty of such instants will be the period of two finger snaps. The instant for the completion of the work[107] is the longest length of time, which starts at the arousing of mind[108] and goes through to buddhahood, and the shortest length of time is the period of one finger snap, but these extremes of time are not definite.{25} **Function** goes from causing seeing up to causing knowing. **Entity** is from the eye's awareness up to the mental mind's awareness.

The Compendium teaches an eightfold group by adding the two of fundament[109] consciousness and afflicted mind consciousness to the previous six. However, no more will be said here because extensive presentations of those two will be given below in the context of the four summaries of the Great Vehicle.

---

[105](...continued)
times used as an abbreviation of the word for consciousness "rnam par shes pa" and sometimes used simply to indicate an awareness in general as is being done here. One has to watch the context in order to know which of the two meanings is intended.

[106] ... which is one of the mental events defined earlier ...

[107] ... of attaining enlightenment ...

[108] ... for truly complete enlightenment, that is, the enlightenment mind, for the very first time.

[109] For fundament, see the glossary.

2. Igniters

Now, the second topic in which one is to become expert consists of a presentation of the igniters.

The etymological definition of āyatana is that it provides the doorway to the birth and flaring of consciousness; therefore it is called "igniter".[110]

Igniters are divided into the six outer igniters and six inner igniters.

2.1. *Outer Igniters*

The visual form igniter is the same in meaning as the object of eye consciousness, the visual forms of colour and shape. The sound igniter is the same in meaning as the object of ear consciousness, sounds with and without knowing. The smell igniter is the same in meaning as the object of smell consciousness, smells both unified and mixed. The taste igniter is the same in meaning as the object of tongue consciousness, the tastes of sweet, and so on. The touch igniter is the same in meaning as the object of body consciousness, the touches of elements and what arises from the elements. The dharma igniter is the same in meaning as the objects of mental consciousness, the dharmas.

Moreover, *The Treasury* says:

> Those three, together with the non-revelatory and{26}
> Not compounded ones,
> Are called "the dharma igniter dhātu".

According to that, the three of feelings, perceptions, and formatives,

---

[110] See *About Key Terms* in the introduction for an explanation of āyatana.

non-revelatory forms, space and the two cessations, altogether seven, are called "dharma igniter" and "dharma dhātu"[111].

2.2. Inner Igniters

Eye igniter means the same as the eye faculty. Ear igniter is the same as the ear faculty. Nose igniter is the same as the nose faculty. Tongue igniter is the same as the tongue faculty. Body igniter is the same as the body faculty. Mental igniter is the same as the sixfold group which is contained by the consciousness aggregate, together with the mental faculty.

When these are enlarged on, there is a presentation of the twenty-two faculties: the eye faculty, ear faculty, nose faculty, tongue faculty, body faculty, mental faculty, male faculty, female faculty, unsatisfactoriness faculty, good faculty, good mind faculty, not good mind faculty, neutral faculty, faith faculty, perseverance faculty, mindfulness faculty, samādhi faculty, prajñā faculty, faculty that causes total knowing, faculty of total knowing, faculty having total knowing, and life faculty.

The five faculties from eye to body having form have already been explained above. **Mental faculty**{27} is the extremely subtle absence of thought which occurs immediately the sixth consciousness passes[112]. The **male faculty** is comparable to a thumb. The **female faculty** is comparable to the cavity of a drum. The **unsatisfactoriness faculty** is the experiencing of unhappy body together with its consciousness and faculty whereas **good faculty** is the experiencing of being happy in that. **Good mind faculty** is the experiencing of joy in the mental consciousness. **Not good mind faculty** is that

---

[111] See *About Key Terms* in the introduction for an explanation of dhātu and dharmadhātu. "Dhātu" here means element or basic constituent, not basic zone.

[112] ... it is the faculty for the production of the next moment of mind.

suffering has arisen in regard to that. **Neutral faculty** is there has been no production at all of either happiness or unsatisfactoriness in both body and mind. **Faith faculty** is trust in and admiration[113] for the existence and good qualities of karma and its fruit and the truths and the Jewels. **Perseverance faculty** is not allowing there to be an interruption to listening, contemplating, meditating, and so on—the side of virtue. **Mindfulness faculty** is not forgetting even for an æon the words and meanings to which one has listened and heard. **Samādhi faculty** is not falling away from mind abiding one-pointedly on the object of meditation. **Prajna faculty** is unmistaken knowledge of the self and general characteristics of dharmas. **Faculty that causes total knowing** is that, at the time of abandoning what is to be abandoned on the path of seeing, if the set of nine consisting of the five from faith to prajñā and happy, happy mind, neutral, and mental faculties are used to totally abandon what is to be abandoned on the path of seeing,{28} then what was previously not known is made totally known. **The faculty of total knowing** is that at the time the afflictions which are to be abandoned by meditation have been abandoned, the things which are not conducive to that set of nine faculties have had their specific antidotes provided. **The faculty having total knowing** is that at the time of obtaining arhathood, those faculties altogether have caused the knowledge of the abandonment and ending of every single one of the afflictions of the three realms and cause the wisdom of unborn awareness to become manifest. **Life faculty** is that which holds the life and life force for as long as one has not died.

Additionally, those when summed up are five: mind's basis, discursively thinking about that, total affliction, complete purification's assemblage[114], and complete purification. In that, the six from eye

---

[113] … these are the first two kinds of faith in the threefold classification of faith.

[114] Assemblage here is an ancient Indian way of talking which means (continued...)

to mental faculty and the life faculty are mind's support. Man and woman are discursive thinking about that, so there is its production; another person knows "It is a woman". Good and good mind ones create desire; unsatisfactoriness and not good mind ones create anger; and the neutral ones create delusion, all of which is on the side of total affliction. The five of faith and so on, being the cause of nirvāṇa, are on the side of complete purification. The three total knowledges are complete purification.

3. Dhatus

Now, for the third topic in which one is to become expert, the dhātus.

The etymological definition of dhātu is a class of things which become the source of something else[115]{29}, therefore, they are called dhātu.

They are divided into: six dhātus of outer objects, six dhātus of inner faculties, and six dhātus of intervening consciousness, making eighteen.

Form dhātu and visual form which are that which becomes the eye's domain are the same in meaning. Sound dhātu and sound become ear's domain are the same in meaning. Smell dhātu and smell become the nose's domain are the same in meaning. Taste dhātu and taste become the tongue's domain are the same in meaning.

---

[114](...continued)
"the needs or requisites for something assembled".

[115] This is a slightly rough definition. According to the Buddha, the āyatanas are like sources, being the sources of consciousness, and the dhātus are like the elements or basic constituents of the whole process of samsaric perception.

Touch dhātu and touch become the body's domain are the same in meaning. Dharma dhātu and dharmas become the domain of mental mind are the same in meaning.

And, eye dhātu and eye faculty are the same in meaning. Ear dhātu and ear faculty are the same in meaning. Nose dhātu and nose faculty are the same in meaning. Tongue dhātu and tongue faculty are the same in meaning. Body dhātu and body faculty are the same in meaning. Mental mind dhātu and mental mind faculty are the same in meaning.

And, eye consciousness dhātu and eye consciousness are the same in meaning. Ear consciousness dhātu and ear consciousness are the same in meaning. Nose consciousness dhātu and nose consciousness are the same in meaning. Tongue consciousness dhātu and tongue consciousness are the same in meaning. Body consciousness dhātu and body consciousness are the same in meaning. Mental mind consciousness dhātu and mental mind consciousness are the same in meaning.{30}

That set of eighteen dhātus also can be summarized according to whether they can be shown or not, in which case the ones that can be show to the eye are the form dhātu alone and the ones that can not be shown to the eye are the rest.

If summarized according to whether or not they have impedance, the set of ten dhātus which are included within form aggregate have impedance, and the other eight do not have impedance. The meaning of having impedance is that it gets in the way, preventing further movement. There are three types of impedance: impedance in relation to obscuration, impedance in relation to object, and impedance in relation to reference. 1) This is being an obstructor in its own place of something produced in another, as in a hand impeding a stick[116]. 2) The eye and so on are impeded in relation to the object, as in when one object is seen, others are obscured. 3) Minds and mental events themselves impede in relation to their reference, as in not being able to reference all objects at one time.

Of those, these should be known as ones which cause impedance in relation to obscuration. Moreover, these are summed up within the three of virtuous, non-virtuous, and indeterminate as follows. For the indeterminate case, the five faculties and the three dhātus of smell, taste, and touch, make eight. The other ten are viewed as existing as all three of virtuous, and so on. And, for the seven mind dhātus, the ones having equivalence with non-attachment and so on, are virtuous, the ones having equivalence with attachment and so on, are non-virtuous, and the others are indeterminate. For dharma dhātu[117],{31} the ones having equivalence with an essential nature of non-attachment and so on, and those of motivated occurrence[118], and the ones of analytical cessation are virtuous. The ones having equivalence with an essential nature of attachment and so on, and the ones that are motivated occurrences are non-virtuous. The others are indeterminate.

Visual form and sound dhātus included in the revelatory forms of body and speech which have been motivated by virtuous and non-virtuous minds, are virtuous and non-virtuous, and otherwise indeterminate.

---

[116] In English, we would say that the hand holds a stick, though the meaning is that, in holding the stick, it is preventing it from going elsewhere; it is obstructed or impeded in such a way as to be held in the hand. This then provides the explanation of why the Tibetan word being used here "thogs", which actually means to impede or to hold up, is also used to mean "to hold" in the hand.

[117] The meaning here is the dharmas' element.

[118] Motivated occurrences were explained in an earlier note. They are body and speech which result from an earlier motivation.

The need for the threefold ascertainment of aggregates, and so on[119] is, as *The Treasury* says:

> Because of the three of misunderstanding, faculty, and
> desire,
> The three of aggregates, and so on, were taught.

In other words, the three—the aggregates, and so on—have been taught in order to overcome three types of misunderstanding—that of one faction which says they are held within mental events, that of some others who say that they are held within form, and that of yet others who say that they are held within both form and mind—and in order to accommodate the three degrees of faculty—sharp, middle and dull—and in order to comply with the needs of those who like fewer, more, and many words.

Thus, all knowable dharmas are incorporated within the three of the form aggregate, the mental mind igniter, and the dharma dhātu[120].

4. Interdependent Origination

Now, for the fourth topic in which one is to become expert, interdependent origination[121].

The etymological definition as the Buddha taught it[122] is:

---

[119] … that is, the aggregates, igniters, and dhātus.

[120] … meaning dharmas' element.

[121] The very clear explanation of the twelve links found in Tsongkhapa's *Great Stages of the Path*, which will be invaluable in understanding this fourth section, is available in a free publication on the PKTC web-site.

[122] … in sūtra …

> Dependent on something, something originates, so there is dependent origination; this existing, this originates, this having been produced, this is produced.

It has two divisions:{32} the interdependencies of the sides of total affliction and complete purification.

4.1. *Interdependent Origination of the Side of Total Affliction*

This consists of both external interdependent origination and internal interdependent origination.

4.1.1. External interdependent origination

This consists of being in relation to cause and relation to conditions.

4.1.1.1. *In relation to cause*

> Seeds give rise to sprouts,
> Sprouts given rise to leaves,
> Leaves give rise to stalks,
> Stalks give rise to trunks,
> Trunks give rise to sap,
> Sap gives rise to flowers,
> Flowers give rise to seeds.[123]

4.1.1.2. *In relation to conditions*

This is the external earth element, water element, fire element, wind element, space element, and time element, making six.

4.1.2. Internal interdependency

This consists of being in relation to cause and in relation to conditions.

---

[123] This is a quote from a sūtra.

4.1.2.1 In relation to cause

> It is like this: due to the condition of ignorance, there is formative; due to the condition of formative, there is consciousness; due to the condition of consciousness, there is name and form[124]; due to the condition of name and form, there is igniter; due to the condition of igniter, there is contact; due to the condition of contact, there is feeling; due to the condition of feeling, there is craving; due to the condition of craving, there is appropriation[125]; due to the condition of appropriation, there is becoming; due to the condition of becoming, there is birth; due to the condition of birth, there is old age and death, misery, lamenting, suffering, unhappiness, and upset—in this way the great aggregates of unsatisfactoriness are fully produced.[126]

They are identified as follows. *The Treasury* says:

> Ignorance and affliction are a previous situation.
> The formatives are of previous karma.{33}
> Consciousness is the aggregates at conception.
> Name and form are from that point forwards.
> The six igniters standing for that are what comes next.
> Contact goes up as far as having the ability

---

[124] The Buddha defined name as the four aggregates without form and form as the form aggregate.

[125] For appropriation, see the glossary.

[126] This is the Buddha speaking in a Lesser Vehicle sūtra. A very clear explanation of the twelve links which will be invaluable in understanding this can be found in the free publication on the PKTC web-site called *Contemplation by Way of The Twelve Interdependent Arisings An Excerpt From The Great Stages of the Path to Enlightenment By Lord Tsongkhapa.*

To make causal consciousness with pleasant, unpleasant, and so on.
Feeling goes up to sexual union and is followed by craving which is that,
Having become involved with enjoyments
There is appropriation and in order
To gain enjoyments one is completely running.
In relation to that craving, the one that performs the action
Of making the result arise is becoming.
At the point of conception there is birth.
Up through feeling there is old age and death.

In accordance with that, ignorance is some situation of affliction in a previous life. Formative is in some situation of meritorious, and so on, karma in a previous life. Consciousness is the five aggregates occurring at the instant of conception in the mother's womb. Name and form are from the mind of conception onwards for as long as the six igniters have not stood in for them. The igniters, having stood in, go for as long as the three of faculty, object, and consciousness have not assembled. Contact is the assembly of the three; it is a circumstance in which there is not the capacity to thoroughly establish the cause of the three feelings. Feeling goes from being able to engage in the desire of sexual union up to the point immediately before doing so. Craving goes for as long as one has not engaged the object that one is wholly engaged in seeking, whether it be a desirable thing in general or the sexual union of desire{34}. Appropriation is that, having engaged in wholly seeking in order to get the object, whatever its circumstance might be, one is running towards it. Becoming is that, having run after an object like that in order to get it, a later becoming has definitely been established. Birth is that, death and transference from this life that has been karmically produced having occurred, there is connection with the conception of a later birth. Old age and death follows on from birth, which lasts for as long as there is feeling. In this life there are the four of name and form, igniter, contact, and feeling, and in another life there is birth and death.

Followers of the Great Vehicle have a different way of identifying these. For them, ignorance is having become obscured to seeing the nature of karma and karmic result, truth, the Jewels, and dharmas; that is to say, the stupidity of not knowing. Formatives are that which causes the formation of the various types of karma—virtuous, non-virtuous, and indeterminate—in the three realms. Consciousness is individually knowing and being aware of the differing objects of forms, and so on. Name and form are the four name aggregates and the form aggregate which have a developmental sequence of quivering mass, and so on[127], so are a like row of temporary housings. Igniters are like a door for the production of mind and mental events, being the six faculties of eye, and so on. Contact is the assembling of the three: object, faculty, and consciousness. Feeling is that those three having assembled, there is experiencing of the three of good, unsatisfactory, and neutral.{35} Craving is wanting to be free of unsatisfactory feelings such as those of suffering due to thirst and wanting to connect with good ones. Appropriation is desire appropriation, views appropriation, discipline and yogic acts appropriation, and advocating self appropriation. Becoming is that the cause of being born into the three realms, the latencies of karma and affliction, have grown in strength to the point that they will produce a later life. Birth is that one now has a new body, such as that of god, man, etcetera, which one did not have previously. Old age is to become white haired and wrinkled. Death is that the time of staying in the bodily corpse having reached its end, warmth and consciousness leave, then it falls apart. The misery which becomes part of the link of old age and death is the suffering that comes with the anxieties over becoming separated from relatives, friends, possessions, and so on. Lamenting is to tell the story in words of one's misery and how it has come about. Unsatisfactoriness is that the

---

[127] "Quivering mass, and so on" refers to the sequence of developmental forms defined for a human embryo in Indian and Tibetan medicine. At the beginning, when consciousness has entered conjoined sperm and egg, there is a jelly-like quivering mass. That evolves into "an elongate shape", and so on.

body is degenerating and not happy. Unhappy mind is that mind has degenerated and is not happy. Upset is that, having full memory of the various bad things that one has done previously, the mind is filled with dread.

> How many lives will it be completed in?
> That involves twelve limbs of interdependent
> origination
> In three parts.

And,

> Two of two former (ignorance and formatives) and later
> (birth and old age and death) limits[128]
> With eight in between{36} is a completion.

That teaches total completion in three lives.

It is also taught in the Great Vehicle that there is completion in two lives which has to be understood as six causes (three afflictions and three karmas) and six results (the rest included up to birth). If the links are summarized within total affliction, the three that are the particular ignorance, craving, and appropriating involved are included in the affliction aspect of total affliction. The particular formatives, consciousness, and becoming involved are included in the karma aspect of total affliction. The remainder, name and form, igniter, contact, feeling, birth, and old age and death are included in the birth aspect of total affliction. Why is the consciousness in that included in the karma aspect of total affliction? The master

---

[128] A limit in Sanskrit refers to several things, including a life. This is saying that the shortest time for the completion of a set of links is three lives: two links in a former life, followed by two links in a later life, with eight in a life between the two, making twelve links in three lives in total. Note that vast numbers of lives which are not part of that particular set of links can also be in between the three lives involved.

Conquerors' Son Infinitely[129] taught, "It is because it has been categorized as a latency of the formatives."

Furthermore, the set of twelve links of interdependency is contained within a set of five meanings. Ignorance acts as the field for becoming. Both formatives and becoming act as the farmer. Consciousness acts as the seed.{37} Both craving and appropriation act as the rain. The rest, the six of name and form, and so on, act as the ripeners of the sprout.

4.1.2.2 *In relation to condition*

These are the internal earth element, water element, fire element, wind element, space element, and consciousness element, making six.

4.2 *Interdependent Origination of the Side of Complete Purification*

Interdependency of the side of complete purification has the two divisions of interdependency of path and interdependency of fruition.

4.2.1 Interdependency of path

Examination of where old age and death arose from leads to its having arisen from birth, then, examination of where formatives arose from leads to their having arisen from ignorance. When this forward sequence of interdependency is comprehended, prajñā which realizes absence of self uproots the ignorance which has become the root of becoming. Thereby, ignorance ceases, causing the formatives to cease, causing birth to cease, causing old age and death to cease, and so on, so the matter has then been determined

---

[129] This refers to Zhanphen Thaye who was most commonly called Gyalsay Zhanphen Thaye or Conquerors' Son Who Benefits Others Infinitely.

through the mode of the reverse order of interdependency. In that way, the primary path truth which has become the actual antidote to ignorance is prajñā without outflows; *The Complete Commentary* says:

> Loving kindness and so on, because they do not directly oppose stupidity,
> Do not entirely eliminate badness.
> Because the view of emptiness is its direct opposite,
> It utterly opposes
> All badness arising from that.

Its[130] basis is the training[131] of samādhi; without it there might be vipaśhyanā but, as with a lamp in wind, it will not remain steady.{38} Its basis in turn is the higher training of discipline; without it, there will be clinging and attachment to desirables resulting in there being no chance for the accomplishment of śhamatha[132]. Because of that, the path is included within the three higher trainings, nevertheless, master Vasubandhu pointed out that:

> The one abiding in discipline who has hearing and contemplation,
> Will utterly join with meditation[133].

---

[130] … meaning the prajñā's …

[131] … meaning the higher training …

[132] For śhamatha see the glossary.

[133] Theoretically speaking, the path to be followed is included in the three higher trainings, but, practically speaking, a person takes up discipline, develops the samādhi that goes with hearing and contemplation, and then gets on with doing nothing but the meditation which will develop the prajñā without outflows needed to reverse the twelve links of interdependency.

4.2.2. Interdependency of fruition

The path is used to abandon the entirety of the things to be abandoned on the paths of seeing and meditation. Having done so, the ultimate fruition has been manifested and then the deeds of permanence, pervasiveness, and spontaneous existence are equal to the dharmadhātu[134].

The explanation which up to here has been of the four doors of seeing the truth is now finished.

5 and 6. Topics and Non-Topics

Now, there will be the presentations of the fifth and sixth topics in which one is to become expert, topics and non-topics respectively. Expertise in the topics and non-topics of the śhrāvaka level is classed as being expert in certain details of interdependent origination. Specifically, expertise in topics and non-topics of the "this exists" type brings knowledge of different causes[135], and with that, the

---

[134] Deeds of permanence, pervasiveness, and spontaneous existence are the deeds of an actual buddha with permanent and pervasive dharmakāya and form kāyas of spontaneous existence. Dharmadhātu here refers to the basic zone of dharmas, not to the dharma element of the eighteen dhātus. Since this dharmadhātu is the space encompassing all dharmas, this is saying that a buddha's activity will encompass everything that there is.

[135] When the Buddha taught the Lesser Vehicle to the śhrāvakas and pratyekabuddhas, he taught that a personal self did not exist but he also taught that all phenomena do exist, as part of his skilful means for gradually bringing his disciples along the path. "This exists" here is in reference to this type of teaching. Because phenomena are considered to exist in this kind of teaching, causes and effects become important and are taught extensively at this level. Therefore, this level of teaching is advantageous for learning about cause and effect.

results of the full-ripening of virtuous and non-virtuous karmas. Now, as has been said[136]:

> We desire the result of the full ripening of virtuous karmas. We do not desire the result of the full ripening of non-virtuous karmas.

That being so, for this there is a synopsis of the presentation of karmic cause and effect, and{39} a detailed explanation of the presentation of the four truths.

5-6.1. *Synopsis of the Presentation of Karmic Cause and Effect*

5-6.1.1. General Presentation

In general, karma consists of body karma, speech karma, and mind karma. Alternatively, it consists of meritorious karma, non-meritorious karma, and unfluctuating karma. Alternatively again, there are the three of virtuous karma, non-virtuous karma, and indeterminate karma.

5-6.1.1.1. Virtuous karma

For virtuous karma, there are the four of: that which is consistent with merit (what causes one to actually obtain the upper realms, like the ten virtues); that which is consistent with emancipation (the path of accumulation of the three vehicles); that which is consistent with the factor of definite opening (the path of connection of the three vehicles); and virtue without outflows (which goes from the path of seeing of the three vehicles). Alternatively, there are the four of: essential nature virtue (the eleven virtuous mental events); equivalence virtue (like the faith and so on of the omnipresent retinue);

---

[136] ... by the Buddha ...

motivated virtue (the actions of body and speech created by faith, and so on); and superfactual virtue (nirvāṇa)[137].

5-6.1.1.2. Non-virtuous karma

For non-virtuous karma, there are the four of: essential nature non-virtue (the root and proximate afflictions); equivalence non-virtue (like their retinue, the omnipresent mental events); motivated non-virtue (the actions of body and speech created by affliction); and superfactual non-virtue (saṃsāra in its entirety).

5-6.1.1.3. Indeterminate karma

For indeterminate karma, there are the four of the minds of the full ripened birth, actor, artisan, and manifestation[138].

5-6.1.2. Detailed Presentation

This has the three parts of detailed presentations of cause, condition,{40} and result.

5-6.1.2.1. Cause

There are six causes: the operative cause, the co-occurring cause, the having equivalence cause, the same lot cause, the omnipresent cause, and the full-ripening cause. The **operative cause** is that any dharma whatever it might be has no obstruction made to its production. For example, if no obstruction has been made by something else to the production of a sprout, then, because there has been no obstructing of it, it is given the name "operative cause". Because in the production of such as a sprout, there is the presence within one thing of all four of earth, water, fire, and wind complete, it is de

---

[137] For superfact, see the glossary.

[138] These are the four ways that the supreme nirmāṇakāya of a world-leading buddha manifests.

another, which is the **co-occurring cause**. Because each mind and mental event is not capable of holding an object on its own, it is dependent occurrence where there is mutual dependence of being done by one thing assisted by another, which is called the "**having equivalence cause**". If a virtuous mind has been produced, the mental events also are virtuous, and if a non-virtuous mind has been produced, the mental events also are non-virtuous, which is the **same lot cause**. There having been a production previously in the three realms—desire, form, and formless—there will later be the production of an afflicted dharma, so it is **omnipresent cause**. Virtuous and non-virtuous karmas propel into the upper levels and bad migrations, causing birth in good and bad bodies, which is the **full-ripening cause**.

5-6.1.2.2. Conditions

There are four types of condition: causal condition, governing condition, immediate condition, and referential condition.{41} The fundament consciousness works as a cause and also becomes a condition, therefore, it is a **causal condition**. The five sense faculties of eye and so on, because each functions to govern its own type of consciousness, are the **governing condition**. Immediately the sixth has ceased, that is called "the mental mind consciousness' **immediate condition**". The objects of form, sound, and so on, are the **referential condition**.

5-6.1.2.3. *Fruitions*

The five fruitions are: the result consistent with the cause; the result of the governor; the result which is production of being; the result which is full-ripening; and the result which is separation.

Those who created virtue in the past will want again in this life to create virtue, and those who created non-virtue in the past will want again in this life to create non-virtue, which is the **result consistent with the cause**. Creation of non-virtue in past lives will lead to birth in bad places in this life and the creation of virtue will cause birth in good places; governing places good and bad, it is the **result of the governor.** Like farming fields causes the increase of grain production, there is a steady increase of the results belonging to karma which has been made, which is called "the **result which is production of being**". Generosity causing the acquisition of goods, killing causing a short life, and the like are the **result which is full-ripening**. Cultivation of the noble ones' path abandons the afflictions, which is called the **result which is separation.**{42}

5-6.2. *Detailed Explanation of the Presentation of the Four Truths*

The etymological definition is that the teaching has no discordance[139], therefore it is truth.

There are, as *The Highest Continuum* says, four divisions:

> Just as sickness is to be understood, the cause of sickness
> is to be abandoned, and,
> In order to gain a healthy situation there is reliance on
> medicine,
> So the unsatisfactoriness and its cause, its cessation, and
> likewise its path are
> That to be known, to be abandoned, to be contacted,
> and be relied upon.

5-6.2.1. Truth of unsatisfactoriness

There are four divisions of the truth of unsatisfactoriness: where it ripens, the places of unsatisfactoriness; for whom it ripens, the sentient beings with unsatisfactoriness; what it ripens as, the enumerations of unsatisfactoriness; and the way in which it ripens, the steps of entering suffering.

---

[139] This feature of the dharma teaching is fully explained in *Unending Auspiciousness*.

It has four aspects as follows. Because it is born and dies in each moment, it is impermanent. Because the three and eight unsatisfactorinesses uninterruptedly cause harm, it is unsatisfactoriness. Because there is within the five aggregates no permanent self of the sort thought of by the Tīrthikas, it is empty. Because this set of five aggregates, moreover, is not the self of the sort thought of by the Tīrthikas, it is self-less.

5-6.2.2. Truth of source

There are two divisions of source: source which is karma and source which is affliction.

It has four aspects as follows. The afflictions of desire, and so on, and the virtues and non-virtues created by them turn into causes of becoming, therefore, it is cause. Their latencies in the mind stream, etcetera, are present as seeds{43} which will produce the three realms, so it is source. Virtuous karmas of a later life cause the latencies of virtue to grow and happy fruitions to ripen and non-virtuous ones cause the latencies of non-virtue to grow and unsatisfactory fruitions to ripen, therefore, it is condition. In that way, both causes and conditions are assembled and the latencies individually grow, then the aggregates of unsatisfactoriness are actually produced in the abodes of the higher and lower levels, therefore, it is full production.

5-6.2.3. Truth of cessation

There are two divisions of cessation: individually examined cessation and not individually examined cessation.

It has four aspect as follows. The afflictions of desire, and so on, and the karmas of the evil deeds of killing, and so on, having been abandoned do not re-occur, so it is cessation. The unsatisfactory fruitions produced by karma and afflictions do not ever arise again, therefore, it is peace. Because a place of unchanging definite bliss has been obtained, it is most excellent. Emancipation from the prison-like three realms has been obtained and the bliss of nirvāṇa has been obtained, therefore, it is definite occurrence[140].

5-6.2.4. Truth of the path

There are four divisions of the path: it is the path by which unsatisfactoriness is totally comprehended, the source is abandoned, cessation is made manifest, and the path is cultivated. Alternatively, it can be divided into: the path of accumulation, the path of connection, the path of seeing, the path of meditation, and the path of finalization.

It has four aspects, as follows. It goes from the level of individualized beings{44} to the abode of the noble ones, therefore it is path. It becomes the antidote which abandons ignorance and the afflictions, therefore, it is tenable. Wrong mind having been abandoned, it connects with not-wrong, therefore, it is accomplishment. It causes one to be definitely separated from the badness of saṃsāra and to arrive at the place of nirvāṇa, therefore, it is definite occurrence.

Furthermore, the entities of the dharmas of the four types being correctly determined also includes the path into truth. The four types are: relation type, action type, proving type, and dharmatā type. 1) In production of the eye-consciousness, it is the type of thing which arises in relation to both the eye faculty and object, visual form; others can be connected in a similar way, with sprouts arising in relation to seeds, formatives arising in relation to ignorance, and so on, which is the relation type. 2) That eye-con-

---

[140] Tib. nges par 'byung ba. This is usually translated as renunciation. However, the term itself means that, having understood already that one is in a bad situation, one has gone forward to a solution that is a definite solution and one which definitely happens. The latter part is what the Buddha intended and is the meaning here.

sciousness having arisen, it does the work of viewing form, it does not do the work of listening to sounds. The eye-faculty, moreover, creates eye-consciousness, it does not create another consciousness, such as that of the ear, and so on. All the others can be connected in a similar way, with the seed of barley creating barley and not creating something else such as buckwheat or beans, which is the action type. 3) Proving has three parts: inference is like knowing from smoke that there is fire and knowing from water fowl that{45} there is water; direct perception is the unconfused seeing done with the six consciousnesses and the seeing done with the mind of the yogin; and authoritative statement[141] is the non-deceptive words spoken from the mouth of Buddha—as a sūtra says:

> Authoritative statement is words which are trustworthy
> Because, everything bad having ended,
> There is no cause for false words to be spoken.
> Authoritative statement is to be understood as badness ended.

Those are valid cognizer or proving type. 4) The general and self-characteristics of solid earth, wet water, and so on, and dharmas being empty and without self, and karmic fruition being infallible, which are primordially present like that are the dharmatā[142] type.

Then the reason for referring to these truths as "the truths of the noble ones" is given in a sūtra:

> The placement of a single hair on the hand's palm

---

[141] For authoritative statement, see the glossary.

[142] General and self-characteristics are explained in Followers of Sūtra school teachings. Essentially general characteristics are those in relation to a conception of the thing involved and self-characteristics are those of the object itself, without concept intervening. In short, general and self-characteristics covers all characteristics of everything. These are dharmatā type because dharmatā actually means the quality of any given thing; see dharmatā in the glossary for more.

Will go un-noticed by humans,
Though if it were in the eye, it
Would give them discomfort and harm.
Just so, the childish ones, comparable to the hand's
palm,
Do not notice the hair of formative unsatisfactoriness,
Whereas the experts[143], comparable to the eye,
Have extreme renunciation arising because of it.

In accordance with what it says there, the ones who know the natures of the four truths exactly as they are are the noble ones, therefore, the truths are named using that phrase[144].

Moreover, when summed up, they fall into the two categories of the causes and results of the side of total affliction and the causes and results of the side of complete purification{46}. Alternatively, they fall into the two categories of fictional truth and superfactual truth[145]; it is as a sūtra says:

The Knower of the World[146] did not hear the two truths
From someone else, but knew them for himself.
The world is fiction and likewise superfact—
No third truth is invoked at all.

If they are summarized even further, then, as it says in a sūtra:

---

[143] ... experts meaning the noble ones, the ones who are expert in knowing truth. This is an epithet of the noble sangha. A full explanation of it is contained in *Unending Auspiciousness*.

[144] Although Westerners usually speak of "the four noble truths" in fact, the Buddhist tradition has always understood them according to the Buddha's explanation of them, an example of which is given here, as "the four truths of the noble ones".

[145] For fictional and superfactual, see the glossary.

[146] ... is one of the nine principal epithets of the Buddha taught by the Buddha. A full explanation of it is contained in *Unending Auspiciousness*.

> The unborn is one truth itself
> In regard to which one group states it is "four truths"[147].
> If one has entered the heart of enlightenment[148] and not
> even one truth is established there,
> How could four be seen?

In accordance with that, they are included in the dharmatā superfactual truth[149] alone.

---

[147] That one group is the followers of the Lesser Vehicle.

[148] "The heart of enlightenment" is a standard phrase of the Buddhist tradition meaning "enlightenment itself".

[149] "Dharmatā superfactual truth" means the superfactual truth of reality as it is.

Chapter 2

An Explanation of the Four Dharma Summaries of the Great Vehicle

The explanation of the four dharma summaries of the Great Vehicle is in two parts: overall, how the Great Vehicle is special compared to the Lesser vehicle; and, in detail, an explanation of the Great Vehicle which is special in that way.

1. How the Great Vehicle is Special Compared to the Lesser Vehicle

The Ornament of the Sūtra Section says:

> A greater degree of reference,
> Similarly for the two accomplishings,
> Wisdom, the starting perseverance,
> And become skilled in means,
> And the great accomplishment of limbs,
> And great buddha enlightened activity;
> Because it possesses these greats,
> It is definite that it is to be expressed as "Great Vehicle".

According to that: it references an unfathomably great, vast number of dharmas in the sūtras, and so on; it will accomplish the two purposes of self and others; it is wisdom which realizes the lack of self of dharmas and persons;{47} it starts at the devoted and perpetual perseverances of three countless æons[150]; it has skilful means of not simply abandoning saṃsāra yet being in it without total affliction; it accomplishes the strengths, fearlessness, and eighteen unmixed dharmas[151]; and it again and again totally shows manifest complete enlightenment and the great nirvāṇa. These exist for Great Vehicle followers, not for Lesser Vehicle followers.

2. An Explanation of the Great Vehicle With Those Differences

This has two parts: determining the Great Vehicle through ten meanings, and those summed up into four.

2.1. *Determining it Through Ten Meanings*

The Compendium of the Vehicle says:

> The abode of the knowable, its characteristics, entering them,
> Its causes and results, that utterly divided,
> The three higher trainings, to have abandoned that fruition,
> And wisdom are the vehicle supreme and special.
> This teaching is like this: seeing these which are not seen elsewhere
> Becomes the cause of supreme enlightenment;
> That which the ten topics show up as special[152] is what

---

[150] These two types of perseverance are explained in *The Treasury of Abhidharma.* The point here is that the perseverance involved is not concerned with personal liberation but with the attainment of a truly complete buddha.

[151] ... of a truly complete buddha.

[152] ... or unique or different from all others, including the Lesser Vehicle.

The Great Vehicle is asserted to be in the Buddha
Word.

According to that[153], the abode of the knowable is that place called the fundament[154], which is the cause of the characteristics of the knowable, the three essential natures. The characteristics of the knowable means "the entity of the knowable", that is, its three essential natures. What it is that one will enter those characteristics by is consciousness only. The{48} causes and results of doing that are as follows. The cause is that entering into consciousness only means that the worldly actions of generosity, and so on, will have turned into pāramitā. The fruition is those having become manifest and transcendent over the world. That cause and result fully divided according to meditation is the specifics of the levels of familiarization that the meditation brings, that is, the ten levels. At that time, there is the thorough purification of the higher trainings of discipline and samādhi and prajñā[155]. The non-abiding nirvāṇa which comes from abandoning the śhrāvakas' obscurations through personal self-knowing[156] is to have abandoned its fruition[157]. The

---

[153] This chapter is a statement of the Great Vehicle from the Mind Only perspective based on the presentation found in *The Compendium of the Vehicle*.

[154] Skt. ālaya.

[155] "Thorough purification of the three higher trainings" means that that the three higher trainings each have to be thoroughly perfected through practise. Note that each of the three higher trainings is counted as one of the ten topics.

[156] In personal self-knowing, "self-knowing" refers to wisdom and "personal" refers to the fact that each person has their own wisdom. An extensive explanation of the term can be found in *Unending Auspicious*.

[157] ... the fruition of the three higher trainings.

three kāyas are its fruition, wisdom. In that way the entirety of Great Vehicle is contained within those ten topics.

2.1.1. The abode of the knowable

To begin with, the fundament consciousness, which was spoken of as "the abode of the knowable", is established using authentic statement and reasoning.

2.1.1.1 *Authoritative statement*

The Bhagavat said in the *Abhidharma Sūtra*:

> The beginningless time's dhātu[158]
> Is the place of all dharmas;
> Because it exists, being a migrator and
> Also nirvāṇa will be obtained[159].

And,

> The consciousness having
> Every seed of all dharmas is the fundament;
> Therefore that fundament consciousness
> Is what I explain to the holy ones.

And, it is as stated in the *Unravelling the Intent Sūtra*:{49}

> The receiving consciousness is profound and subtle.
> All seeds descend like a river (all seeds enter it by the instant).
> Declaring that "It would not be suitable to think of it as a self",
> This is something I have not taught to the childish.

In regard to that, moreover, because it is the cause of the place of all faculties being present and because it becomes the place of appropriation of all bodies, it is called "the receiving consciousness".

---

[158] Dhātu here means the basic space which contains something.

[159] Because that space exists, both saṃsāra and nirvāṇa come to exist.

2.1.1.2 *Reasoning*

A Complete Summation of Determinations says:

> Receipt, and initial, clear, and
> Seed, karma, and body feeling, and
> Equilibration in absence of mind, and
> Likewise, death and transference would not be all right.

According to that, if it were the case that there were no fundament consciousness, then a receiving place would not be possible, initial engagement would not be possible, engagement in clearness would not be possible, seeds would not be possible, karma would not be possible, body feelings would not be possible, equilibration of absence of mind would not be possible, and death and transference of consciousness would not be possible. Thus, eight types of fault would accrue.

2.1.1.2.1 First fault

In regard to receiving a body, because of the necessity of a steady stream of full-ripening which has been engaged by prior karma, the fundament consciousness arises due to prior karma. In regard to that then, the six engaging consciousnesses would arise from various conditions of the present{50}; also the six consciousnesses, indeterminately fully ripening, would appear as virtue and non-virtue within a vacuum; also the awarenesses of the six-fold group, because of having arisen from a definite place, would be maintained in their own places, but the remainder would not be so maintained; and where paybacks[160] were occurring, paybacks would not be occurring. Thus there would be fault after fault in relation to the fundament being the receiving place.

2.1.1.2.2 Second fault

[160] … meaning karmic paybacks …

You might ask, "If, according to that, two consciousnesses were to arise as one factor, then at the time of consciousness being present, the fundament would be uninterrupted, wouldn't it?" In the case of such an assertion, the fundament consciousness would only arise together with the other consciousnesses of eye, and so on. If it were not so, assertions of it being viewed by some would be assertions as far as consciousness, in which case it would not be all right for the initial engagement into a consciousness whatever it might be, because there would be none of the particulars of mentation, faculty, and object of the six having become manifest.

2.1.1.2.3 Third fault

The mental consciousness when recollecting an object experienced in the past engages the object in a way which is unclear. For objects of the present moment, engagement of the mental mind simultaneous with the faculty awareness is clear, so, if there were no sudden occurrence in that, then mental consciousness also would not exist as clearness.

2.1.1.2.4 Fourth fault

It would not be all right for a seed of one set of the sixfold group{51} to be one. It is like this: virtuous minds concluded by non-virtuous minds, and non-virtuous minds concluded by virtuous minds, and both concluded by indeterminate ones, and so on, are a mutual discordance, and, the stream of mind having stopped, if it were to be that way for a long period, it would not be all right for it to arise once again.

2.1.1.2.5 Fifth fault

It is like this: the revelatory ones which appear as places, facts, and body, appear as a sudden occurrence, so, if this were to become without simultaneous occurrence, at the first instant of the time of one consciousness, various karmas and so on, would simply be non-existent.

2.1.1.2.6 Sixth fault

Mind doing examination and analysis as it is, or as it is not, or alternatively, mind being settled into equipoise, could be all right, but the occurrence of various feelings of that body would not be all right because the mental consciousness as it should be is mind, and so on, yet if there were no fundament, the cause of the many feelings would not exist.

2.1.1.2.7 Seventh fault

It is like this: at the time of having entered into the equilibrium of absence of perception or cessation, the consciousness involved being separated from a body, there would be death.

2.1.1.2.8 Eighth fault

It is like this: at the time of death and transference there is the disappearance of heat from the upper or lower parts of the body because there is a separation simply from the fundament consciousness which took receipt of a body definite as perpetual rise and fall; it is not that{52} it is separation from non-definite mental consciousness.

2.1.2. The characteristics of the knowable

This has three parts[161].

---

[161] The three characteristics of the knowable are very clearly explained in a book available free from the Padma Karpo Translation Committee web-site called *The Three Characters Of Mind Only School An Explanation by Khenpo Tsultrim Gyatso.*

2.1.2.1. *Total thought*[162]

The Ornament of the Sūtras says:

> Name and meaning is the meaning as it is
> And its appearance as a name which,
> For the reason of being non-authentic thought,
> Has the characteristic of being total thought.

That is saying that names appearing for the meaning as it is and the meaning as it is appearing as names are what non-authentic total thought references.

2.1.2.2. *Other-powered*[163]

From the same source:

> Three superficies and that which has the appearance of
> three superficies,

---

[162] Tib. kun tu brtags pa. This term literally means "nothing but being known through thought". It has also been translated as "all-labelling", "totally conceptualizing", and so on. It is often translated with "the imaginary", which conveys very well the pejorative sense of the term. However, if that is used, it becomes difficult in a text like this to couple the name with the constant references to it being nothing but thought. In all levels of Buddhist teaching it is the general name for the final level of ignorance in the production of samsaric mind. It is the final wall which samsaric mind builds around itself; with it in place, all things are known only through thoughts about those things. In the Mind Only school, it is one of the three characteristics of the knowable, with the same meaning of all that can be known understood only through thinking about it. The term is translated as "total thought" in this book.

[163] Tib. gzhan gyi dbang. This refers to something which is under the control not of itself but something else. Thus it is also referred to as that which is not independent but dependent. Therefore, this term is also translated as "the dependent". The way that it is dependent on, or under the control of, other is that it is interdependent origination.

> The characteristic of grasped and grasping,
> Non-authentic total thought,
> Is the characteristic of being under the control of
> other[164].

The three superficies are: appearing as place, appearing as fact, and appearing as body. Or, the three are: afflicted mind; grasping, the awarenesses of the five doors[165]; and thought, mental consciousness. Of those, the former three have the characteristic of being the grasped at[166] and the latter three have the characteristic of being the grasping.

2.1.2.3. *Wholly-existent*[167]

From the previous source:

> What itself is not existent and existent,
> The equality of existent and not existent,
> Not peace and peace, and no discursive thought
> Is the characteristic of the wholly existent.

The reasons why it is so are, according to that, that in suchness: the dharmas of total thought do not exist, and that non-existence exists; the absence of duality of that existent and non-existent is equality;{53} the adventitious stains are not peace and their essential nature is itself peace and the absence of elaboration is not the domain of discursive thinking.

---

[164] ... dependent.

[165] ... the five senses.

[166] ... the objects side which are grasped at by the subject side, the grasping mind. See grasped-grasping in the glossary.

[167] Tib. yongs grub. This term means that aspect of mind "which really does exist". It has been translated as "thoroughly established" but that is too philosophical and misses the point of the practical meaning which this term embodies.

2.1.3. How that is entered

Who enters is the bodhisatvas. The place where they enter is the level of intentional conduct[168] of the Great Vehicle, the path of seeing, the path of meditation, and the path of finalization. The way they enter is through the creation of the force of virtue, the three types of mind training, abandonment of the four places, and the perseverances of devoted application and perpetual application to the meditation of śhamatha and vipaśhyanā which references dharmas and their meaning.

Of those, the three mind trainings are the following ways of thinking. 1) Thinking "It is the case that unfathomable sentient beings who have become humans within the various world realms are in every moment becoming manifest complete buddhas", one will not shrink from the task. 2) "I have heard the thoughts, whatever they are, through which one fully enacts the pāramitās of generosity, and so on, so I will complete the pāramitās with little difficulty." 3) "It might be a fruition with outflow, but if I obtain the body of my wishes in the higher levels immediately upon death, then why would I, possessing as I do virtue without outflow, not obtain perfections of not-mentating and{54} dharmas?"

Then, the four places to be abandoned are like this. 1) By abandoning mentation[169], there is the non-mentation of the śhrāvaka and pratyekabuddha vehicles. 2) By abandoning doubt and hesitations, there is no doubting the Great Vehicle. 3) By abandoning all overt clinging to dharma, at the time of hearing and contemplating there will be no grasping at I and mine. 4) By abandoning discursive thinking, all of the concept tokens concerned with that which is put before one will not be mentated and will not be discursively thought about.

---

[168] For intentional conduct, see the glossary.

[169] For mentation and non-mentation, see the glossary.

The others are easy to understand.

2.1.4. Showing the causes and results of that

For this, the bodhisattvas have total detachment in regard to possessions, have no downfalls in regard to discipline, have no upset in regard to unsatisfactory occurrences, have no laziness in regard to meditation, do not engage in the causes of distraction, and having developed one-pointedness of mind engage simply in being fully connected to the six pāramitās in which dharmas are utterly distinguished in accordance with how they actually are. The bodhisatva who has entered that has obtained the pure set of six pāramitās held wholly through a pure form of the extra thought[170]. *The Ornament of the Great Vehicle Sūtra Section* says:

> The generosity of the bodhisatvas:
> Was not attached (to possessions), is not attached (postponement), and has no attachment (has satisfied mind),
> And not attachment itself (as a payback) even.
> Was not attached (full ripening){55}, is not attached (avarice and subtle), and has no attachment (distraction).

This provides the capacity to train in the path of the six pāramitās through abandonment of the seven attachments.

2.1.5. The utter division of meditation

The utter division of meditation is the ten levels of the bodhisatvas. To take that further, the *Compendium of the Great Vehicle* says:

---

[170] "Extra thought" is a thought associated with enlightenment mind (see the glossary) in which one is utterly determined to finally attain enlightenment for the sake of sentient beings.

Ignorance in regard to the dharmadhātu[171],
Not that which has affliction, the ten obscurations,
Those not conducive to the ten levels'
Antidotes are the levels.

According to that, when the antidotes to the not conducive side, the ten ignorances, manifest the ten knowables of the dharmadhātu, there are what are called "the levels", which are as follows.

The first level, Utter Joy, is so called because the bodhisatva at the beginning of this level has obtained the ability to accomplish the sakes of himself and others, so is at a place of special joy.

The second, Stainless, is so called because he distances himself from the stains of loose discipline.

The third, Light Maker, is so called because, being a place where there is no degeneration of samādhi and equilibria, it has become a place of great illumination of dharma.

The fourth, Radiant Light, is so called because the dharmas of the side of enlightenment which are like light burn up all stains of the two obscurations.

The fifth, Difficult Training, is so called because, having no degeneration of samādhi and completely ripening sentient beings, but also doing that uninterruptedly, he is perpetually abiding in a place which has that sort of difficult activity.{56}

The sixth, Become Manifest, is so called because he is abiding in knowledge of interdependent origination, so the Prajñāpāramitā has become manifest.

The seventh, Gone Far, is so called because of having arrived at the end of all concept tokens.

---

[171] Dharmadhātu here means the basic space containing all dharmas.

The eighth, Unmoving, is so called because he is not propelled by any of all the concept tokens and manifestation-producing formatives.

The ninth, Good Intellect, is so called because he has the four individual authentic knowledges: of dharmas, of meaning, of etymology of words, and of knowledgeability.

The tenth, Cloud of Dharma, is so called because all doors of dhāraṇī and samādhi have been comprehended and the dharmakāya has been wholly completed.

Moreover, from the standpoint of the three countless great æons[172]: in the first one there will be intentional conduct; in the second one up as far as the beginning of the seventh level will be accomplished; and in the third one, the remaining levels will be done and the path of meditation will be completed.

2.1.6. Higher training of discipline

Those which restrain the bad conduct not-conducive to the vowed disciplines, that is, the vows, are twenty-fold. The way that they have been taught here are the pāramitās of the discipline which gathers virtuous dharmas and the discipline of working for sake of sentient beings in which one makes efforts for the sake of migrators through the four things of magnetizing.

The four things of magnetizing are: giving which brings them in one's circle;{57} explaining the holy dharma to them; entering them into conduct whose meaning is the three higher trainings; and oneself also acting in a way that is consistent with that meaning.

---

[172] The Buddha taught that the sūtra journey to truly complete enlightenment took three countless great æons, with each æon being involved with the levels as shown here.

2.1.7. Higher training of mind[173]

This is to be known through six divisions as follows.

1) The utter division according to reference is referencing only the dharma of the Great Vehicle.

2) The utter division according to variety is as follows. Where one will enter equilibrium will be a samādhi which illuminates the entirety of the Great Vehicle. And, where one enters will be the preservation of an excellent king of samādhis, which sees the tathāgatas of the ten directions in direct perception. And having entered into such, there will be the Going Like a Hero[174], and so on, which are able to defeat all māra hordes.

3) The utter division of antidote is so called because wisdom which references the mixture of all dharmas draws out, in the manner of extracting the leader of the leaders, all of the bad things taken on which obscure the fundament consciousness.

4) The utter division according to workability is so called because, due to having totally captured birth in whichever places one wishes via good dhyānas, samādhi provides workabilility.

5) The utter division according to making manifest is that the good qualities of samādhi have resulted in the creation of awareness in which something is made manifest[175] which is without obstruction to fathomless world realms.

In regard to that, the transformations of moving, and so on{58}, occur because of making movement, making blazing, making

---

[173] Higher training of mind is another name for higher training of samādhi.

[174] These are four samādhis of a Buddha.

[175] Awareness in which something is made manifest refers to the five extrasensory perceptions taught in Buddhism.

pervasive, showing, the making of transformation into others' things, going, coming, retracting, expanding, setting out all the form bodies, going via same lot, making illumination and also making non-illumination, making control over, making utterly setting out others' miracles, knowledgability, mindfulness, giving happiness, manifestly accomplishing the great miracle of giving off light, and manifestly accomplishing the ten types of hardship in which all hardships are contained.

The ten types of hardship are like this: 1) proclaimed hardships are so called because they are the proclaiming of prayers made for great enlightenment; 2) the hardship of not turning back is so called because one is not turned back by the sufferings of saṃsāra; 3) the hardship of not changing direction is that one does not change one's direction on account of sentient being's efforts to turn one aside; 4) the hardship of manifest direction is so called because of manifest direction towards activities done for all sakes of sentient beings who create harm; 5) the hardship of not being cloaked is so called because although one is born in the world, one is not cloaked by the dharmas of the world; 6) the hardship of aspiration is so called because one aspires to the absence of thoughts{59} or the vastness and the profundity of the Great Vehicle; 7) the hardship of thought is so called because of the realizing of non-self in persons and phenomena; 8) the hardship of totally taking into the mind is so called because of totally taking into one's mind the profundity that the tathāgatas have understood then expressed in their speech; 9) the hardship of being, without distinction, without total affliction, is so called because in it saṃsāra has not been simply rejected yet there is no total affliction through having done so; 10) the hardship of connection is so called because the buddhas who are seated in complete liberation from all obscurations spontaneously, through to the limit of cyclic existence, connect to the enactments of all sakes of sentient beings.

6) The utter division through activity is that, because pāramitā is to be cultivated, and sentient beings are to be wholly ripened, and a

buddha-field is to be wholly purified, and all buddha dharmas are to be thoroughly accomplished, the samādhis of bodhisatvas are viewed as the utter division through activity.

2.1.8. Higher training of prajna

In the higher training of prajñā, non-discursively-thinking wisdom is the actual prajñā, so the unmistaken methods for accomplishing it are taking into one's being the meaning found in the Great Vehicle sūtras. It is necessary to determine those at this point, so, according to the *Ornament of the Sūtra Section of the Great Vehicle*,

> Covert intent regarding what is to be entered,
> Covert intent regarding characteristics{60},
> Covert intent regarding the antidote, and
> Covert intent regarding a change.

it is to be understood that the covert intents[176] in the Buddha's speech are fourfold. The bases of the intents and needs for them are as follows. The same source says:

> Śhrāvakas, essential nature, and
> Likewise taming badness
> And profundity of expression,
> Are the four covert intents.

1) According to that, for the purpose of entering the śhrāvakas into the teaching of the Great Vehicle, form, and so on were taught to be existent so as not to scare them, which is the covert intent regarding what is to be entered. 2) With the intent that in total thought the characteristic has no essential nature, that in the other-powered the production has no essential nature, and that in the wholly-existent the superfactual has no essential nature, the Buddha's teaching that all dharmas have no essential nature, are unborn, and so on is covert intent regarding characteristics. 3) His teaching the Great Vehicle as the antidote to the eight obscurations is the

---

[176] For intent, see the glossary.

covert intent regarding the antidote, which is as follows. It is like for an antidote to the obscurations which get in the way of buddhahood, his saying, "I myself at that time completely saw truly complete buddhahood." It is like for an antidote to the obscurations - which get in the way of dharma, his saying, "If one has respected and honoured the buddhas who are equal in number to the sands of the Ganges, then a realization of the primal Great Vehicle will now be produced." It is like for an antidote to the obscuration of laziness, his saying, "Merely saying out loud the name of the tathāgata Chandraprabhavimala, will certainly result in unsurpassed enlightenment."{61} It is like for an antidote to the obscuration of grasping at being satisfied with only something small, the Bhagavat condemned some for being generous, and so on, yet praised others. It is like for an antidote to the obscuration of acting out desire, the Bhagavat praised the wealth of buddha-fields and connections with them. It is like for an antidote to the obscuration of acting out pride the Bhagavat highly praised the perfections of some buddhas. It is like for an antidote to the obscuration of regret, his saying, "Those who harm the buddhas and bodhisatvas will go to[177] the higher levels." It is like for an antidote to the obscuration of the uncertain family which reverts to the Lesser Vehicle, he gave the great śhrāvakas a prophecy for buddhahood and taught them one ultimate vehicle. 4) The Buddha's speech which relates to profound expressions is the covert intent regarding change. It is like this: it was said in the sūtra section,

> If he were to kill father and mother, and
> Both the king and those of ritual purity, and
> The people of the country together with their circles,
> That person would be pure.

which refers to the two parents, father and mother, who created the body, and the king who protects, and the brahman priests who have the practices of ritual purity, and the people of the country together with their circles of horses, bulls, camels, and so on{62}. These,

---

[177] ... be born in.

changed into the meaning "the authentic" are to be understood, in order, in this way: the two of craving and appropriation, the view of holding as supreme, holding disciplines and yogic acts as supreme, and the six igniters together with their objects. Moreover:

> Not trusting, and not remembering a past deed,
> Breaking into someone's home,
> Bringing someone down, and eating vomit;
> That is a supreme being.

which refers to not trusting in the existence of a next birth, not remembering a kindly deed done in the past, being a thief who breaks into a home, telling lies to bring someone down, and eating vomit like a dog would do. These changed into the meaning "supreme", referring to an arhat, are to be seen, in order, as follows: having sight of the wisdom of complete liberation, he trusts in himself; he knows non-composite nirvāṇa; he has abandoned the causes of appropriation which make for further becoming; he does not cause suffering for any migrator; and in terms of seen dharmas[178], he has taken a body which can be used, but has no hankering after life and possessions. Moreover:

> Who knows absence of essence as essence,
> Strongly abides in perversion,
> And whose affliction occurs as utter total affliction,
> Will attain holiness.

That also has to be taken like this. Essence is complete distracted mind. Absence of that is understood to be the essence.{63} Perversion is purity, happiness, self, and permanence, the reverse of all of which is abiding in impurity, suffering, absence of self, and impermance. Afflictions cause the suffering of weariness because of long-term engagement in what is difficult. That and the rest of it is unfathomably deep.

---

[178] "Seen dharmas" means the things which have karmically manifested in this life.

Now, in regard to those four types of intent, the earlier source says:

> Equality, other meaning, and
> Similarly other time, and
> Persons' thoughts
> Are to be known as four types of intent.

Of the four given that way, 1) the intent in regard to equality is, as in "I myself at that time completely saw truly complete buddhahood", the intent[179] of dharmakaya equality. 2) Intent in regard to other meaning is, as in "all dharmas have no essential nature, are unborn", that the words are not exactly the same as the fact of it. 3) As for the intent in regard to other time, this comes due to the intent that saying aloud the name of tathāgata Chandraprabhavimala means definitely having enlightenment, though it will be a long time ahead. 4) Intent in regard to persons' thoughts comes due to the intent of praising some for things like generosity while condemning others for being satisfied with small things, which was done to reverse grasping at supreme[180].

Those are the cause of no-thought wisdom. Actual no thought is, according to *The Compendium of the Vehicle* like this:{64}

> The awareness of bodhisatvas
> Is referencing without discursive thought:
> It is the inexpressibility of dharmas (it is this way because expressions are total thought),
> Non-self, suchness ... (those are its enumerations)

---

[179] ... here meaning "the understanding had by" ...

[180] "Grasping at supreme" is one of the five wrong views, views which are mentioned in several places in the text. This wrong view is "grasping at the wrong view which sees wrong religious practices as supreme or true religious practices".

2.1.9. The particulars of abandoning

The bodhisatvas' abandoning is that they do not abide in the extremes of saṃsāra and nirvāṇa in the way that worldly ones and śhrāvakas do, therefore, they have "non-dwelling nirvāṇa". With this, they wholly engage the places of total affliction but, driven by compassion and using the other-powered, their power of working for the sake of migrators for as long as saṃsāra is not emptied means that they are without its experiences.

2.1.10. The particulars of wisdom

The particulars of the wisdom are the particulars of the svabhāvakikāya, the saṃbhogakāya, and nirmāṇakāya. The svabhāvakikāya is the dharmakāya of the tathāgatas, being the place of all of the good qualities of the buddha level. The saṃbhogakāya is the kāya which has for its use the dharmas of the Great Vehicle; working for the sake of the bodhisatvas dwelling on the levels, it is considered to arise in dependence on the dharmakāya. The nirmāṇakāya is that it, which depends on the dharmakāya, having stayed in the abode of Tuṣhita, then shows the acts of complete enlightenment; as *The Highest Continuum* says:{65}

> The deeds of transference from the Tuṣhita abode,
> Entering the womb, being born,
> Expertise in the ways of artisans,
> Enjoying a retinue of queens,
> Renunciation, asceticism,
> Going to the heart of enlightenment,
> Defeating the armies of māra, complete
> Enlightenment, turning the wheel of dharma,
> And going to nirvāṇa are shown
> In fields totally without impurity
> For as long as becoming remains.

2.2. Those Summed up into Four

According to *Descent into Laṅka* there are four:

> The five dharmas, three natures,
> And the set of eight consciousnesses, those and
> The two absences of self—in these things
> All of the Great Vehicle is summed up.

2.2.1. The Five Dharmas

The five dharmas are: name, concept token, discursive thinking, suchness, and no-discursive-thinking wisdom. 1) It does not appear in the domain of consciousness and is inexpressible but, because it is designated and illustrated by a name, it is name[181]. 2) The seven consciousnesses and the fundament consciousness being present in the mode of mutual cause and effect is concept token. 3) There is relation to the self- and generally-characterized dharmas of the eight consciousnesses, therefore, it is discursive thinking. 4) All dharmas are not substantially existent, so they are suchness. 5) The unperverted wholly-existent wisdom is{66} the no-discursive-thinking wisdom.[182]

---

[181] We use the conventions of conceptual names and verbal labels out of necessity. If we did not use conventions to represent actual things, we would not be able to talk about them or study the dharma.

[182] First we agree on a name, then we produce concept tokens to have concepts about the thing we have named, then we think about the thing. All the dharmas thought about are in fact suchness. Wisdom, which is the wholly-existent character, knows that suchness.

2.2.2. The Three Natures

The three natures have already been extensively shown above, so are given here in brief. It is as *The Treatise Differentiating the Middle and Extremes* says:

> Non-authentic total thought (mind and mental events of three realms included in the other-powered) exists.
> The duality of two (grasped-grasping) in it does not exist.
> Empti(wholly-existent)ness(the base of emptiness, other-powered) exists in this.
> In that (emptiness) also that (base of emptiness) exists.

2.2.3. The Eight Consciousnesses

The six engaging consciousnesses from eye up to mental consciousness stated earlier and the fundament consciousness and the afflicted mental consciousness make eight.

For the fundament, *The Thirty Verses* says:

> Of them, the fundament consciousness
> Is not obscured by all of the seeds
> Of full-ripening, is indeterminate.
> Contact, and so on, also are like that.

According to that, it is the basis infected with all the latencies of full-ripening's consciousnesses, an indeterminate entity, one which has equivalence with the retinue of omnipresent ones. Also:

> Nature, characteristic, reference, superfice, retinue,
> Engagement mode, time of reversal,
> Divisions, enumerations, terms explained, and meaning
> To be known through the pure valid cognizers.

According to that, its nature is indeterminate, its characteristic is that it appears as the variety, its reference is the vast containers and contents[183]{67}, its superfice is non-distinction by the dividing line of object, and its retinue is that it is together with the five omnipresent ones. For its engagement mode, there is which mindstream it is engaged in: generally it is engaged in the mind stream of every sentient being; and in particular it is engaged as far as the śhrāvakas and the pratyekabuddhas not having gone into the nirvāṇa without remainder of the aggregates and is engaged in bodhisatvas up to the end of the line. For which consciousnesses it simultaneously engages with: in the contexts of absence of perception, its equilibrium, heavy sleep, and fainting, it is with the afflicted mentality alone. In the formless case, it is together with the afflicted mentality and mental consciousness both. In the form case, there is no nose and tongue consciousness, so it is together with the other five. In the desire case, because the seven-fold group exists, there is engagement together with those, though in the case of cessation equilibrium it engages with another, matchless mind. At the time of turning away, there is the turning away of śhrāvakas and pratyekas into nirvāṇa without remainder and the turning away of bodhisatvas into manifest buddhahood. There are two divisions: the factor of seed and the factor of full ripening. Enumeration of names: it is known as "receiving consciousness", "all seeds consciousness", "fundament consciousness", and "full-ripening's consciousness". The terms explained are:{68} it is called "receiving consciousness" because it becomes the cause of taking a body again and again; it is called "all seeds consciousness" because it becomes the base of all latencies; it is called "fundament consciousness" because, under the influence of the pure and impure, all of nirvāṇa and saṃsāra occur due to it; and it is called "full-ripening's consciousness" because of having arisen from previous karmas. The faults of there being no fundament, and so on, can also be established through pure valid cognizers which make logical proofs.

---

[183] For containers and contents, see the glossary.

The afflicted mentality looks inwardly at the fundament and then looks at a self, and takes pride in a self, and is attached to the self, and is stupid in regard to the self, making four. With that and the five omnipresent ones, it has a retinue of nine. And it always has equivalence. This is the consciousness which is the place of total affliction: first it creates consciousness, and second it makes them into that which has an affliction. The first is it being the mental mind which is the immediate condition and the second is it being the mind that grasps at I.

If there were no afflicted mentality, five faults would accrue. 1) There would be the fault of there initially being no unmixed ignorance, as follows. Ignorance has the nature of delusion which is an obstructor of the production of knowledge of thatness. It does not exist in the five consciousnesses nor the non-afflicted mental consciousness and also is not in the afflicted one, because it is not accomplished as something other than that. {69}There, "unmixed" means "ignorance which is independent[184]".

2) There would be the fault of being not comparable to the group of five, because there would be no common place of simultaneous production of the five consciousnesses of the eye, and so on and the mental consciousness, in which case there would not be a governing condition for the mental consciousness going with the production of the five consciousnesses of the eye, and so on. Therefore there is also the problem that the name "mental consciousness" would become inexpressible.

3) There would be the fault of being without the particulars in the two equilibria because in the equilibrium of absence of perceptions in which there is no afflicted mentality there would be afflicted mind, so it would be non-peace there and because the cessation equilibrium would become non-existent, meaning that the distinction "this is peace" could not be made.

---

184 ... or has self-control.

4) There would be the fault of no etymological definition because what is referred to as "exists because of grasping at I" would not exist in the six consciousnesses so there would always be absence of grasping at I.

5) There would be the fault of being no grasping at I in the continuum produced in absence of perception, because for the gods without perception mind and mental events have ceased, so, at that time there also would be no grasping at I.

2.2.4. *The Two Types of Non-Self*

There are two types of non-self: non-self of persons and non-self of phenomena.

1) From form is not self, self does not have form{70}, form does not belong to self, and self is not abiding in form, up to self is not abiding in consciousness, is the meditation on the antidote to the twenty views of the perishable.

2) According to *The Compendium of the Vehicle*:

> You must utterly realize absence of the grasped!
> Because of that you realize the absence of grasping,
> Because of which you contact absence of referencing.

According to that, to begin with it is necessary to determine absence of the grasped, so the previous text continues:

> For the classes, whatever they are like,
> Such as pretas, animals, men, and gods,
> One thing, different minds, because of which
> We assert that facts are not established.

That is saying that pretas, animals, men, and gods knowing the superfice of one thing see it in different ways. Thus, these things they see are totally thought up, so are viewed as not existing in fact.

> Likewise if there is no grasped, there will be no grasping
> at that.

This is saying "In accordance with the grasped at being false, the mind grasping at it could not be true" which means that both of them are empty. That being the case, it is also not the case that an awareness empty of both grasped at and grasping, a mere self-knowing self-illumination, does not exist; as *The Compendium of the Vehicle* says:

> If the other-powered and wholly-existent
> Were to be at all times not existent,
> Then the complete purification of the totally afflicted
> Would at all times become non-existent.

And as *Descent into Laṅka* says:

> That dharmas are without essential nature, dharmas are
> unborn,
> Dharmas do not cease, dharmas from the very beginning
> are peace, and
> All dharmas are the nature of nirvāṇa
> Will be advocated by anyone expert in the intent,
> absence[185].
> That "characteristics are without essential nature, birth
> is without essential nature, and
> Superfact is without essential nature" certainly is
> explained!
> Anyone who, expert in this, understands the intent[186]
> Does not go down a path which would lead to utter ruin.

---

[185] … or understanding of the Buddha, that things are without or absent of essential nature, unborn …

[186] Anyone who understands the intent of the Buddha will be able to follow this path in which a fundamental mind that exists is asserted without that person being ruined because of mis-understanding the word "exists" and falling into the extreme of permanence because of it.

In this chapter, I have drawn together into a single summary the various treasured matters found within the texts of the noble one Asaṅga and his brother.

Chapter 3

The Way to Engage in the Path of the Middle Way

{71}Now, for the mind secret[187] of all conquerors of the three times, the highest thing sought by the conquerors' sons, the bodhisatvas, the unmistaken determination of all dharmas' actuality. This third main topic, the explanation of the way to engage in the path of the Middle Way free of extremes, has three parts: identifying the nature of what is to be entered, the Middle Way; the way to enter that; and the result of having entered into it.

1. Identifying the Nature of What is to be Entered, the Middle Way

Because it is free of extremes, it is the middle way. As the glorious lord who is the father of his lineage, the noble one Nāgārjuna, said,

> What interdependently arises
> Is explained to be emptiness.
> That when given a designation
> Is itself the path of Middle Way.

[187] This is one of the three secrets of the conquerors, not a secret in their minds. See three secrets in the glossary.

And, Jetsun Āryadeva taught:

> Not existent, not non-existent, not existent and non-existent,
> And also not neither[188]—{72}
> The Middle Way liberated from the four extremes
> Is the experts' just-that-ness.

That is saying that arriving at a determination of interdependent origination's entity as emptiness and emptiness's entity as freedom from every extreme of elaboration is the superfactual; because there is freedom from extremes within that, it is expressed as "the Middle Way".

2. The Way to Enter That

It is necessary to enter that through use of the great treatises. Therefore, the master[189] personally said that *The Root Prajna* is the grandmother text of all his treatises on the Middle Way, like the body[190]. Following on from that and like its limbs, there are: the *Refutation of Objections*, the *Seventy Verses on Emptiness*, the *Finely Woven Sūtra* which negates sixteen words and meanings of philosophers asserted in the texts containing the proofs of the Tīrthikas, and the *Sixty Verses on Reasoning*, which primarily teaches the cessation of the wrong ideas contained in the lower tenets of our own side. Those are categorized as the Fivefold Collection of Reasonings. The same talk also appears in the *Jewelled Lamp of the Middle Way* which says:

> The ones called *Root Middle Way*, *Refutation of Objections*,
> *Seventy on Emptiness*, *Sixty on Reasoning*,

---

188 … meaning not both either …

189 … Nāgārjuna …

190 … with all the others being appendages to that central body …

And *Finely Woven*,
Are the actual ones used to determine birthlessness.

Furthermore, because of the various ways of unravelling the intent that have appeared in the many treatises of the Middle Way side, two main types of Middle Way—Consequence and Autonomy[191]—and many divisions of them have come about, so that the Middle Way itself has come to have various levels, higher and lower, within it. However, here we rely on and involve ourselves with the explanations of the one who is like the crowning jewel of all the masters of the Consequence school{73}, glorious Chandrakīrti, who made unsurpassedly good explanations greater in value for those wanting emancipation than even the gems of this world. In general, he made unfathomably deep commentaries on the intent of guardian Nāgārjuna and in particular he made the *Clear Words*—a commentary on the words of the *Root Middle Way*—and two roots and commentaries which become commentaries on its meaning, and the great commentaries on *Sixty Verses on Reasoning* and Āryadeva's *Four Hundred*. As the later All-knowing One[192] said:

This, by examining and analysing all of the lower ones' features,
Does not reveal mistakes in the higher ones.
The fictional is viewing the things of the other-powered with desire
But a limit of accomplishment for it is not proclaimed.
That is the feature of the expert above all others,
The establisher of the system of the Consequence chariot, Chandrakīrti.

---

[191] … meaning Prāsaṅgika and Svatantrika …

[192] The "later All-Knowing One" is Longchen Rabjam.

Furthermore, the stainless system of the main texts created by the scholars of the Noble Land, master Vimala[193], Conquerors' Son Śhāntideva, supreme expert Buddhapalita, and so on, is a place which can be relied upon.

3. The Result of Having Entered into it

Non-ultimately speaking, for our own sake there can be no occurrence of the rational mind which grasps at truth in the confused appearances of saṃsāra and for others' sake it is possible to remain for as long as an æon in working for the purposes of migrators in accordance with their wishes; Āryadeva said:

> Those of small merit will not
> Develop doubts because of this.{74}
> By entertaining the merest doubt,
> Becoming will be worn down[194].

And, as it says in *Entering into the Bodhisatvas' Conduct*:

> … for the sake of those who have unsatisfactoriness
> because of stupidity,
> They accomplish liberation from attachment and fear
> While abiding in saṃsāra;
> This is the result of emptiness.

Ultimately speaking, the fruition is to have manifested the holy rank of complete enlightenment.

---

[193] … Vimalamitra …

[194] Those of greater merit will hear the Great Vehicle teachings on emptiness and will start to doubt their solidified reality because of it. Even a small doubt leads to saṃsāra starting to wear out and fall into tatters. This quote is given with the first part, non-ultimate results of engaging in the Middle Way, because it shows that there are degrees to the destruction of saṃsāra.

Chapter 4

The Way to Meditate on Luminosity Great Completion

Rongzom[195], the lion among men, said:

> Generally speaking, in Great Completion there are three sections, nine great internal spaces, twenty-one thousand volumes, ten thousand tantra sections, eighty great protections, five hundred and eighty nails, sixteen thousand foremost instructions of key points, one thousand nine hundred introductions, thirty thousand oral advices on bypassing, and nine thousand oral instructions on differentiation, all in six million four hundred thousand verses.

In relation to that, beings who have held the teaching have appeared during the course of time as expert and accomplished ones who dwelt on the level of a noble one. In this degenerate time[196], it was Lhatsun's assertion that the one referred to in the root tantra *Sound Breakthrough* with the words,

> Then, one expert in terms filled with glory …

---

[195] … Rongzom Paṇḍita who was one of the very learned ones of the Nyingma tradition in the eleventh century C.E.

[196] Tib. dus snyigs ma. Literally meaning the time of the dregs, the time when what is good is only a minute fraction of what it has been in the past.

"was the great All-knowing One"[197]. Our guide, the Dharma Lord, the glorious holy lama[198] said{75}:

> The one referred to with "the one below him, the
> glorious monk"
> Is understood to mean the vidyādhara Kumārāja
> And then the one of supreme intellect.

which is saying that it is the All-Knowing guru[199]. Whatever the case, in accordance with the prophecy made by the conqueror Vajradhara himself that All-Knowing Lord of Speech Longchen Rabjam would be an owner of the Great Completion teaching, Longchen Rabjam summed up the meaning of the entirety of the tantra section of Great Completion in his *Seven Great Treasuries*, *Four Quintessences*, *Trilogy of Resting up*, and so on. Their words and meanings having been blessed with great wisdom, fortunate ones quickly have the mind lineage transmitted and devoted ones merely on meeting with the foremost instructions have a self-introduction to co-emergent wisdom. The father of the vidyādhara lineage transmits it, those with a karmic connection receive it, and the oral instructions of buddha held in the hand are transmitted. Those who rely on the texts of the dharma of Nature Great Completion of the all-knowing king of dharma and the sons in his lineage discover the dharmakāya in its own place, so they only ever find the meaning they seek in a spacious and happy way.

---

[197] Dzogchen master Lhatsun Namkha Jigmey [1597–1653] said that he thought the words quoted in the root tantra of the Seventeen Tantras referred to Longchen Rabjam, who is called "the great All-Knowing One" within the Nyingma tradition.

[198] This refers to Orgyan Tenzin Norbu.

[199] Kumārāja was one before Longchenpa and the one of supreme intellect refers to Longchenpa himself. The "All-Knowing guru" is Longchenpa.

Epilogue

I would like to say the following here.

The hundreds of great minds who were noble ones
Did indeed open up the dharma doors of the three
  vehicles
But what the unripened, new intellects had to sell
Was not enough to gain the jewel of all-knowing.

There are thousands of good explanations of the holy
  ones who appeared in the past
And the authoritative statements of the vidyādharas who
  gained accomplishment
But if one does not consider this point of the childish
  ones of this time,{76}
What value will be gained from the elaborate
  explanation in these huge textbooks?

The conquerors and conquerors' sons, however many
  they are,
Do not set them aside as objects of prayers for the
  development of enlightenment mind
But the failings of this degenerate time cause all the
  suffering beings
Each to work out his own karmic lot.

Therefore, although the way of thinking of childish ones
like myself,
Is not enough to set migrators on the path of benefit and
ease
Because the enlightened understanding of the sun
amongst teachers, Conquerors' Son Lord of
Dharma[200]
Has ended with his passing away, I have written this.

Any and every fault in here due to not comprehending
or wrongly understanding
Is admitted before the assembly of experts.
Valid cognition of the mode of the holy dharma
Is not arrived at by anyone other than the assembly of
noble ones.

I roll into one the merit created here and the other roots
of merit
Nicely created by myself and others
And dedicate it to becoming the cause
Of the precious teaching of the conqueror remaining
without degeneration for a long time.

This was composed to open the door of intellect of those new to hearing and contemplating by Zhanphen Nangwa, a monk whose crown touches the dust at the feet of the great expert, Orgyan Tenzin Norbu. Let there be goodness![201]

---

[200] This refers to Zhanphen Thaye.

[201] Following this, which is the actual colophon, some editions continue with"a printer's aspiration" added during a later reprinting of the text. The edition that we used had a printer's aspiration but it is neither part of the original text nor important to it, so it has not been included in the translation.

List of Texts Cited

The following is an exhaustive list of the texts mentioned in this book. The name in English is given first followed by the name in Tibetan or Sanskrit.

A Complete Summation of Determinations, Skt. yogacāra bhūmi niraṇaya saṃgrāha: one of the five texts by Asaṅga on the levels of the bodhisatvas. The Tibetan edition is available in the Tibetan *Translated Treatises.*

A Marvelous Garland of Rare Gems By Nyoshul Khenpo, translated by Richard Barron, published by Padma Publishing, 2005, ISBN: 1-881847-41-1.

Abhidharma Sūtra, Tib. chos mngon pa'i mdo: one of the seven texts comprising the Abhidharma section of the Buddha's sūtras. The Tibetan edition is available in the Tibetan *Translated Word.*

Clear Words, Skt. prasannapada: a major commentary on Nāgārjuna's *The Root Prajñā* by Chandrakīrti. The Tibetan edition is available in the Tibetan *Translated Treatises.*

Descent into Laṅka, Skt. laṅkāvatāra sūtra: a sūtra of the third turning of the wheel of dharma, generally classified as Mind Only. The Tibetan edition is available in the Tibetan *Translated Word.*

Entering into the Bodhisatvas' Conduct, Skt. bodhisatva caryāvatāra: by Śhāntideva. The Tibetan edition is available in the Tibetan *Translated Treatises.*

Finely Woven Sūtra, Skt. vaidalyasūtra: a text on reasoning by Nāgārjuna classified as one of his five texts on reasoning. The Tibetan edition is available in the Tibetan *Translated Treatises.*

Four Hundred, Skt. madhyamaka catuṣhaṭaka śhāstrikārikā: a text by Āryadeva on the meaning of emptiness according to the Middle Way. The Tibetan edition is available in the Tibetan *Translated Treatises.*

Four Quintessences: Tib. snying thig ya bzhi by Longchen Rabjam, a set of several native Tibetan works on Great Completion. The set is classified as Dzogchen teaching primarily for the practitioner. It includes the source texts for the Quintessence Great Completion teachings passed down through Vimalamitra and Padmasambhava and commentaries on each of them, making the four parts mentioned in the name.

Jewelled lamp of the Middle Way, Tib. dbu ma'i rin chen sgron me.

Refutation of Objections, Skt. vigraha vyāvartanī kārikā: a text on reasoning by Nāgārjuna classified as one of his five texts on reasoning. The Tibetan edition is available in the Tibetan *Translated Treatises.*

Root Middle Way, Skt. mula prajñā: a text on reasoning by Nāgārjuna classified as one of his five texts on reasoning. The Tibetan edition is available in the Tibetan *Translated Treatises.*

Seventy Verses on Emptiness, Skt. śhūnyatā saptakārikā: a text on reasoning by Nāgārjuna classified as one of his five texts on reasoning. The Tibetan edition is available in the Tibetan *Translated Treatises.*

Sixty Verses on Reasoning, Skt. yukti ṣhāsṭikārikā: a text on reasoning by Nāgārjuna classified as one of his five texts on reasoning. The Tibetan edition is available in the Tibetan *Translated Treatises.*

Sound Breakthrough, Tib. sgra thal 'gyur: the root tantra of the seventeen tantras of innermost unsurpassed Great Completion.

The Compendium, Skt. abhidharmasamuccaya: a grand compendium of the Abdhidharma according to the Mind Only school by

Asaṅga. It is one of two Indian texts on Abhidharma studied in Tibetan Buddhism, the other being *The Treasury* q.v. The Tibetan edition is available in the Tibetan *Translated Treatises.*

The Compendium of the Vehicle: same as *The Compendium of the Great Vehicle.*

The Compendium of the Great Vehicle, Skt. mahāyānasaṃuccaya: a grand compendium of the teachings of the Great Vehicle. The Tibetan edition is available in the Tibetan *Translated Treatises.*

The Complete Commentary, Skt. pramāṇavārttika: a complete commentary by Dharmakīrti on valid cognition. The Tibetan edition is available in the Tibetan *Translated Treatises.*

The Highest Continuum, Tib. rgyud bla ma: one of the Five Dharmas of Maitreya by Asaṅga. The Tibetan edition is available in the Tibetan *Translated Treatises.*

The Ornament of the Sūtra Section: same as *The Ornament of the Great Vehicle Sūtra Section.*

The Ornament of the Sūtras: same as *The Ornament of the Great Vehicle Sūtra Section.*

The Ornament of the Great Vehicle Sūtra Section, Skt. mahāyāna sūtrālaṅkāra: one of the Five Dharmas of Maitreya by Asaṅga. The Tibetan edition is available in the Tibetan *Translated Treatises.*

The Root Prajna, Skt. mulaprajñā: a text on reasoning by Nāgārjuna classified as one of his five texts on reasoning. The Tibetan edition is available in the Tibetan *Translated Treatises.*

The Seven Treasuries, Tib. mdzod bdun: by Longchen Rabjam, a set of several native Tibetan works on Great Completion. The set is classified as Dzogchen teaching primarily for the scholar.

The Thirty Verses, Skt. trimśhika kārikā: a text by Vasubandhu presenting the Mind Only system. The Tibetan edition is available in the Tibetan *Translated Treatises.*

The Treasury, Skt. abhidharmakoṣha: a text by Vasubandhu presenting the Abdhidharma according to the Particularist school. It is one of two Indian texts on Abhidharma studied in Tibetan Buddhism, the other being *The Compendium* q.v. The

Tibetan edition is available in the Tibetan *Translated Treatises*. The key difference between the two texts is that this text presents Abhidharma according to the fundamental Lesser Vehicle teachings where the other presents it according to the Great Vehicle Mind Only teachings.

The Treatise Differentiating the Middle and Extremes, Skt. madhyanta vibhanga: one of the Five Dharmas of Maitreya by Asaṅga. The Tibetan edition is available in the Tibetan *Translated Treatises*.

Trilogy of Resting up, Tib. ngal gso skor gsum: by Longchen Rabjam, a set of several native Tibetan works on Great Completion. The trilogy is classified as Dzogchen teaching midway between that only for the scholar and that only for the practitioner.

Unending Auspiciousness, The Sūtra of the Recollection of the Noble Three Jewels with Commentaries by Ju Mipham, Taranatha, and Tony Duff by Tony Duff, published by Padma Karpo Translation Committee, 2010, 978-9937-8386-1-0.

Unravelling the Intent Sūtra, Skt. saṃdhi nirmocana sūtra: a major sūtra of the third turning of the wheel of dharma. The sūtra is generally classified as Mind Only. The Tibetan edition is available in the Tibetan *Translated Word*.

Glossary of Terms

Actuality, Tib. gnas lugs: A key term in both sūtra and tantra and one of a pair of terms, the other being "apparent reality" (Tib. snang lugs). The two terms are used when determining the reality of a situation. The actuality of any given situation is how (lugs) the situation actuality sits or is present (gnas); the apparent reality is how (lugs) any given situation appears (snang) to an observer. Something could appear in many different ways, depending on the circumstances at the time and on the being perceiving it but, regardless of those circumstances, it will always have its own actuality of how it really is.

Adventitious, Tib. glo bur: This term has the connotations of popping up on the surface of something and of not being part of that thing. Therefore, even though it is often translated as "sudden", that only conveys half of the meaning. In Buddhist literature, something adventitious comes up as a surface event and disappears again precisely because it is not actually part of the thing on whose surface it appeared. It is frequently used in relation to the afflictions because they pop up on the surface of the mind of buddha-nature but are not part of the buddha-nature itself.

Affliction, Skt. kleśha, Tib. nyon mongs: This term is usually translated as emotion or disturbing emotion, etcetera, but the Buddha was very specific about the meaning of this word. When the Buddha referred to the emotions, meaning a movement of mind, he did not refer to them as such but called them "kleśha" in Sanskrit, meaning exactly "affliction". It is a basic part of the Buddhist teaching that emotions afflict beings, giving them problems at the time and causing more problems in the future.

Alertness, Tib. shes bzhin: Alertness is a specific mental event that occurs in dualistic mind. It and another mental event, mindfulness, are the two functions of mind that must be developed in order to develop śhamatha or one-pointedness of mind. In that context, mindfulness is what remembers the object of the concentration and holds the mind to it while alertness is the mind watching the situation to ensure that the mindfulness is not lost. If distraction does occur, alertness will know it and will inform the mind to re-establish mindfulness again. The mental event called "unalertness" is its opposite.

All-Knowing One, Tib. kun mkhyen: Every century in Tibet, there were just a few people who seemed to know everything so were given the title "All-Knowing One". Moreover, of all the All-Knowing ones, Longchenpa was regarded as the greatest, therefore, he is also frequently referred to as the "great" or "greatest" All-Knowing One. Note that "All-Knowing" does not mean "omniscient one".

Appropriation, Skt. upādāna, Tib. nye bar len pa: This is the name of the ninth of the twelve links of interdependent origination. It is the crucial point in the process at which a karma that has been previously planted is selected and activated as the karma that will propel the being into its next existence. In other words, it is the key point in a being's existence when the next type of existence is selected.

Ati, Skt. mahāti, Tib. shin tu chen po: Mahā Ati or Ati Yoga is the name of the ninth and last of the nine vehicles taught in the Nyingma system of nine vehicles. The name "ati" literally means that it is the vehicle at the end of the sequence of all other vehicles. It is not only the final vehicle at the end of the sequence but the peak of all vehicles given that it presents reality more directly than any of the vehicles below it. It is therefore also called the king of vehicles.

"Mahāsaṅdhi"—"Dzogpa Chenpo" in the Tibetan language and "Great Completion" in the English language—is the name of the teachings on reality contained in the Maha Ati vehicle and also of the reality itself. Great Completion and Maha Ati are often used interchangeably even though their references are slightly different. See Great Completion in the glossary for more.

Authoritative statement, Skt. āgama, Tib lung. Although often translated as "scripture", authentic statement means statement made by someone who has the true knowledge needed to make fully reliable statements about a subject. It is often used to indicate dharma taught by the Buddha or his disciples which is authoritative because of its source. It is also used in the pair "authoritative statement and realization" which, the Buddha explained, summed up the ways of transmitting his realization.

Awareness, Skt. jñā, Tib. shes pa: "Awareness" is always used in our translations to mean the basic knower of mind or, as Buddhist teaching itself defines it, "a general term for any registering mind", whether dualistic or non-dualistic. Hence, it is used for both samsaric and nirvanic situations; for example, consciousness (Tib. rnam par shes pa) is a dualistic form of awareness, whereas wisdom (Tib. ye shes) is a non-dualistic forms of awareness.

Becoming, Skt. bhāvanā, Tib. srid pa: This is another name for samsaric existence. Beings in saṃsāra have a samsaric existence but, more than that, they are constantly in a state of becoming—becoming this type of being or that type of being in this abode or that, as they are driven along without choice by the karmic process that drives samsaric existence.

Bliss, Skt. sukha, Tib. bde: The Sanskrit term and its Tibetan translation are usually translated as "bliss" but refer to the whole range of possibilities of everything on the side of good as opposed to bad. Thus, the term will mean pleasant, happy, good, nice, easy, comfortable, blissful, and so on, depending on context. In this text, the term is mostly translated as "good" because it is mostly used as the direct opposite to duḥkha, meaning unsatisfactory.

Bodhisatva, Tib. byang chub sems dpa': A bodhisatva is a person who has engendered the bodhichitta, enlightenment mind, and, with that as a basis, has undertaken the path to the enlightenment of a truly complete buddha specifically for the welfare of other beings. Note that, despite the common appearance of "bodhisattva" in

Western books on Buddhism, the Tibetan tradition has steadfastly maintained since the time of the earliest translations that the correct spelling is bodhisatva; see under satva and sattva.

Clinging, Tib. zhen pa: In Buddhism, this term refers specifically to the twofold process of dualistic mind mis-taking things that are not true, not pure, as true, pure, etcetera and then, because of seeing them as highly desirable even though they are not, attaching itself to or clinging to those things. This type of clinging acts as a kind of glue that keeps a person joined to the unsatisfactory things of cyclic existence because of mistakenly seeing them as desirable.

Complete Purification: See under total affliction.

Concept tokens, Tib. mtshan ma: This is the technical name for the structures or concepts which function as the words of conceptual mind's language. They are the very basis of operation of the third skandha and hence of the way that dualistic mind communicates with its world. For example, a table seen in direct visual perception will have no concept tokens involved with knowing it. However, when thought becomes involved and there is the thought "table" in an inferential or conceptual perception of the table, the name-tag "table" will be used to reference the table and that name tag is the concept token.

Although we usually reference phenomena via these concepts, the phenomena are not the dualistically referenced things we think of them as being. The actual fact of the phenomena is quite different from the concept tokens used to discursively think about them and is known by wisdom rather than concept-based mind. Therefore, this term is often used in Buddhist literature to signify that dualistic samsaric mind is involved rather than non-dualistic wisdom.

Confusion, Tib. 'khrul pa: In Buddhism, this term mostly refers to the fundamental confusion of taking things the wrong way that happens because of fundamental ignorance, although it can also have the more general meaning of having lots of thoughts and being confused about it. In the first case, it is defined like this "Confusion is the appearance to rational mind of something being present when it is not" and refers, for example, to seeing an object, such as a table, as being truly present, when in fact it is present only as mere, interdependent appearance.

Consciousness, Skt. vijñāna, Tib. rnam shes: The Sanskrit term means "awareness of superficies". A consciousness is a dualistic (jñā) awareness which merely registers a certain type of (vi) superfice, for example, an eye consciousness by definition registers only the superficies belonging to visual form. The addition of the "vi" to the basic term for awareness conveys a sense of less than perfect. This is not a wisdom awareness which can know every superfice but a limited type of awareness which is restricted to knowing one kind of superfice or another. Note that this definition, which is a crucial part of understanding the meaning of consciousness, is fully conveyed by the Sanskrit (and Tibetan) terms but not at all by the English term.

Containers and contents, Tib. snod bcud: Containers are the outer worlds and environment and their contents are the beings living in them. This phrase is sometimes extended to "outer and inner, containers and contents" with the same meaning. It usually means "the entirety of saṃsāra", though sometimes means "the entirety of saṃsāra and nirvāṇa".

Cyclic existence: See under saṃsāra.

Dharmadhatu, Skt. dharmadhātu, Tib. chos kyi dbyings: This is the name for the *dhātu* meaning range or basic space in which all *dharmas*, meaning all phenomena, come into being. If a flower bed is the place where flowers grow and are found, the dharmadhātu is the dharma or phenomena bed in which all phenomena come into being and are found.

Dharmadhatu, Skt. dharmadhātu, Tib. chos kyi khams: This is the name for one of the eighteen elements. It is the element of that which is known by mental faculty and mental consciousness—dharmas or phenomena. It is not the same as the other dharmadhātu mentioned immediately above.

Dharmakaya, Skt. dharmakāya, Tib. chos sku: In the general teachings of Buddhism, this refers to the mind of a buddha, with "dharma" meaning reality and "kāya" meaning body.

Dharmata, Skt. dharmatā, Tib. chos nyid: This is a general term meaning the way that something is, and can be applied to anything at all; it is similar in meaning to "actuality" *q.v.* For example, the dharmatā of water is wetness and the dharmatā of the becoming bardo is a place where beings are in a samsaric, or becoming mode, prior to entering a nature bardo. It is used frequently in Tibetan Buddhism to mean "the dharmatā of reality" but that is a specific case of the much larger meaning of the term. To read texts which use this term successfully, one has to understand that the term has a general meaning and then see how that applies in context.

Dhyana, Skt. dhyāna, Tib. bsam gtan: A Sanskrit term technically meaning all types of mental absorption. Mental absorptions cultivated in the human realm generally result in births in the form realms which are deep forms of concentration in themselves. The practices of mental absorption done in the human realm and the godly existences of the form realm that result from them both are named "dhyāna". The Buddha repeatedly pointed out that the dhyānas were a side-track to emancipation from cyclic existence. In a more general way, the term also means meditation in general where one is concentrating on something as a way of developing oneself spiritually.

Direct Crossing, Tib. thod rgal: The name of one of the two main practices of the innermost level of Great Completion. The other one is Thorough Cut *q.v.*

Discursive thought, Skt. vikalpa, Tib. rnam rtog: This means more than just the superficial thought that is heard as a voice in the head. It includes the entirety of conceptual process that arises due to mind contacting any object of any of the senses. The Sanskrit and Tibetan literally mean "(dualistic) thought (that arises from the mind wandering among the) various (superficies *q.v.* perceived in the doors of the senses)".

Elaboration, Tib. spro ba: This is a general name for what is given off by dualistic mind as it goes about its conceptual business. The term is pejorative in that it implies that a story has been made up, unnecessarily, about something which is actually nothing, which is empty. Elaborations, because of what they are, prevent a person from seeing emptiness directly.

Freedom from elaboration or being elaboration-free implies direct sight of emptiness. It is important to understand that these words are used in a theoretical or philosophical way in the second turning sūtra teachings but are used in an experiential way in the final teachings of the third turning sūtras and in the tantras of Great Completion and Mahāmudrā. In the former, being free of elaborations is a definition of what could happen according to the tenets of the Middle Way, and so on; in the latter it is a description of a state of being, one which, because it is empty of all the elaborations of dualistic being, is the actual sphere of emptiness.

Enlightenment mind, Skt. bodhicitta, Tib. byang chub sems: This is a key term of the Great Vehicle. It is the type of mind that is connected not with the lesser enlightenment of an arhat but the enlightenment of a truly complete buddha. As such, it is a mind which is connected with the aim of bringing all sentient beings to that same level of buddhahood. A person who has this mind has entered the Great Vehicle and is either a bodhisatva or a buddha.

It is important to understand that "enlightenment mind" is used to refer equally to the minds of all levels of bodhisatva on the path to buddhahood and to the mind of a buddha who has completed the path. Therefore, it is not "mind striving for enlightenment" as is so often translated, but "enlightenment mind", meaning that kind of mind which is connected with the full enlightenment of a truly complete buddha and which is present in all those who belong to the Great Vehicle. The term is used in the conventional Great Vehicle and also in the Vajra Vehicle. In the Vajra Vehicle, there are some special uses of the term where substances of the pure aspect of the subtle physical body are understood to be manifestations of enlightenment mind.

Entity, Tib. ngo bo: The entity of something is just exactly what that thing is. In English we would often simply say "thing" rather than entity. However, in Buddhism, "thing" has a very specific meaning rather than the general meaning that it has in English. It has become common to translate this term as "essence" *q.v.* However, in most cases "entity", meaning what a thing is rather than an essence of that thing, is the correct translation for this term.

Exaggeration, Tib. skur 'debs pa: In Buddhism, this term is used in two ways. Firstly, it is used in general to mean misunderstanding from the perspective that one has added more to one's understanding of something than needs to be there. Secondly, it is used specifically to indicate that dualistic mind always overstates or exaggerates whatever object it is examining. Dualistic mind always adds the ideas of solidity, permanence, singularity, and so on to everything it references via the concepts that it uses. Severing of exaggeration either means removal of these un-necessary understandings when trying to properly comprehend something or removal of the dualistic process altogether when trying to get to the non-dualistic reality of a phenomenon.

Fact, Skt. artha, Tib. don: "Fact" is that knowledge of an object that occurs to the surface of mind or wisdom. It is not the object but what the mind or wisdom understands as the object. Thus there are two usages of "fact": fact known to dualistic and non-dualistic minds. The higher tantras especially use "fact" to refer to the actual fact known in direct perception of actuality. Thus, there are phrases such as "in fact" which do not mean that the author is speaking truly about something but that whatever is about to be said is referring to actual fact as known to wisdom. A further complexity is that phrases such as "in fact" in those contexts are often abbreviations of "in superfact" *q.v.* This brings a further difficulty for the reader because "superfact" can be used in a general way to indicate directly perceived non-samsaric fact or can be used according to its specific definition (for which see superfact). In Buddhist tradition, problems like this are solved by having the text explained by one's teacher. That might not be possible for some readers, so uses of the word "fact" should be looked at carefully to see whether they are indicating fact in general or the factual situation of knowing reality in direct perception.

Fictional, Skt. saṃvṛtti, Tib. kun rdzob: This term is paired with the term "superfactual" *q.v.* In the past, these terms have been translated as "relative" and "absolute" respectively, but those translations are nothing like the original terms. These terms are extremely important in the Buddhist teaching so it is very important that they be corrected, but more than that, if the actual meaning of these terms is not presented, then the teaching connected with them cannot be understood.

The Sanskrit term saṃvṛtti means a deliberate invention, a fiction, a hoax. It refers to the mind of ignorance which, because of being obscured and so not seeing suchness, is not true but a fiction. The things that appear to that ignorance are therefore fictional. Nonetheless, the beings who live in this ignorance believe that the things that appear to them through the filter of ignorance are true, are real. Therefore, these beings live in fictional truth.

Fictional and superfactual: Fictional and superfactual are our greatly improved translations for "relative" and "absolute" respectively. Briefly, the original Sanskrit word for fiction means a deliberately produced *fiction* and refers to the world projected by a mind controlled by ignorance. The original word for superfact means "that *super*ior *fact* that appears on the surface of the mind of a noble one who has transcended saṃsāra" and refers to reality seen as it actually is. The terms "relative" and "absolute" do not convey this meaning at all and, when they are used, the meaning being presented is simply lost.

Fictional truth, Skt. saṃvṛtisatya, Tib. kun rdzob bden pa: See under fictional.

Foremost instruction, Skt. upadeśha, Tib. man ngag: There are several types of instruction mentioned in Buddhist literature: there is the general level of instruction which is the meaning contained in the words of the texts of the tradition; on a more personal and direct level there is oral instruction which has been passed down from teacher to student from the time of the buddha; and on the most profound level there are foremost instructions which are not only oral instructions provided by one's guru but are special, core instructions that come out of personal experience and which convey the teaching concisely and with the full weight of personal experience.

Fortune, fortunate person, Tib. skal ldan: To meet with any given dharma teaching, a person must have accumulated the karmic fortune needed for such a rare opportunity, and this kind of person is then called "a fortunate one" or "fortunate person". This term is especially used in the Vajra Vehicle, whose teachings and practices are generally very hard to meet with.

Fundament (consciousness), Skt. ālaya, Tib. kun gzhi: This term, if translated, is usually translated as "all-base" or something similar. The Sanskrit term means a range that underlies and forms the basis for something above it. In Buddhist teaching, it means a particular level of awareness that sits beneath all other levels of awareness. It is a fundamental awareness which is the basis for all of saṃsāra and nirvāṇa.

Grasped-grasping, Tib. gzung 'dzin: When mind is turned outwardly as it is in the normal operation of dualistic mind, it has developed two faces that appear simultaneously. Special names are given to these two faces: mind appearing in the form of the external object being referenced is called "that which is grasped" and mind appearing in the form of the consciousness that is registering it is called the "grasper" or "grasping" of it. Thus, there is the pair of terms "grasped-grasper" or "grasped-grasping". When these two terms are used, it alerts one to the fact that a Mind Only style of presentation is being discussed. This pair of terms pervades Mind Only, Middle Way, and tantric writings and is exceptionally important in all of them.

Note that one could substitute the word "apprehended" for "grasped" and "apprehender" for "grasper" or "grasping" and that would reflect one connotation of the original Sanskrit terminology. The solidified duality of grasped and grasper is nothing but an invention of dualistic thought; it has that kind of character or characteristic.

Great Completion, Tib. rdzogs pa chen po: Two main practices of reality developed in the Buddhist traditions of ancient India and then came to Tibet: Great Completion (Mahāsaṅdhi) and Great Seal (Mahāmudrā). Great Completion and Great Seal are names for reality and names for a practice that directly leads to that reality. Their ways of describing reality and their practices are very similar. The Great Completion teachings are the pinnacle teachings of the tantric teachings of Buddhism that first came into Tibet with Padmasambhava and his peers and were later kept alive in the Nyingma (Earlier Ones) tradition. The Great Seal practice came into Tibet later and was held in the Sakya and Kagyu lineages. Later again, the Great Seal was held by the Gelugpa lineage, which obtained its transmissions of the instructions from the Sakya and Kagyu lineages.

It is popular nowadays to call Great Completion by the name Great Perfection, though that is a mistake. The original name Mahāsaṅdhi refers to that one space of reality in which all things come together. Thus it means "completeness" or "completion" as the Tibetans chose to translate it and does not imply or contain the sense of "perfection".

Great Vehicle, Skt. mahāyāna, Tib. theg pa chen po: The Buddha's teachings as a whole can be summed up into three vehicles where a vehicle is defined as that which can carry a person to a certain destination. The first vehicle, called the Lesser Vehicle, contains the teachings designed to get an individual moving on the spiritual path through showing the unsatisfactory state of cyclic existence and an emancipation from that. However, that path is only concerned with personal emancipation and fails to take account of all of the beings that there are in existence. There used to be eighteen schools of Lesser Vehicle in India but the only one surviving nowadays is the Theravāda of south-east Asia. The Greater Vehicle is a step up from that. The Buddha explained that it was great in comparison to the Lesser Vehicle for seven reasons, which are explained in chapter two of this book. The Great Vehicle has two divisions: a conventional form in which the path is taught in a logical, conventional way, and an unconventional form in which the path is taught in a very direct way. This latter vehicle is called the Vajra Vehicle because it takes the innermost, indestructible (vajra) fact of reality of one's own mind as the vehicle to enlightenment.

Intent, Tib. dgongs pa: This is the honorific form of (Tib. sems pa) meaning "to think, to comprehend", so is used to refer to an enlightened person's understanding, though the Gelugpa school is even more restrictive and uses it only for wisdom understanding of the Buddha. In some places "intent" meaning the intended meaning based on an enlightened person's understanding and in other places simply "understanding" should be understood for this term.

Intentional conduct, Tib. mos spyod: A name in the Great Vehicle for the path activities done at levels of both accumulation and connection. At this level, one is still intending to directly realize emptiness. Note that intention is the name of one of the fifty-one mental events. Thus this name implies that it is conduct still at the level of dualistic being, though it is a good mind because it intends to reach non-dualistic being. Also, by definition there is no real accomplishment until the path of seeing is reached, so there is no real accomplishment at the level of intentional conduct. Intentional conduct as non-accomplishment followed by the three paths which are levels of accomplishment is a general presentation contained in the common vehicle.

Kaya, Skt. kāya, Tib. sku: The Sanskrit term means a functional or coherent collection of parts, similar to the French "corps", and hence also comes to mean "a body". It is used in Tibetan Buddhist texts specifically to distinguish bodies belonging to the enlightened side from ones belonging to the samsaric side.

Enlightened being in Buddhism is said to be comprised of one or more kāyas. It is most commonly explained to consist of one, two, three, four, or five kāyas, though it is pointed out that there are infinite aspects to enlightened being and therefore it can also be said to consist of an infinite number of kāyas. In fact, these descriptions of enlightened being consisting of one or more kāyas are given for the sake of understanding what is beyond conceptual understanding so should not be taken as absolute statements.

The most common description of enlightened being is that it is comprised of three kāyas: dharma, saṃbhoga, and nirmāṇakāyas. Briefly stated, the dharmakāya is the body of truth, the saṃbhogakāya is the body replete with the good qualities of enlightenment, and the nirmāṇakāya is the body manifested into the worlds of saṃsāra and nirvāṇa to benefit beings.

Dharmakāya refers to that aspect of enlightened being in which the being sees the truth for himself and, in doing so, fulfils his own needs for enlightenment. The dharmakāya is purely mind, without form. The remaining two bodies are summed up under the heading of rūpakāyas or form bodies manifested specifically to fulfil the needs of all un-enlightened beings. "Saṃbhogakāya" has been mostly translated as "body of enjoyment" or "body of rapture" but it is clearly stated in Buddhist texts on the subject that the name refers to a situation replete with what is useful, that is, to the fact that the saṃbhogakāya contains all of the good qualities of enlightenment as needed to benefit sentient beings. The saṃbhogakāya is extremely subtle and not accessible by most sentient beings; the nirmāṇakāya is a coarser manifestation which can reach sentient beings in many ways. Nirmāṇakāya should not be thought of as a physical body but as the capability to express enlightened being in whatever way is needed throughout all the different worlds of sentient beings. Thus, as much as it appears as a supreme buddha who shows the dharma to beings, it also appears as anything needed within sentient beings' worlds to give them assistance.

The three kāyas of enlightened being is taught in all levels of Buddhist teaching. It is especially important in Mahāmudrā and Great Completion and is taught there in a unique and very profound way.

Latency, Skt. vāsanā, Tib. bag chags: The original Sanskrit has the meaning exactly of "latency". The Tibetan term translates that inexactly with "something sitting there (Tib. chags) within the environment of mind (Tib. bag)". Although it has become popular to translate this term into English with "habitual pattern", that is not its meaning. The term refers to a karmic seed that has been imprinted on the mindstream and is present there as a latency, ready and waiting to come into manifestation.

Lesser Vehicle, Skt. hīnayāna, Tib. theg pa dman pa: See under Great Vehicle.

Luminosity, Skt. prabhāsvara, Tib. 'od gsal ba: The core of mind has two aspects: an emptiness factor and a knowing factor. The Buddha and many Indian religious teachers used "luminosity" as a metaphor for the knowing quality of the core of mind. If in English we would say "Mind has a knowing quality", the teachers of ancient

India would say, "Mind has an illuminative quality; it is like a source of light which illuminates what it knows".

This term has been translated as "clear light" but that is a mistake that comes from not understanding the etymology of the word. It does not refer to a light that has the quality of clearness (something that makes no sense, actually!) but to the illuminative property which is the nature of the empty mind.

Note also that in both Sanskrit and Tibetan Buddhist literature, this term is frequently abbreviated just to Skt. "vara" and Tib. "gsal ba" with no change of meaning. Unfortunately, this has been thought to be another word and it has then been translated with "clarity", when in fact it is just this term in abbreviation.

Mara, Skt. māra, Tib. bdud: The Sanskrit term is closely related to the word "death". Buddha spoke of four classes of extremely negative influences that have the capacity to drag a sentient being deep into saṃsāra. They are the "māras" or "kiss of death": of having a samsaric set of five skandhas; of having afflictions; of death itself; and of the son of gods, which means being seduced and taken in totally by sensuality.

Mentation, Skt. manaskāra, Tib. yid la byed pa: Mentation is the act of using the mental mind in general and is also one of the omnipresent mental events q.v. Its use implies the presence of dualistic mind. Non-mentating could be simply not using the dualistic mind but is usually used to imply the absence of dualistic mind, that is, the presence of wisdom.

Migrator, Tib. 'gro ba: Migrator is one of several terms that were commonly used by the Buddha to mean "sentient being". It shows sentient beings from the perspective of their constantly being forced to go here and there from one rebirth to another by the power of karma. They are like flies caught in a jar, constantly buzzing back and forth. The term is often translated using "beings" which is another general term for sentient beings but doing so loses the meaning entirely: Buddhist authors who know the tradition do not use the word loosely but use it specifically to give the sense of beings who are constantly and helplessly going from one birth to another, and that is how the term should be read.

Mind, Skt. chitta, Tib. sems: There are several terms for mind in the Buddhist tradition, each with its own, specific meaning. This term is the most general term for the samsaric type of mind. It refers to the type of mind that is produced because of fundamental ignorance of enlightened mind. Whereas the wisdom of enlightened mind lacks all complexity and knows in a non-dualistic way, this mind of un-enlightenment is a very complicated apparatus that only ever knows in a dualistic way.

The Mahāmudrā and Great Completion teachings use the terms "entity of mind" and "mind's entity" to refer to what this complicated, samsaric mind is at core—the enlightened form of mind.

Noble one, Skt. ārya, Tib. 'phags pa: In Buddhism, a noble one is a being who has become spiritually advanced to the point that he has passed beyond cyclic existence. According to the Buddha, the beings in cyclic existence were ordinary beings, spiritual commoners, and the beings who had passed beyond it were special, the nobility.

Outflow, Skt. āsrāva, Tib. zag pa: The Sanskrit term means a bad discharge, like pus coming out of a wound. Outflows occur when wisdom loses its footing and falls into the elaborations of dualistic mind. Therefore, anything with duality also has outflows. This is sometimes translated as "defiled" or "conditioned" but these fail to capture the meaning. The idea is that wisdom can remain self-contained in its own unique sphere but, when it loses its ability to stay within itself, it starts to have leakages into dualism that are defilements on the wisdom. See also under un-outflowed.

Prajna, Skt. prajñā, Tib. shes rab: The Sanskrit term, literally meaning "best type of mind" is defined as that which makes correct distinctions between this and that and hence which arrives at correct understanding. It has been translated as "wisdom" but that is not correct because it is, generally speaking, a mental event belonging to dualistic mind where "wisdom" is used to refer to the non-dualistic knower of a buddha. Moreover, the main feature of prajñā is its ability to distinguish correctly between one thing and another and hence to arrive at a correct understanding.

Preserve, Tib. skyong ba: In general, it means to defend, protect, nurture, maintain. It is also used in meditation instructions to mean the maintaining or nurturing of a particular state of mind through the practice of meditation.

Rational mind, Tib. blo: Rational mind is one of several terms for mind in Buddhist terminology. It specifically refers to a mind that judges this against that. With rare exception it is used to refer to samsaric mind, given that samsaric mind only works in the dualistic mode of comparing this versus that. Because of this, the term is mostly used in a pejorative sense to point out samsaric mind as opposed to an enlightened type of mind.

This term has been commonly translated simply as "mind" but that fails to identify this term properly and leaves it confused with the many other words that are also translated simply as "mind". It is not just another mind but is specifically the sort of mind that creates the situation of this and that (*ratio* in Latin) and hence upholds the duality of saṃsāra. In that case, it is the very opposite of the essence of mind. Thus, this is a key term which should be noted and not just glossed over as "mind".

Realization, Tib. rtogs pa: Realization has a very specific meaning: it refers to correct knowledge that has been gained in such a way that the knowledge does not abate. There are two important points here. Firstly, realization is not absolute. It refers to the removal of obscurations, one at a time. Each time that a practitioner removes an obscuration, he gains a realization because of it. Therefore, there are as many levels of realization as there are obscurations. Maitreya, in the *Ornament of Manifest Realizations*, shows how the removal of the various obscurations that go with each of the three realms of samsaric existence produces realization.

Secondly, realization is stable or, as the Tibetan wording says, "unchanging". As Guru Rinpoche pointed out, "Intellectual knowledge is like a patch, it drops away; experiences on the path are temporary, they evaporate like mist; realization is unchanging".

Reference and Referencing, Tib. dmigs pa: Referencing is the name for the process in which dualistic mind references an actual object by using a conceptual token instead of the actual object. Whatever is referenced is then called a reference. Note that these terms imply the presence of dualistic mind and their opposites, non-referencing and being without reference imply the presence of non-dualistic wisdom.

Refuge, Skt. śharaṇaṃ, Tib. bskyab pa: The Sanskrit term means "shelter", "protection from harm". Everyone seeks a refuge from the unsatisfactoriness of life, even if it is a simple act like brushing the teeth to prevent the body from decaying un-necessarily. Buddhists, after having thought carefully about their situation and who could provide a refuge from it which would be thoroughly reliable, find that three things—buddha, dharma, and saṅgha—are the only things that could provide that kind of refuge. Therefore, Buddhists take refuge in those Three Jewels of Refuge as they are called. Taking refuge in the Three Jewels is clearly laid out as the one doorway to all Buddhist practice and realization.

Samsara, Skt. saṃsāra, Tib. 'khor ba: This is the most general name for the type of existence in which sentient beings live. It refers to the fact that they continue on from one existence to another, always within the enclosure of births that are produced by ignorance and experienced as unsatisfactory. The original Sanskrit means to be constantly going about, here and there. The Tibetan term literally means "cycling", because of which it is frequently translated into English with "cyclic existence" though that is not quite the meaning of the term.

Satva and sattva: According to the Tibetan tradition established at the time of the great translation work done at Samye under the watch of Padmasambhava not to mention one hundred and sixty-three of the greatest Buddhist scholars of Sanskrit-speaking India, there is a difference of meaning between the Sanskrit terms "satva" and "sattva", with satva meaning "an heroic kind of being" and "sattva" meaning simply "a being". According to the Tibetan tradition established under the advice of the Indian scholars mentioned above, satva is correct for the words Vajrasatva and bodhisatva, whereas sattva is correct for the words samayasattva, samādhisattva, and jñānasattva, and is also used alone to refer to any or all of these three satvas.

All Tibetan texts produced since the time of the great translations conform to this system and all Tibetan experts agree that this is correct, but Western translators of Tibetan texts have for last few hundreds of years claimed that they know better and have "satva" to "sattva" in every case, causing confusion amongst Westerners confronted by the correct spellings. Recently, publications by Western Sanskrit scholars have been appearing in which these great experts finally admit that they were wrong and that the Tibetan system is and always has been correct!

Shamatha, Skt. śhamatha, Tib. gzhi gnas: The name of one of the two main practices of meditation used in the Buddhist system to gain insight into reality. This practice creates a foundation of one-pointedness of mind which can then be used to focus the insight of the other practice, vipaśhyanā. If the development of śhamatha is taken through to completion, the result is a mind that sits stably on its object without any effort and a body which is filled with ease. Altogether, this result of the practice is called "workability of body and mind".

Superfactual, Skt. paramārtha,Tib. don dam: This term is paired with the term "fictional" *q.v.* In the past, the terms have been translated as "relative" and "absolute" respectively, but those translations are nothing like the original terms. These terms are extremely important in the Buddhist teaching so it is very important that their translations be corrected but, more than that, if the actual meaning of these terms is not presented, the teaching connected with them cannot be understood.

The Sanskrit term literally means "the fact for that which is above all others, special, superior" and refers to the wisdom mind possessed by those who have developed themselves spiritually to the point of having transcended saṃsāra. That wisdom is *superior* to an ordinary, un-developed person's consciousness and the *facts* that appear on its surface are superior compared to the facts that appear on the ordinary person's consciousness. Therefore, it is superfact or the holy fact, more literally. What this wisdom knows is true for the beings who have it, therefore what the wisdom sees is superfactual truth.

Superfactual truth, Skt. paramārthasatya, Tib. don dam bden pa: See under superfactual.

Superfice, superficies, Tib. rnam pa: In discussions of mind, a distinction is made between the entity of mind which is a mere knower and the superficial things that appear on its surface and which are known by it. In other words, the superficies are the various things which pass over the surface of mind but which are not mind. Superficies are all the specifics that constitute appearance—for example, the colour white within a moment of visual consciousness, the sound heard within an ear consciousness, and so on.

Three higher trainings, Tib. bslabs pa gsum: The three trainings of the Buddhist path are śhīla, samādhi, and prajñā—discipline, concentration, and correct discernment.

Three secrets, Tib. gsang ba: This term is usually defined as a path term which refers to the body, speech, and mind of a person who is on the way to buddhahood. When a person becomes a buddha, he has reached his full state of enlightenment and at that point the three secrets have become unchanging so are now referred to as "the three vajras" of a tathāgata. This path term is used to mean the three vajras of the fruition state of buddhahood.

Three Vehicles, theg pa gsum: The entire teachings of the Buddha can be summed up into three "vehicles". Each vehicle is a complete set of teachings that will take a person to a particular level of spiritual attainment. The first one, the Lesser Vehicle, is a set of teachings that will take a person out of cyclic existence but will not lead the person to full enlightenment. The second one, the Great Vehicle, is "great" relative to the Lesser Vehicle because it can lead a person to full enlightenment. The third vehicle, the Vajra Vehicle, also can lead a person to full enlightenment. The difference between the Great and Vajra Vehicles is that the first consists of exoteric teachings that are suitable for anyone whereas the second consists of esoteric teachings which are not. The Great Vehicle and the Vajra Vehicle both lead to the same attainment, but the first proceeds very gradually whereas the second is very fast. The Great Vehicle proceeds using the sūtra teachings of the Buddha whereas the Vajra Vehicle proceeds using the tantric teachings.

Tirthika, Skt. tīrthika, Tib. mu stegs pa: This is very kind name adopted by the Buddha for those who did not follow him but who, because they followed some other spiritual path, had at least started on the path back to enlightenment. The Sanskrit name means "those who have arrived at the steps at the edge of the pool". A lengthy explanation is given in the *Illuminator Tibetan-English Dictionary* by Tony Duff and published by Padma Karpo Translation Committee.

Total affliction and complete purification, Tib. kun nas nyon mongs pa dang rnam par byang ba: The Buddha divided all types of existence into two: enlightened existence and un-enlightened existence. He taught his disciples that their unenlightened existence was total (through and through) affliction, but if they followed the path to enlightenment, they would arrive, through the practice of purification of that affliction, at the state of enlightened existence, which he then referred to as "complete purification". In this way, he made the character of these two types of existence clear and at the same time goaded his disciples to get on the path and reach the point of complete purification.

Un-outflowed, Skt. anāśhrāva, Tib. zag pa med pa: Un-outflowed dharmas are ones that are connected with wisdom that has not lost its footing and leaked out into a defiled state; it is self-contained wisdom without any taint of dualistic mind and its apparatus. See also outflowed.

Unsatisfactoriness, Skt. duḥkha, Tib. sdug bngal: This term is usually translated into English with "suffering" but there are many problems with that. When the Buddha talked about the nature of samsaric existence, he said that it was unsatisfactory. He used the term "duḥkha", which includes actual suffering but means much more than that. Duḥkha is one of a pair of terms, the other being "sukha", which is usually translated as, but does not only mean, bliss. The real meaning of duḥkha is "everything on the side of bad"—not good, uncomfortable, unpleasant, not nice, and so on. Thus, it means "unsatisfactory in every possible way". The real meaning of its opposite, sukha, is "everything on the side of good"—not bad, comfortable, pleasant, nice, and so on. Therefore, that he is completely liberated from the sufferings actually means that he has completely liberated himself from the unsatisfactoriness of saṃsāra, which includes all types of suffering and happiness, too.

Vajra Vehicle, Skt. vajrayāna, Tib. rdo rje'i theg pa: See under Great Vehicle.

Valid cognizer, valid cognition, Skt. pramāṇa, Tib. tshad ma: The Sanskrit term "pramāṇa" literally means "best type of mentality" and comes to mean "a valid cognizer". Its value is that is can be used to validate anything that can be known. The Tibetans translated this term with "tshad ma" meaning an "evaluator"—something which can be used to evaluate the truth or not of whatever it is given to know. It is the term used in logic to indicate a mind which is knowing validly and which therefore can be used to validate the object it is knowing.

Valid cognizers are named according to the kind of test they are employed to do. A valid cognizer of the conventional or a valid cognizer of the fictional tests within conventions, within the realm of rational, dualistic mind. A valid cognizer of the ultimate or valid cognizer of superfact tests for the superfactual level, beyond dualistic mind.

Vipashyana, Skt. vipaśhyanā, Tib. lhag mthong: This is the Sanskrit name for one of the two main practices of meditation needed in the Buddhist system for gaining insight into reality. The other one, śhamatha, keeps the mind focussed while this one looks piercingly into the nature of things.

Wisdom, Skt. jñāna, Tib. ye shes: This is a fruition term that refers to the kind of mind, the kind of knower possessed by a buddha. Sentient beings do have this kind of knower but it is covered over by a very complex apparatus for knowing, that is, dualistic mind. If they practise the path to buddhahood, they will leave behind their obscuration and return to having this kind of knower.

The Sanskrit term has the sense of knowing in the most simple and immediate way. This sort of knowing is present at the core of every being's mind. Therefore, the Tibetans called it "the particular type of awareness which is there primordially". Because of the Tibetan wording it has often been called "primordial wisdom" in

English translations, but that goes too far; it is just "wisdom" in the sense of the most fundamental knowing possible.

Wisdom does not operate in the same way as samsaric mind; it comes about in and of itself without depending on cause and effect. Therefore it is frequently referred to as "self-arising wisdom" *q.v.*

Supports for Study

I have been encouraged over the years by all of my teachers to pass on the knowledge I have accumulated in a lifetime dedicated to study and practice, primarily in the Tibetan tradition of Buddhism. On the one hand, they have encouraged me to teach. On the other, they are concerned that, while many general books on Buddhism have been and are being published, there are few books that present the actual texts of the tradition. Therefore they, together with a number of major figures in the Buddhist book publishing world, have also encouraged me to translate and publish high quality translations of individual texts of the tradition.

My teachers always remark with great appreciation on the extraordinary amount of teaching that I have heard in this life. It allows for highly informed, accurate translations of a sort not usually seen. Briefly, I spent the 1970's studying, practising, then teaching the Gelugpa system at Chenrezig Institute, Australia, where I was a founding member and also the first Australian to be ordained as a monk in the Tibetan Buddhist tradition. In 1980, I moved to the United States to study at the feet of the Vidyadhara Chogyam Trungpa Rinpoche. I stayed in his Vajradhatu community, now called Shambhala, where I studied and practised all the Karma Kagyu, Nyingma, and Shambhala teachings being presented there and was a senior member of the Nalanda Translation Committee. After the vidyadhara's nirvāṇa, I moved in 1992 to Nepal, where I have been continuously involved with the study, practise, translation, and teaching of the Kagyu system and especially of the Nyingma system of Great Completion. In recent years, I have spent extended times in Tibet with the greatest living Tibetan masters of Great Completion, receiving very pure transmissions of the ultimate levels of this teaching directly in Tibetan and practising them there in retreat. In that way, I have studied and practised extensively not in one Tibetan tradition as is usually done, but in three of the four Tibetan traditions—Gelug, Kagyu, and Nyingma—and also in the Theravada tradition, too.

With that as a basis, I have taken a comprehensive and long-term approach to the work of translation. For any language, one first must have the lettering needed to write the language. Therefore, as a member of the Nalanda Translation Committee, I spent some years in the 1980's making Tibetan word-processing software and high-quality Tibetan fonts. After that, reliable lexical works are needed. Therefore, during the 1990's I spent some years writing the *Illuminator Tibetan-English Dictionary* and a set of treatises on Tibetan grammar, preparing a variety of key Tibetan reference works needed for the study and translation of Tibetan Buddhist texts, and giving our Tibetan software the tools needed to translate and research Tibetan texts. During this time, I also translated full-time for various Tibetan gurus and ran the Drukpa Kagyu Heritage Project—at the time the largest project in Asia for the preservation of Tibetan Buddhist texts. With the dictionaries, grammar texts, and specialized software in place, and a wealth of knowledge, I turned my attention in the year 2000 to the translation and publication of important texts of Tibetan Buddhist literature.

Padma Karpo Translation Committee (PKTC) was set up to provide a home for the translation and publication work. The committee focusses on producing books containing the best of Tibetan literature, and, especially, books that meet the needs of practitioners. At the time of writing, PKTC has published a wide range of books that, collectively, make a complete program of study for those practising Tibetan Buddhism, and especially for those interested in the higher tantras. All in all, you will find many books both free and for sale on the PKTC web-site. Most are available both as paper editions and e-books.

It would take up too much space here to present an extensive guide to our books and how they can be used as the basis for a study program. However, a guide of that sort is available on the PKTC web-site, whose address is on the copyright page of this book; we recommend that you read it to see how this book fits into the overall scheme of PKTC publications. One book that will be particularly helpful as a support for this book will be:

- *Unending Auspiciousness, The Sūtra of the Recollection of the Noble Three Jewels with Commentaries by Ju Mipham, Taranatha, and Tony Duff*, which includes many basic definitions and teachings of the Lesser and Greater Vehicle.

Other books that present the view and would be of interest are:

- *The Other Emptiness, Entering Wisdom Beyond Emptiness of Self*, a major exposition on the view of other emptiness;
- *A Juggernaut of the Non-Dual View, Ultimate Teachings of the Second Drukchen Gyalwang Je*, a set of sixty-six teachings on the ultimate view by one of the early masters of the Drukpa Kagyu;
- *Maitrīpa's Writings on the View*, several teachings on the view from the "father of other emptiness";
- *Theory and Practice of Other Emptiness Taught Through Milarepa's Songs*, a complete explanation of the view of other emptiness given through two songs of Milarepa which are famous for their expositions of the non-dual view;

- *"Instructions for Practising the View of Other Emptiness", A Text of Oral Instructions by Jamgon Kongtrul*;
- *The Lion's Roar That Proclaims Zhantong (Other Emptiness)* by Ju Mipham

We make a point of including, where possible, the relevant Tibetan texts in Tibetan script in our books. We also make them available in electronic editions that can be downloaded free from our web-site, as discussed below. The Tibetan text for this book has been included in the book. A digital edition, together with the software needed to read it, is available on the PKTC web-site.

Electronic Resources

PKTC has developed a complete range of electronic tools to facilitate the study and translation of Tibetan texts. For many years now, this software has been a prime resource for Tibetan Buddhist centres throughout the world, including in Tibet itself. It is available through the PKTC web-site.

The wordprocessor TibetDoc has the only complete set of tools for creating, correcting, and formatting Tibetan text according to the norms of the Tibetan language. It can also be used to make texts with mixed Tibetan and English or other languages. Extremely high quality Tibetan fonts, based on the forms of Tibetan calligraphy learned from old masters from pre-Communist Chinese Tibet, are also available. Because of their excellence, these typefaces have achieved a legendary status amongst Tibetans.

TibetDoc is used to prepare electronic editions of Tibetan texts in the PKTC text input office in Asia. Tibetan texts are often corrupt so the input texts are carefully corrected prior to distribution. After that, they are made available through the PKTC web-site. These electronic texts are not careless productions like so many of the Tibetan texts found on the web, but are highly reliable editions useful to non-scholars and scholars alike. Some of the larger collections of these texts are for purchase, but most are available for free download.

The electronic texts can be read, searched, and even made into an electronic library using either TibetDoc or our other software, TibetD Reader. Like TibetDoc, TibetD Reader is advanced software with many capabilities made specifically to meet the needs of reading and researching Tibetan texts. PKTC software is for purchase but we make a free version of TibetD Reader available for free download on the PKTC web-site.

A key feature of TibetDoc and Tibet Reader is that Tibetan terms in texts can be looked up on the spot using PKTC's electronic dictionaries. PKTC also has several electronic dictionaries—some Tibetan-Tibetan and some Tibetan-English—and a number of other reference works. The *Illuminator Tibetan-English Dictionary* is renowned for its completeness and accuracy.

This combination of software, texts, reference works, and dictionaries that work together seamlessly has become famous over the years. It has been the basis of many, large publishing projects within the Tibetan Buddhist community around the world for over thirty years and is popular amongst all those needing to work with Tibetan language or deepen their understanding of Buddhism through Tibetan texts.

Tibetan Text

༄༅། །མཁས་པར་བྱ་བའི་གནས་དྲུག་བསྟན་པ་ཤེས་བྱ་གསལ་བའི་མེ་ལོང་
ཞེས་བྱ་བ་བཞུགས་སོ།།

[ཤོག་བུ་༢] ༄༅། །བླ་མ་དང་ལྷག་པའི་ལྷ་ལ་ཕྱག་འཚལ་ལོ། །ཤེས་བྱ་མཐའ་མེད་མཁའ་དབྱིངས་ཁྱབ་པར་མཁྱེན་རབ་ཉི་མའི་སྙིང་པོ་བརྙེས། །སོ་སོ་ཡང་དག་རིག་བཞིའི་ཚུལ་གྱིས་འགྲོ་ལ་ཆོས་ཚུལ་སྟོང་མཛད་དེ། །ཞུ་ཆེན་སྒྱུར་བྱེད་མཆན་བུའི་གནས་འདུག་མཁས་པ་པཻ་རོ་ཙ་ན་གང་། །ཐུན་མོངས་མཆོག་གི་དངོས་གྲུབ་བརྙེས་ནས་མཁའ་ལ་འཛའ་བཞིན་ཡལ་ལ་འདུད། །དེ་ཉིད་སླར་ཡང་སྙིགས་མའི་སྐབས། །བསལ་མཛད་མཁྱེན་རབ་ཟླ་བ་ནི། །གཞན་ཕན་ཆོས་ཀྱི་སྣང་བ་ཅན། །མཐའ་ཡས་སྐྱེ་དགུའི་དཔལ་དུ་ཤར། །དམ་པ་གང་གི་ལེགས་པར་བཤད་པ་ཡི། །ཆ་ཙམ་སུ་ཡི་རྣ་བར་སོན་པ་ཡང་། །གཞན་ལ་མི་འཇིགས་སྤོབས་པའི་ལམ་རླེད་ན། །འདི་ལ་རབ་དགའ་མི་སྐྱེ་གང་ཞིག་ཡོད། །དེ་ཕྱིར་རྒྱལ་དང་[ཤོག་བུ་༣] རྒྱལ་བའི་སྲས། །ཀུན་གྱིས་གཤེགས་པའི་ལམ་བཟང་པོ། །ཐོས་པ་རིན་ཆེན་སྐྱེ་དགུའི་མིག །འདི་ལ་ཐོག་མར་འཇུག་པར་རིགས། །དེ་ལ་འདིར་སྐྱབས་མགོན་རྒྱལ་བའི་སྲས་པོ་གཞན་ཕན་མཐའ་ཡས་འོད་ཟེར་གྱི་ཞལ་སྔ་ནས། ། སྐལ་ལྡན་ཚེ་འདིར་བློ་འདོད་རྣམས། །མཁས་པར་བྱ་བའི་གནས་དྲུག

སློབས། །མཁས་བྱའི་གནས་དྲུག་མི་ཤེས་པས། །ཆོས་ཀྱི་རྣམ་དབྱེ་མི་ཤེས་སོ། །ཆོས་ཀྱི་རྣམ་དབྱེ་མི་ཤེས་པས། །ཕྱི་ནང་བདེན་རྫུན་མི་ཤེས་སོ། །ཕྱི་ནང་བདེན་རྫུན་མི་ཤེས་པས། །ཕྱི་དོན་བདེན་གྲུབ་མི་འགོག་གོ །ཕྱི་དོན་བདེན་གྲུབ་མི་འགོག་པས། །ནང་ལ་འཇུག་པ་མི་ཤེས་སོ། །ནང་ལ་འཇུག་པའི་མི་ཤེས་པས། །སྣང་བ་སེམས་སུ་མི་ཤེས་སོ། །སྣང་བ་སེམས་སུ་མི་ཤེས་པས། །ཀུན་[ཤོག་བུ་༤]གཞིའི་རྣམ་ཤེས་མི་ཤེས་སོ། །ཀུན་གཞིའི་རྣམ་ཤེས་མི་ཤེས་པས། །ཀུན་གཞིའི་གསང་གནད་མི་ཤེས་སོ། །ཀུན་གཞིའི་གསང་གནད་མི་ཤེས་པས། །སྦྱོར་གྲོལ་བློ་འདས་མི་ཤེས་སོ། །སྦྱོར་གྲོལ་བློ་འདས་མི་ཤེས་པས། །དབུ་མའི་ལྟ་བ་མི་ཤེས་སོ། །དབུ་མའི་ལྟ་བ་མི་ཤེས་པས། །སྟོང་པའི་འོད་གསལ་མི་ཤེས་སོ། །སྟོང་པའི་འོད་གསལ་མི་ཤེས་པས། །སྣང་བའི་འོད་གསལ་མི་ཤེས་སོ། །སྣང་བའི་འོད་གསལ་མི་ཤེས་པས། །སྣང་སྟོང་འཇུག་འཇུག་མི་ཤེས་སོ། །སྣང་སྟོང་ཟུང་འཇུག་མི་ཤེས་པས། ཟུང་འཇུག་འོད་གསལ་མི་ཤེས་སོ། །ཟུང་འཇུག་འོད་གསལ་མི་ཤེས་པས། །རྫོགས་པ་ཆེན་པོ་མི་ཤེས་སོ། །རྫོགས་པ་ཆེན་པོ་མི་ཤེས་པས། །ཚེ་འདིར་སངས་རྒྱས་མི་ཐོབ་བོ། །དེ་ཕྱིར་མི་ཚེ་འདི་ཉིད་ལ། །རྫོགས་པའི་སངས་རྒྱས་ཐོབ་འདོད་རྣམས། །དང་པོ་མཁས་བྱའི་གནས་དྲུག་སློབས། །དེ་རྗེས་ཐེག་ཆེན་སྡོམ་བཞི་སློབས། །དེ་ནས་དབུ་མ་ལ་འཇུག་སྟེ། །འོད་གསལ་རྫོགས་པ་ཆེན་པོ་སྒོམས། །ཞེས་གསུངས་པའི་དོན་གཏན་ལ་འབེབས་པ་ལ་བཞི་སྟེ། མཁས་པར་བྱ་བའི་གནས་དྲུག །ཐེག་ཆེན་ཆོས་ཀྱི་སྡོམ་བཞི། མཐའ་བྲལ་དབུ་མའི་ལམ་ལ་ཇི་ལྟར་འཇུག་པའི་ཚུལ། །འོད་གསལ་རྫོགས་པ་ཆེན་པོ་ཇི་ལྟར་སྒོམ་ཚུལ་བཤད་པའོ། །དང་པོ་ནི། མདོ་ལས། རིགས་ཀྱི་བུ་ཁྱོད་ཕུང་པོ་ལ་མཁས་པར་བྱའོ། །སྐྱེ་མཆེད་ལ་མཁས་པར་བྱའོ། །ཁམས་ལ་མཁས་པར་བྱའོ། །རྟེན་ཅིང་[ཤོག་བུ་༥]འབྲེལ་བར་འབྱུང་བ་ལ་མཁས་པར་བྱའོ། །གནས་ལ་མཁས་པར་བྱའོ། །གནས་མ་ཡིན་པ་ལ་མཁས་པར་བྱའོ། །ཞེས་པ་ལྟར་དྲུག་ལས། དང་པོ་ཕུང་པོ་ལ་ངེས་ཚིག་ནི། དུ་མ་

སྤུང་བས་ན་ཕུང་པོའོ། །དབྱེ་ན་ལྔ་སྟེ། གཟུགས་ཀྱི་ཕུང་པོ། ཚོར་བའི་ཕུང་པོ། འདུ་ཤེས་ཀྱི་ཕུང་པོ། འདུ་བྱེད་ཀྱི་ཕུང་པོ། རྣམ་པར་ཤེས་པའི་ཕུང་པོའོ། །དང་པོ་ལ་གཉིས། མཚན་ཉིད་དང་། དབྱེ་བའོ། །དང་པོ་ནི། གཟུགས་སུ་རུང་བ་གཟུགས་ཀྱི་མཚན་ཉིད་དོ། །གཉིས་པ་ལ་གཉིས། རྒྱུ་གཟུགས་དང་། འབྲས་གཟུགས་སོ། །རྒྱུ་གཟུགས་ལ་བཞི་སྟེ། ས་ཆུ་མེ་རླུང་ངོ་། །འབྲས་གཟུགས་ལ་བཅུ་གཅིག་སྟེ། དབང་པོ་ལྔ། ཡུལ་ལྔ། རྣམ་པར་རིག་བྱེད་མ་ཡིན་པའི་གཟུགས་སོ། །དེ་ལ་དབང་པོ་ལྔ་ནི་བྱེ་སྒྲ་རྣམས་གཟུགས་ཅན་དུ་འདོད་དོ། །དེའང་མིག་གི་དབང་པོ་ཟར་མའི་མེ་ཏོག་ལྟ་བུ། །རྣ་བའི་དབང་པོ་གྲོག་གཙུས་པ་ལྟ་བུ། །སྣའི་དབང་པོ་ཟངས་དུང་གཤིབས་པ་ལྟ་བུ། ལྕེའི་དབང་པོ་ཟླ་བ་གམ་པ་ལྟ་བུ། ལུས་ཀྱི་དབང་པོ་བྱ་རེག་ན་འཇམ་གྱི་པགས་པ་ལྟ་བུའོ། །ཞེས་ཟེར་རོ། །མདོ་སྡེ་བདག་དབང་རྟེན་འདི་ལ་ཡུལ་འཛིན་རུང་གི་ནུས་པ་ཁྱད་པར་ཅན་དུ་ཡོད་པ་ལ་དབང་པོ་ཞེས་འདོད་དོ། །ཡུལ་ལྔ་ནི། གཟུགས་སྒྲ་དྲི་རོ་རེག་བྱའོ། །དེ་ཡང་མཛོད་ལས། །གཟུགས་རྣམ་གཉིས་ཏེ་རྣམ་ཉི་ཤུ། ། སྒྲ་ནི་རྣམ་པ་བརྒྱད་ཡོད་དེ། །དྲི་ནི་རྣམ་བཞི་རོ་རྣམ་དྲུག །རེག་[ཤོག་བུ་༦]བྱ་བཅུ་གཅིག་བདག་ཉིད་དོ། །ཞེས་པ་ལྟར་ལས། དང་པོ་གཟུགས་ལའང་དབྱེ་ན་དབྱིབས་གཟུགས་བརྒྱད་དང་། ཁ་དོག་གི་གཟུགས་བཅུ་གཉིས་ཏེ་བསྡོམས་པས་ཉི་ཤུའོ། །དེ་ལ་དབྱིབས་གཟུགས་བརྒྱད་ནི། རིང་པོ་དང་ཐུང་དུ། །མཐོ་བ་དང་དམའ་བ། ཟླུམ་པོ་དང་ལྷམ་པ། ཕྱལ་ལེ་བ་དང་། ཕྱལ་ལེ་བ་མ་ཡིན་པའོ། །ཁ་དོག་གི་གཟུགས་བཅུ་གཉིས་ལའང་རྩ་བའི་ཁ་དོག་བཞི་དང་ཡན་ལག་གི་ཁ་དོག་བརྒྱད་ཡོད་པ་ལས། དང་པོ་ནི། སྔོ་སེར་དཀར་དམར་དག་གོ །ལྗང་གུ་ནི་ཁ་དོག་འདུས་པ་ཡིན་པས་འདིར་ལོག་པ་མེད་དོ། །གཉིས་པ་ལ། སྤྲིན་དང་དུ་བ། རྡུལ་དང་ཁུག་རྣ། སྣང་བ་དང་མུན་པ། ཉི་ཟེར་དང་གྲིབ་མ་རྣམས་སོ། །ཀུན་བཏུས་ལས་ནི། དེ་དག་གི་སྟེང་དུ་དབྱིབས་ལ་རྡུལ་ཕྲ་མོ་དང་རགས་པ་གཉིས་དང་ཁ་དོག་ལ་མངོན་...ཐོག་པའི་རིག་དང་བྲལ་བའོ། པར་སྐབས་ཡོད་པ་དང་།

རྣམ་པར་…རྣམ་འགྱུར། རིག་བྱེད་དང་ནམ་མཁའ་…སྟེང་ན་སྔོན་པོར་སྣང་བའོ། ཁ་དོག་གཅིག་པའོ་ཞེས་ལྔ་བསྟན་པས་ཉེར་ལྔའི་བར་དུ་གསུངས་སོ། །གཉིས་པ་སྒྲ་ཡའང་། ཟིན་པའི་འབྱུང་བ་ལས་གྱུར་པའི་སྒྲ་བཞི་དང་། མ་ཟིན་པའི་འབྱུང་བ་ལས་གྱུར་པའི་བཞི་སྟེ་བརྒྱད་དོ། །དེའང་དང་པོ་ལ་སེམས་ཅན་དུ་སྟོན་མི་སྟོན་གཉིས། དེ་རེ་རེ་ལ་སྙན་མི་སྙན་གཉིས་ཏེ་བཞིའོ། །དེ་དག་གི་དཔེར་བརྗོད་ནི་རིམ་པ་བཞིན། ཆོས་སྟོན་པ་དང་། ཚིག་རྩུབ་སྨྲ་བ་དང་། ཐེག་རྡོབ་པ་དང་། ཁྲུ་ཚུར་བརྡེག་པ་རྣམས་ [ཤོག་བུ་ ༧] སོ། །ཕྱི་མ་ཡའང་སེམས་ཅན་དུ་སྟོན་མི་སྟོན་གཉིས་དང་། དེ་རེ་རེ་ལ་སྙན་མི་སྙན་གཉིས་རེ་སྟེ་བཞི་ཡོད་དོ། །དེ་དག་གི་དཔེར་བརྗོད་ཀྱང་རིམ་པ་བཞིན། སྤྲུལ་པའི་གང་ཟག་གིས་ཆོས་སྟོན་པ་དང་། དེས་ཚིག་རྩུབ་སྨྲ་བ་དང་། རོལ་མོའི་སྒྲ་དང་། བྲག་རལ་བའི་སྒྲ་ལྟ་བུ་རྣམས་སོ། །འདི་ལ་ཀུན་བཏུས་ལས་ནི། ཡིད་དུ་འོང་བ་དང་། མི་འོང་བ་དང་། གཉིས་ཀ་དང་། ཟིན་པའི་དང་། མ་ཟིན་པའི་འབྱུང་བ་ཆེན་པོའི་རྒྱུ་ལས་བྱུང་བ་དང་། དེ་གཉིས་ཀ་དང་།…ལག་པ་དང་རྫ་རྔའི་ལྟ་བུ། འཇིག་རྟེན་གྱི་གྲགས་པ་དང་།…ཐལ་པའི་སྐད་ཀྱིས་བསྒྲུས་པའོ། །གྲུབ་པས་…འཕགས་པ་རྣམས་ཀྱིས་བསྟན་པའོ། བསྟན་པ་དང་། ཀུན་…མུ་སྟེགས་ཅན་གྱིས་བསྟན་པའོ། བརྟགས་པ་དང་། འཕགས་པས་ཐ་སྙད་བརྟགས་པ་དང་…ཕྱི་མ་གཉིས་མཐོང་བ་ལ་སོགས་པའི་ཐ་སྙད་ཀྱི་དབང་དུ་བྱས་སོ། །འཕགས་པ་མ་ཡིན་པས་བརྟགས་པའོ། །ཞེས་རྣམ་གྲངས་བཅུ་གཅིག་ཏུ་གསུངས་སོ། །གསུམ་པ་དྲི་ཡའང་ལྷན་སྐྱེས་དང་སྦྱོར་བྱུང་གཉིས། རེ་རེ་ལ་ཞིམ་མི་ཞིམ་གཉིས་གཉིས་ཀྱིས་ཕྱེ་བས་བཞིའོ། །དེ་དག་གི་དཔེར་བརྗོད་ཀྱང་རིམ་པ་བཞིན། ཨ་ག་རུའི་དྲི་དང་། སྒོག་སྐྱའི་དྲི་དང་། སྤོས་རེང་གི་དྲི་དང་། དྲི་ང་བ་དུམ་འདུས་པའི་དྲི་རྣམས་ལྟ་བུའོ། །ཀུན་བཏུས་ལས་ནི། དྲི་བཟང་དང་། དྲི་ང་བ་དང་། དྲི་མཉམ་པ་དང་།…ཨ་ག་རུ་ལྟ་བུའོ། ལྷན་ཅིག་སྐྱེས་པ་དང་། སྦྱར་བ་ལས་བྱུང་བ་དང་། འགྱུར་བ་ [ཤོག་བུ་ ༨] ལས་ཤིང་ཐོག་སྨིན་པ་ལྟ་བུའོ། བྱུང་བའོ། །ཞེས་དྲུག་ཏུ་གསུངས་སོ། ། བཞི་པ་རོ་ཡའང་དབྱེ་ན་རྣམ་པ་དྲུག་སྟེ། མངར་བ་དང་། སྐྱུར་བ་དང་། ཁ་བ་

དང་། བསྐ་བ་དང་། ཚ་བ་དང་། ལན་ཚྭ་བའོ། །དེ་དག་གི་དཔེར་བརྗོད་ཀྱང་རིམ་བཞིན། བུ་རམ། སྐྱུ་རུ་ར། ཏིག་ཏ། ཨ་རུ་ར། ཙི་ཏྲ་ཀ། ལན་ཚྭ་རྣམས་ཀྱི་རོ་ལྟ་བུའོ། །ཀུན་བཏུས་ལས་ནི། དེ་དག་གི་སྟེང་དུ། ཡིད་དུ་འོང་བ་དང་མི་འོང་བ་དང་། དེ་གཉིས་ཀ་མ་ཡིན་པ་དང་། ལྷན་ཅིག་སྐྱེས་པ་དང་། སྦྱར་བ་ལས་བྱུང་བ་དང་། འགྱུར་བ་ལས་བྱུང་བའོ། འདི་ནི་དྲི་ལས་དཔག་པར་བྱའོ། །ཞེས་རྣམ་གྲངས་བཅུ་གཉིས་སུ་གསུངས་སོ། །ལྔ་པ་རེག་བྱ་ལའང་། འབྱུང་བའི་རེག་བྱ་བཞི། འབྱུང་འགྱུར་གྱི་རེག་བྱ་བདུན་དང་བཅུ་གཅིག་གོ །དང་པོ་བཞི་ནི། ས་སྲ་བ། ཆུ་གཤེར་བ། མེ་དྲོ་བ། རླུང་ཡང་བའོ། །ཕྱི་མ་བདུན་ནི། མེ་ཆུ་འདུས་པའི་རིགས་ འཇམ་རྩུབ་ ས་རླུང་འདུས་པ། གཉིས། ས་ཆུ་འདུས་བ་ ལྗི་ཡང་གཉིས་ མེ་རླུང་འདུས་པ། བཀྲེས་ ས་མེ་འདུས་པ། སྐོམ་གཉིས་ མེ་རླུང་འདུས་པ། གྲང་བ་དང་ ཆུ་རླུང་འདུས་པའི་རིགས་བྱ། བཅས་པའོ། །ཀུན་བཏུས་ལས་ནི། འདི་ལྟར། འཇམ་པ་ཉིད་དང་། རྩུབ་པ་ཉིད་དང་། ཡང་བ་ཉིད་དང་། ལྗི་བ་ཉིད་དང་། མཉེན་པ་ཉིད་དང་། ལྷོད་པ་ཉིད་དང་། ལྷོད་པ་མ་ཡིན་པ་དང་། གྲང་བ་དང་། བཀྲེས་པ་དང་། སྐོམ་པ་དང་། ཚིམ་པ་(ཤོག་བུ་༩)དང་། ཉམས་ཡོད་པ་དང་། ཉམས་ཆུང་བ་དང་། བརྒྱལ་བ་དང་། གཡའ་བ་དང་། འཁྲེད་པ་དང་། ན་བ་དང་། རྒ་བ་དང་། འཆི་བ་དང་། ངལ་བ་དང་། ངལ་སོས་པ་དང་། སྤྱུང་ཆེ་བའོ། མི་འཇིགས་པའོ། ཕྱི་མ་གཉིས་ཁམས་སློམས་པ་དང་། ཚིམ་པ་ནི་གཉིས་ཀ་གཞན་མི་སློམས་པར་བལྟའོ། ཞེས་རྣམ་གྲངས་ཉེར་གཉིས་ཀྱི་བར་དུ་གསུངས་སོ། །རྣམ་པར་རིག་བྱེད་མ་ཡིན་པའི་གཟུགས་ནི་མཛོད་ལས། གཡེངས་དང་ གནས་སྐབས་ཀྱི་ཁྱད་པར། སེམས་མེད་པ་ཡི་ཡང་། ངོ་བོའི་ཁྱད་པར་ དགེ་དང་མི་དགེ་ དུས་ཀྱི་ཁྱད་པར་རྒྱུན། རྗེས་འབྲེལ་གང་། །འབྱུང་བ་རྒྱུ་ཁྱད་པར་ ཆེ་རྣམས་རྒྱུར་བྱས་པ། །དེ་ནི་རྣམ་རིག་བྱེད་མིན་བརྗོད། །ཞེས་དང་། པ་རང་ཀུན་ནས་སློང་བྱེད་དེ་གཞན་ལ་རིག་པར་མི་བྱེད་པས་ན་རིག་བྱེད་མ་ཡིན་པའི་གཟུགས་ཞེས་སྔོན་གྱི་ལོ་ཙྪ་བའི་གསུངས་པས་བསྟན་པ། དབྱེ་ན་དེ་ཉིད་ལས། །རྣམ་རིག་མིན་རྣམ་

གསུམ་ཞེས་བྱ། །སྡོམ་དང་སྡོམ་པ་མིན་དང་གཞན། །སྡོམ་པ་སོ་སོར་ཐར་ཞེས་བྱ། །དེ་བཞིན་ཟག་མེད་བསམ་གཏན་སྐྱེས། ཞེས་སོ། །འདི་དག་...མཚན་ཉིད་ནི་སློབ་དཔོན་དབྱིག་གཉེན་གྱི་བཞེད་པ་ལྟར་བྲིས་...པ་ཡིན་ལ་སློབ་དཔོན་འདུན་བཟང་ནི་དེ་ལས་གཞན་དུ་འཆད་པར་མཛད་དོ། །དེ་དག་ཐམས་ཅད་ཀྱང་བསྡུ་ན་བསྟན་ཡོད་ཐོགས་བཅས་ཀྱི་གཟུགས་མིག་གི་སྤྱོད་ཡུལ་དུ་གྱུར་པ་རྣམས་དང་། བསྟན་མེད་ཐོགས་བཅས་ཀྱི་གཟུགས་རྣ་བ་སོགས་བཞིའི་སྤྱོད་ཡུལ་དུ་གྱུར་པ་[ཤོག་བུ་༧༠]རྣམས་དང་། བསྟན་མེད་ཐོགས་མེད་ཀྱི་གཟུགས་རིག་བྱེད་མ་ཡིན་པ་ལྟ་བུ་དང་གསུམ་དུ་འདུས་པ་ཡིན་ནོ། །དེ་ནི་ཚོར་བའི་ཕུང་པོ་ལའང་། མཚན་ཉིད་དང་དབྱེ་བའོ། །དང་པོ་ནི། ཉམས་སུ་མྱོང་པ་ཚོར་བའི་མཚན་ཉིད་དོ། །གཉིས་པ་ནི་གཅིག་ཏུ་བསྡུ་ན། མདོ་ལས། གང་ཅི་ཚོར་བ་ཐམས་ཅད་ནི་སྡུག་བསྔལ་བའོ། །དེ་ཅིའི་ཕྱིར་ཞེ་ན། ཚོར་བ་བདེ་བ་ནི་འགྱུར་བའི་སྡུག་བསྔལ་གྱི་རང་བཞིན་དང་། ཚོར་བ་སྡུག་བསྔལ་ནི་སྡུག་བསྔལ་གྱི་སྡུག་བསྔལ་གྱི་རང་བཞིན་དང་། ཚོར་བ་བར་མ་ནི་ཁྱབ་པ་འདུ་བྱེད་ཀྱི་སྡུག་བསྔལ་གྱི་རང་བཞིན་ནོ། །ཞེས་གསུངས་པས་སོ་སྐྱེའི་རྒྱུད་ཀྱི་ཚོར་བ་ཐམས་ཅད་དངོས་མ་བརྒྱུད་ནས་སྡུག་བསྔལ་བའི་རང་བཞིན་དུ་བསྟན་ཞིང་། གཉིས་སུ་དབྱེ་ན། ལུས་ཚོར་དང་སེམས་ཚོར་རམ། གསུམ་དུ་དབྱེ་ན། བདེ་བ་དང་། སྡུག་བསྔལ་བ་དང་། བར་མའོ། །བཞི་རུ་དབྱེ་ན། ལུས་ཚོར་དང་སེམས་ཚོར་གཉིས། དེ་རེ་རེ་ལའང་ཀུན་ཉོན་ཕྱོགས་དང་། རྣམ་བྱང་ཕྱོགས་ཀྱི་ཚོར་བ་གཉིས་གཉིས་ཡོད་དོ། །ལྔ་རུ་དབྱེ་ན། བདེ་བ་དང་། སྡུག་བསྔལ་བ་དང་། ཡིད་བདེ་བ་དང་། ཡིད་མི་བདེ་བ་དང་། བཏང་སྙོམས་རྣམས་སོ། །དྲུག་ཏུ་དབྱེ་ན། །མིག་གི་དང་། རྣ་བའི་དང་། སྣའི་དང་། ལྕེའི་དང་། ལུས་ཀྱི་དང་། ཡིད་ཀྱི་འདུས་ཏེ་རེག་པའི་རྐྱེན་གྱིས་ཚོར་བའོ། །འདི་དག་ལ་བདེ་སྡུག་བར་མ་གསུམ་གྱི་དབྱེ་བས་བཅོ་བརྒྱད། དེ་རེ་རེ་ལའང་ཀུན་[ཤོག་བུ་༧༡]ཉོན་ཕྱོགས་དང་རྣམ་བྱང་ཕྱོགས་ཀྱི་དབྱེ་བས་སུམ་ཅུ་རྩ་དྲུག །དེ་རེ་རེ་ལའང་དུས་གསུམ་གྱི་དབྱེ་བས་བརྒྱ་དང་བརྒྱད་ཀྱི་བར་དུའང་དབྱེར་ཡོད་དོ། །ཀུན་བཏུས་ལས་ནི།

མིག་གི་འདུས་ཏེ་རེག་པ་ལས་བྱུང་བའི་ཚོར་བ་བདེ་བ་ཡང་རུང་། སྡུག་བསྔལ་ཡང་
རུང་། སྡུག་བསྔལ་ཡང་མ་ཡིན་བདེ་བ་ཡང་མ་ཡིན་པ་ཡང་རུང་བ་དང་། རྣ་བ་
དང་། སྣ་དང་། ལྕེ་དང་། ལུས་དང་། ཡིད་ཀྱི་འདུས་ཏེ་རེག་པ་ལས་བྱུང་
བའི་ཚོར་བ་བདེ་བ་ཡང་རུང་། སྡུག་བསྔལ་ཡང་རུང་། སྡུག་བསྔལ་ཡང་མ་
ཡིན་བདེ་བ་ཡང་མ་ཡིན་པ་ཡང་རུང་བ་སྟེ། བདེ་བ་ལུས་ཀྱི་ཡང་རུང་ རྣམ་ཤེས་ལྔ་དང་
མཚུངས་ལྡན་ནོ། སྡུག་བསྔལ་ལུས་ཀྱི་ཡང་རུང་། སྡུག་བསྔལ་ཡང་མ་ཡིན་བདེ་བ་
ཡང་མ་ཡིན་པ་ལུས་ཀྱི་ཡང་རུང་། བདེ་བ་སེམས་ཀྱི་ཡང་རུང་། སྡུག་བསྔལ་
སེམས་ཀྱི་ཡང་རུང་། སྡུག་བསྔལ་ཡང་མ་ཡིན་བདེ་བ་ཡང་མ་ཡིན་པ་ ཡིད་ཤེས་དང་
མཚུངས་ལྡན་ནོ། སེམས་ཀྱི་ཡང་རུང་། བདེ་བ་ ལུས་ལ་སྲིད་པ་དང་མཚུངས་ལྡན་ནོ།
ཟང་ཟིང་དང་བཅས་པ་ཡང་རུང་། སྡུག་བསྔལ་དང་། སྡུག་བསྔལ་ཡང་མ་ཡིན་
བདེ་བ་ཡང་མ་ཡིན་པ་ཟང་ཟིང་དང་བཅས་པ་ཡང་རུང་། བདེ་བ་ཟང་ཟིང་མེད་པ་
སྲིད་པ་མེད་པའོ། ཡང་རུང་། སྡུག་བསྔལ་དང་། སྡུག་བསྔལ་ཡང་མ་ཡིན་
བདེ་བ་ཡང་མ་ཡིན་པ་ཟང་ཟིང་མེད་པ་ཡང་རུང་། བདེ་བ་ཞེན་པ་བརྟེན་ འདོད་ཡོན་ལ་
སྲིད་པ་དང་ [ཤོག་བུ་༡༢] མཚུངས་ལྡན་ནོ། པ་ཡང་རུང་། སྡུག་བསྔལ་དང་།
སྡུག་བསྔལ་ཡང་མ་ཡིན་བདེ་བ་ཡང་མ་ཡིན་པ་ཞེན་པ་བརྟེན་པ་ཡང་རུང་། བདེ་བ་
མངོན་པར་ འདོད་ཡོན་ལ་སྲིད་པ་དང་མི་ལྡན་པའོ། འབྱུང་བ་བརྟེན་པ་ཡང་རུང་། །
སྡུག་བསྔལ་དང་། སྡུག་བསྔལ་ཡང་མ་ཡིན་བདེ་བ་ཡང་མ་ཡིན་པ་མངོན་པར་
འབྱུང་བ་བརྟེན་པ་ཡང་རུང་བའོ། །ཞེས་གསུངས་པས་ཚོར་བ་དྲུག་ལ་བདེ་སྡུག་བར་
མས་དབྱེ་བས་བཅོ་བརྒྱད། དེ་ཡང་ལུས་སུ་གཏོགས་པ་བཅོ་ལྔ་དང་། སེམས་སུ་
གཏོགས་པ་གསུམ་མོ། །སྔོ་མ་ལ་ཟང་ཟིང་ཡོད་མེད་ཀྱི་དབྱེ་བས་དང་ཕྱི་མ་ལ་ཞེན་
བརྟེན་དང་མངོན་འབྱུང་གི་དབྱེ་བས་ཕྱེ་ན་སུམ་ཅུ་རྩ་དྲུག་གོ །དེ་ནས་འདུ་ཤེས་ཀྱི་
ཕུང་པོ་ལའང་མཚན་ཉིད་དང་དབྱེ་བ་གཉིས། དང་པོ་ནི། མཚན་མར་འཛིན་པ་
འདུ་ཤེས་ཀྱི་མཚན་ཉིད། གཉིས་པ་ནི། མཚན་མར་འཛིན་པ་དང་། མཚན་མ་
མེད་པའི་འདུ་ཤེས་གཉིས་སོ། །དང་པོ་ལ། རྒྱ་ཆེ་ཆུང་ཚད་མེད་པ་དང་གསུམ་

སོ། །གཉིས་པ་ནི། མཚན་མ་མེད་པར་འཛིན་པའོ། །ཀུན་བཏུས་ལས་ནི། མིག་གི་འདུས་ཏེ་རེག་པ་ལ་བྱུང་བའི་འདུ་ཤེས་དང་། རྣ་བ་དང་། སྣ་དང་། ལྕེ་དང་། ལུས་དང་། ཡིད་ཀྱི་འདུས་ཏེ་རེག་པ་ལས་བྱུང་བའི་འདུ་ཤེས་ཏེ། གང་གིས་མཚན་མ་དང་བཅས་པ་ཡང་ ཐ་སྙད་ལམ་བྱུང་བ་དང་མཚན་མ་མེད་པའི་སྙོམས་འཇུག་དང་སྲིད་རྩེའི་སྙོམས་འཇུག་རྣམས་མ་གཏོགས་པའོ། ཡང་དག་པར་ཤེས་ [ཤོག་བུ་ ༡༣] ཤིང་། མཚན་མ་མེད་པ་དང་ མཚན་བཅས་རྣམས་མ་གཏོགས་པའོ། ཆུང་ངུ་ འདོད་པའི་འདུ་ཤེས། དང་། རྒྱ་ཆེན་པོར་གྱུར་པ་དང་། གཟུགས་ཁམས་པའི་འདུ་ཤེས་སོ། ཚད་མེད་པ་དང་ ནམ་མཁའ་དང་རྣམ་ཤེས་གཉིས་སོ། ཅི་ཡང་མེད་དོ་ ཅི་ཡང་མེད་པའི་འདུ་ཤེས་སོགས། སླམ་ནས་ཅི་ཡང་མེད་པའི་སྐྱེ་མཆེད་ཀྱང་ཡང་དག་པར་ཤེས་པའོ། །ཞེས་འདུ་ཤེས་ཀྱི་དབྱེ་བ་བཅུ་གཉིས་སུ་གསུངས་སོ། །འདུ་བྱེད་ཀྱི་ཕུང་པོ་ལ་འང་མཚན་ཉིད་དང་དབྱེ་བ་གཉིས་ལས། དང་པོ་ནི། ཕུང་པོ་བཞི་ལས་གཞན་མངོན་པར་འདུ་བྱེད་པ་འདུ་བྱེད་ཀྱི་མཚན་ཉིད་དང་། གཉིས་པ་ལ་མཚུངས་པར་ལྡན་པའི་འདུ་བྱེད་དང་། །ལྡན་པ་མ་ཡིན་པའི་འདུ་བྱེད་པ་གཉིས་ལས། དང་པོ་ནི། སེམས་དང་སེམས་བྱུང་རྣམས་ཕན་ཚུན་མཚུངས་པ་ལྔས་མཚུངས་པས་ན་དེ་སྐད་ཅེས་བྱའོ། །དེའང་དམིགས་རྣམ་རྟེན་རྫས་དུས་མཚུངས་པའོ། །ཞེས་པ་ལྟར་ལྔ་ལས། དམིགས་པ་མཚུངས་པ་ནི། མིག་ཤེས་ལྷ་བུ་ལ་མཚོན་ན་དེ་ཉིད་གཟུགས་ལ་དམིགས་ནས་སྐྱེས་པའི་ཚེ་འཁོར་གྱི་སེམས་བྱུང་རྣམས་ཀྱང་གཟུགས་ལ་དམིགས་ནས་སྐྱེའོ། །དེ་བཞིན་དུ་རྣམ་ཤེས་སྒྲ་ལ་དམིགས་པ་སོགས་སོ། །རྣམ་པ་མཚུངས་པ་ནི། མིག་ཤེས་ཡུལ་ཀ་བའི་རྣམ་པ་ཅན་དུ་སྐྱེས་པའི་ཚེ་དེའི་འཁོར་གྱི་སེམས་བྱུང་རྣམས་ཀྱང་ཀ་བའི་རྣམ་པ་ཅན་དུ་སྐྱེའོ། །རྟེན་མཚུངས་ [ཤོག་བུ་ ༡༧] པ་ནི། མིག་ཤེས་མིག་དབང་ལ་བརྟེན་ནས་སྐྱེ་བའི་ཚེ་དེའི་འཁོར་གྱི་སེམས་བྱུང་རྣམས་ཀྱང་མིག་དབང་ལ་བརྟེན་ནས་སྐྱེའོ། །རྫས་མཚུངས་པ་ནི། འདིར་སེམས་སེམས་བྱུང་ཐམས་ཅད་རེ་རེ་ལས་མེད་པས་མཚུངས་པ་དང་། དུས་མཚུངས་པ་ནི། སེམས་དང་སེམས་བྱུང་དུས་གཅིག་ཏུ་སྐྱེས་ནས་འགག་པའང་ལྷན་ཅིག་པའོ། །

སེམས་ལས་བྱུང་བ་རྣམས་ནི་མཛོད་ལྟར་ན། །ཚོར་[༡]དང་སེམས་[༢]པ་འདུ་ཤེས་[༣]དང་། འདུན་[༤]དང་རེག་[༥]དང་བློ་[༦]གྲོས་[༧]དྲན།[༨] །ཡིད་དེ་ལ་བྱེད་དང་མོས་[༩]པ་དང་། །ཏིང་ངེ་འཛིན་[༡༠]སེམས་ཐམས་ཅད་ལའོ། །ཞེས་སེམས་ཀྱི་ས་མང་བཅུ་དང་། །དད་དང་བག་ཡོད་ཤིན་དུ་སྦྱངས། །བཏང་སྙོམས་ངོ་ཚ་ཤེས་ཁྲེལ་ཡོད། །རྩ་བ་རྣམ་གཉིས་མི་འཚེ་དང་། །བརྩོན་འགྲུས་རྟག་ཏུ་དགེ་ལ་འབྱུང་། །ཞེས་དགེ་བའི་ས་མང་བཅུ་དང་། །རྨོངས་དང་བག་མེད་ལེ་ལོ་དང་། །མ་དད་པ་དང་རྨུགས་དང་རྒོད། །ཉོན་མོངས་ཅན་ལ་རྟག་ཏུ་འབྱུང་། ། ཞེས་ཉོན་མོངས་ཆེན་པོའི་ས་མང་དྲུག་དང་། །མི་དགེ་ལ་ནི་ཁྲེལ་མེད་དང་། ངོ་ཚ་མེད་པའོ། །ཞེས་མི་དགེ་བའི་ས་མང་གཉིས་དང་། ཁྲོ་བ་དང་། ཁོན་དུ་འཛིན་དང་གཡོ་དང་ནི། །ཕྲག་དོག་འཚིག་འཆབ་སེར་སྣ་དང་། །སྒྱུ་དང་རྒྱགས་དང་རྣམ་འཚེ་ནི། །ཉོན་མོངས་ཆུང་ངུའི་ས་པ་རྣམས། ཞེས་ཉོན་མོངས་ཆུང་ངུའི་ས་མང་བཅུ་དང་། ཡང་བརྩོན་པ་དབྱིག་བཤེས་ཀྱིས། །རྟོག་དང་དཔྱོད་དང་འགྱོད་༼ཤོག་བུ་༡༥༽པ་དང་། །གཉིད་དང་ཁོང་ཁྲོ་ཆགས་རྣམས་དང་། །ང་རྒྱལ་ཐེ་ཚོམ་ཞེས་བྱ་བ། །བརྒྱད་ནི་ངེས་པ་མིན་པར་བཤད། །ཞེས་སྡེ་ཚན་དུ་མ་ངེས་པ་བརྒྱད་གསུངས་པ་དང་བཅས་སེམས་བྱུང་བཞི་བཅུ་རྩ་དྲུག་ཏུ་འདོད་དོ། ། ཀུན་བཏུས་ལས་ནི། དེ་དག་གི་སྟེང་དུ་གཏི་མུག་མེད་པ་དང་། ལྟ་བ་དང་། བརྗེད་ངས་དང་། ཤེས་བཞིན་མ་ཡིན་པ་དང་། རྣམ་པར་གཡེང་བ་དང་ལྔ་བསྣན་ཏེ་སེམས་བྱུང་ལྔ་བཅུ་རྩ་གཅིག་ཏུ་བཞེད་དོ། །དེ་དག་ལས་ཚོར་འདུ་གཉིས་ནི་གོང་དུ་བཤད་ཟིན་ལ། གཞན་རྣམས་ཀུན་བཏུས་ཀྱི་གོ་རིམ་དང་བསྟུན་ཏེ་ཅུང་ཟད་བཤད་ན། སེམས་པ་ནི་སེམས་མངོན་པར་འདུ་བྱེད་པའོ། །དེའི་ལས་ནི་སེམས་ཡུལ་ལ་འཇུག་པར་བྱེད་པའོ། །ཡིད་ལ་བྱེད་པ་ནི་སེམས་ཀྱི་འཇུག་པ་སྣེ་ཡུལ་ལ་གཏོད་པའོ། ། ལས་ནི་དམིགས་པ་ལ་སེམས་འཛིན་པར་བྱེད་དོ། །རེག་པ་ནི་ཡུལ་དབང་ཤེས་གསུམ་འཕྲད་པའོ། །ལས་ནི་ཚོར་བའི་རྟེན་བྱེད་དོ། །དེ་རྣམས་ནི་ཀུན་འགྲོ་ལྔ་སྟེ་སེམས་ཀུན་གྱི་འཁོར་དུ་འགྲོ་བས་ན་དེ་སྐད་ཅེས་གྲགས་སོ། །འདུན་པ་ནི་བསམ་

པའི་དངོས་པོ་ལ་འདོད་པའོ། །ལས་ནི་བརྩོན་འགྲུས་ཀྱི་རྟེན་བྱེད་དོ། །མོས་པ་ནི་ངེས་པའི་དངོས་པོ་ལ་ངེས་པར་འཛིན་པའོ། །ལས་ནི་མི་འཕྲོག་པ་ཉིད་དོ། །དྲན་པ་ནི་འདྲིས་པའི་དངོས་པོ་ལ་བརྗེད་དུ་མེད་པའོ། །ལས་ནི་རྣམ་པར་མི་གཡེང་བའོ། །ཏིང་ངེ་འཛིན་ནི་སེམས་རྩེ་གཅིག་ [ཤོག་བུ་༡༦] པའོ། །ལས་ནི་ཤེས་པའི་རྟེན་བྱེད་དོ། །ཤེས་རབ་ནི་ཆོས་རབ་ཏུ་རྣམ་པར་འབྱེད་པའོ། །ལས་ནི་ཐེ་ཚོམ་བཟློག་པ་ཉིད་དོ། །དེ་དག་ནི་ཡུལ་སོ་སོར་ངེས་པ་ལྔ་སྟེ་ཡུལ་ངེས་བྱེད་ཡིན་པས་དེ་སྐད་ཅེས་བྱའོ། །དད་པ་ནི་སེམས་དྭངས་པ་སྟེ་མངོན་པར་ཡིད་ཆེས་པའོ། །ལས་ནི་འདུན་པའི་རྟེན་བྱེད་དོ། །ངོ་ཚ་ཤེས་པ་ནི་བདག་གི་དབང་དུ་བྱས་ཏེ་ཁ་ན་མ་ཐོབ་ལ་འཛེམ་པའོ། །ལས་ནི་ལེགས་པར་སྡོམ་པའི་རྟེན་བྱེད་དོ། །ཁྲེལ་ཡོད་པ་ནི་འཇིག་རྟེན་གྱི་དབང་དུ་བྱས་ཏེ་ཁ་ན་མ་ཐོབ་ལ་འཛེམ་པའོ། །ལས་ནི་གོང་ལྟར་རོ། །མ་ཆགས་པ་ནི་སྲིད་པ་དང་སྲིད་པའི་ལོངས་སྤྱོད་ལ་ཆགས་པ་མེད་པའོ། །ལས་ནི་ཉེས་པར་སྤྱོད་པ་ལ་མི་འཇུག་པའི་རྟེན་བྱེད་དོ། །ཞེ་སྡང་མེད་པ་ནི་གཞན་ལ་ཀུན་ནས་མནར་སེམས་པ་མེད་པའོ། །ལས་ནི་སྔ་མ་ལྟར་རོ། །གཏི་མུག་མེད་པ་ནི་བདེན་བཞི་སོགས་ལ་ཡིད་ཆེས་པའོ། །ལས་ནི་གོང་ལྟར་རོ། །བརྩོན་འགྲུས་ནི་དགེ་བ་ལ་སེམས་མངོན་པར་སྤྲོ་བའོ། །ལས་ནི་དགེ་བའི་ཕྱོགས་ཡོངས་སུ་རྫོགས་པར་བྱེད་པའོ། །ཤིན་སྦྱངས་ནི་ལུས་སེམས་ལས་སུ་རུང་བའོ། །ལས་ནི་སྒྲིབ་པ་ཐམས་ཅད་སེལ་བར་བྱེད་དོ། །བག་ཡོད་ནི་འཇུག་ལྡོག་གི་གནས་ལ་གཟབ་པ་ལྟར་ལེན་པའོ། །ལས་ནི་ཕུན་སུམ་ཚོགས་པ་རྣམས་ཡོངས་སུ་སྒྲུབ་པར་བྱེད་དོ། །བཏང་སྙོམས་ནི་སེམས་བྱིང་རྒོད་གཉིས་ཀྱི་ཆ་བཏང་བའོ། །ལས་ནི་ [ཤོག་བུ་༡༧] ཀུན་ནས་ཉོན་མོངས་པའི་སྐབས་མི་དབྱེ་བའོ། །རྣམ་པར་མི་འཚེ་བ་ནི་རྣམ་འཚེའི་གཉེན་པོ་སྙིང་རྗེ་བ་ཉིད་དོ། །ལས་ནི་གཞན་ལ་ཐོ་མི་ཚོམ་པའོ། །དེ་རྣམས་དགེ་བ་བཅུ་གཅིག་ཅེས་བྱ་སྟེ། དགེ་བའི་ལས་ཀུན་འདི་དག་གིས་བསྡུས་པས་སོ། །འདོད་ཆགས་ནི་ཁམས་གསུམ་པའི་རྗེས་སུ་ཆགས་པའོ། །ལས་ནི་སྡུག་བསྔལ་སྐྱེད་པར་བྱེད་དོ། །ཁོང་ཁྲོ་ནི་ཀུན་ནས་མནར་སེམས

པའོ། །ལས་ནི་བདེ་བར་མི་གནས་པ་དང་། ཉེས་པར་སྤྱོད་པའི་རྟེན་བྱེད་པ་ཉིད་
དོ། །ང་རྒྱལ་ནི་འཇིག་ལྟ་ལ་བརྟེན་ནས་སེམས་ཁེངས་པའོ། །དབྱེ་ན་ང་རྒྱལ་
དང་། ཆེ་བའི་ང་རྒྱལ་དང་། ང་རྒྱལ་ལས་ཀྱང་ང་རྒྱལ། ངའོ་སྙམ་པའི་ང་རྒྱལ།
མངོན་པའི་ང་རྒྱལ། ཅུང་ཟད་སྙམ་པའི་ང་རྒྱལ། ལོག་པའི་ང་རྒྱལ་དང་བདུན་
ནོ། །ལས་ནི་གཞན་ལ་མི་གུས་པ་དང་། སྡུག་བསྔལ་འབྱུང་བའི་རྟེན་བྱེད་
དོ། །མ་རིག་པ་ནི་ཁམས་གསུམ་པའི་མི་ཤེས་པའོ། །ལས་ནི་མ་རྟོགས་ལོག་རྟོག་
ཐེ་ཚོམ་རྣམས་དང་ཀུན་ནས་ཉོན་མོངས་པ་འབྱུང་བའི་རྟེན་བྱེད་དོ། །ཐེ་ཚོམ་ནི་བདེན་
པ་རྣམས་ལ་ཡིད་གཉིས་ཟ་བའོ། །ལས་ནི་དགེ་བའི་ཕྱོགས་ལ་མི་འཇུག་པའི་རྟེན་བྱེད་
དོ། །ལྟ་བ་ལ་ལྔ་ལས། འཇིག་ལྟས་ནི་ཕུང་པོ་ལྔ་ལ་བདག་དང་བདག་གིར་ཡང་
དག་པར་རྗེས་སུ་བལྟས་ [ཤོག་བུ་༧ཀ] ཏེ་ལྟ་བ་ཐམས་ཅད་ཀྱི་རྟེན་བྱེད་པའི་ལས་ཅན་
ནོ། །མཐར་འཛིན་ལྟ་བ་ནི་ཕུང་པོ་ལ་རྟག་ཆད་དུ་བལྟས་ཏེ་ངེས་པར་འབྱུང་བའི་བར་
དུ་གཅོད་པའི་ལས་ཅན་ནོ། །ལོག་པར་ལྟ་བ་ནི་རྒྱུ་འབྲས་ལ་སྐུར་པ་འདེབས་པ་སྟེ་
དགེ་རྩ་གཅོད་ཅིང་མི་དགེ་བ་དམ་དུ་འཛིན་པའི་ལས་ཅན་ནོ། །ལྟ་བ་མཆོག་ཏུ་འཛིན་
པ་ནི་ལྟ་བ་དེ་དག་ལ་མཆོག་ཏུ་འཛིན་པ་སྟེ། ལྟ་བ་ངན་པ་ལ་མངོན་པར་ཞེན་པའི་
ལས་ཅན་ནོ། །ཚུལ་ཁྲིམས་དང་བརྟུལ་ཞུགས་མཆོག་ཏུ་འཛིན་པ་ནི་ལྟ་བ་དེ་དང་
འབྲེལ་བའི་སྤྱོད་པ་ལ་དག་གྲོལ་ངེས་འབྱིན་དུ་ལྟ་བ་སྟེ་ངལ་བ་འབྲས་མེད་ཀྱི་རྟེན་བྱེད་
པའི་ལས་ཅན་ནོ། །དེ་དག་ལས་འཇིག་ཚོགས་ལ་ལྟ་བ་ནི་དབྱེ་ན་ཉི་ཤུ་སྟེ།
གཟུགས་བདག་ཡིན་པར་ལྟ་བ་དང་། བདག་གཟུགས་དང་ལྡན་པ་དང་།
གཟུགས་བདག་གི་ཡིན་པ་དང་། གཟུགས་ལ་བདག་གནས་པ་དང་། དེ་བཞིན་དུ་
ཚོར་བ་དང་། འདུ་ཤེས་དང་། འདུ་བྱེད་དང་། རྣམ་པར་ཤེས་པ་བདག་ཡིན་
པ་ལ་སོགས་པར་ལྟ་བའོ། །མཐར་ལྟ་ལ་དབྱེ་ན་ཡོད་མཐའ། མེད་མཐའ།
གཉིས་ཀའི་མཐའ། གཉིས་མིན་མཐའ་སྟེ་བཞིའམ་ཡང་ན་འགག་པ་སོགས་མཐའ་
བརྒྱད་དུ་ལྟ་བའོ། །གཞན་ནི་གོ་སླ། །འདི་རྣམས་རྩ་ཉོན་དྲུག་སྟེ་ཉོན་མོངས་པ་
ཐམས་ཅད་ཀྱི་རྩ་བ་ཡིན་པའི་ཕྱིར་རོ། །ཁྲོ་བ་ནི། ཁོང་ཁྲོ་བའི་ཆར་གཏོགས་པའི་

སེམས་ཀྱིས་ཀུན་ནས་མནར་སེམས་པའོ། །ལས་ནི་གནོད་པ་སེམས་པའི་རྟེན་བྱེད་དོ། །འཁོན་དུ་འཛིན་པ་ནི་སྔར་གྱི་མཁོན་ཡིད་ལ་འཛིན་པའོ། །ལས་ནི་མི་བཟོད་པའི་རྟེན་བྱེད་དོ། །འཆབ་བ་ནི་ཁ་ན་མ་ཐོ་བ་འཆྱུད་པའོ། །ལས་ནི་[ཤོག་བུ་༡༩]བདེ་བར་མི་གནས་པའི་རྟེན་བྱེད་དོ། །འཚིག་པ་ནི་ཁོང་ཁྲོ་བའི་ཆར་གཏོགས་པ་ཁྲོ་བ་དང་། ཁོན་དུ་འཛིན་པ་སྔོན་དུ་འགྲོ་བའི་སེམས་ཀྱིས་ཀུན་ནས་མནར་སེམས་པའོ། །ལས་ནི་ཚིག་རྩུབ་ཀྱི་རྟེན་བྱེད་དོ། །ཕྲག་དོག་ནི་རྙེད་བཀུར་ལ་ཆགས་ནས་གཞན་གྱི་ཕུན་ཚོགས་ལ་མི་བཟོད་པའོ། །ལས་ནི་ཡིད་མི་བདེ་བའོ། །སེར་སྣ་ནི་ལོངས་སྤྱོད་རྣམས་ལ་ཀུན་ཏུ་འཛིན་པའི་སེམས་སོ། །ལས་ནི་ལོངས་སྤྱོད་མི་བསླུངས་པའི་རྟེན་བྱེད་དོ། །སྒྱུ་ནི་རྙེད་བཀུར་ལ་ཞེན་ཅིང་ཡོན་ཏན་མེད་ཀྱང་ཡོད་པར་འཆོས་པའོ། །ལས་ནི་ལོག་འཚོའི་རྟེན་བྱེད་དོ། །གཡོ་ནི་རྙེད་བཀུར་ལ་ཆགས་ནས་སྐྱོན་ཡོད་ཀྱང་མེད་པར་བསྒྱུར་བའོ། །ལས་ནི་ཡང་དག་པའི་གདམས་ངག་ལ་བར་དུ་གཅོད་པའོ། །རྒྱགས་པ་ནི་སེམས་ཁེངས་པ་སྟེ། དབྱེ་ན། རིགས་ཀྱི། གཟུགས་ཀྱི། དབང་ཐང་གི། ལང་ཚོའི། ཐོས་པས་རྒྱགས་པ་དང་ལྔའོ། །ལས་ནི་ཉོན་མོངས་དང་ཉེ་བའི་ཉོན་མོངས་པ་ཐམས་ཅད་ཀྱི་རྟེན་བྱེད་དོ། །རྣམ་འཚེ་ན་བརྩེ་བ་མེད་པའོ། །ལས་ནི་ཐོ་འཚམས་པར་བྱེད་དོ། །ངོ་ཚ་མེད་པ་ནི་བདག་གམ་ཆོས་ཀྱི་དབང་དུ་བྱས་ཏེ་ཉེས་པ་ལ་མི་འཛེམ་པའོ། །ལས་ནི་ཉོན་མོངས་པ་དང་ཉེ་ཉོན་ཐམས་ཅད་ཀྱི་གྲོགས་བྱེད་དོ། །ཁྲེལ་མེད་པ་ནི་འཇིག་རྟེན་གྱི་དབང་དུ་བྱས་ཏེ་ཉེས་པ་ལ་མི་འཛེམ་པའོ། །ལས་ནི་སྔ་མ་བཞིན་ནོ། །རྨུགས་པ་ནི་སེམས་མུན་པ་བབ་པའི་རྣམ་པའོ། །ལས་ནི་གོང་ལྟར་རོ། །རྒོད་པ་ནི་[ཤོག་བུ་༢༠]འདོད་ཆགས་ཀྱི་ཆར་གཏོགས་པའི་སེམས་རྣམ་པར་མ་ཞི་བའོ། །ལས་ནི་ཞི་གནས་ལ་བར་གཅོད་པར་བྱེད་དོ། །མ་དད་པ་ནི་དགེ་བའི་ཆོས་རྣམས་ལ་ཡིད་མི་ཆེས་པའོ། །ལས་ནི་ལེ་ལོའི་རྟེན་བྱེད་དོ། །ལེ་ལོ་ནི་དགེ་བ་ལ་སེམས་མི་སྤྲོ་བའོ། །ལས་ནི་བརྩོན་འགྲུས་ཀྱི་བར་དུ་གཅོད་པའོ། །བག་མེད་པ་ནི་ཉེས་པ་ལ་དོགས་ཟོན་མེད་པའོ། །ལས་ནི་མི་དགེ་བ་འཕེལ་བ་དང་། དགེ་བ་འགྲིབ་པའི་

རྟེན་བྱེད་དོ། །བརྗེད་ངས་ནི། སྔར་འདྲིས་ཀྱིས་དགེ་བ་ཡིད་ཡུལ་ནས་བསྐྱུད་པའོ། །ལས་ནི་གཡེང་བའི་རྟེན་བྱེད་དོ། །ཤེས་བཞིན་མ་ཡིན་པ་ནི་བྱ་བ་གང་ལ་ཡང་མི་ཤེས་བཞིན་དུ་འཇུག་པའོ། །ལས་ནི་ལྟུང་བ་འབྱུང་བའི་རྟེན་བྱེད་དོ། །རྣམ་པར་གཡེངས་བ་ནི་དུག་གསུམ་གྱི་ཆར་གཏོགས་པའི་སེམས་རྣམ་པར་འཕྲོ་བའོ། །དབྱེ་ན་ངོ་བོ་ཉིད་ཀྱི་གཡེང་བ་སྒོ་ལྔའི་ཤེས་པ་ལྟ་བུ་དང་། ཕྱི་རོལ་དུ་གཡེང་བ་དགེ་བ་ལ་ཞུགས་ཚེ་དེ་ལས་གཞན་འདོད་པའི་ཡོན་ལ་རྣམ་པར་འཕྲོ་བའོ། །ནང་གི་གཡེང་བ་ཏིང་ངེ་འཛིན་ལ་ཞུགས་ཚེ་བྱིང་རྒོད་རོ་མྱོང་སོགས་ཀྱི་སྐྱོན་བྱུང་བའོ། །མཚན་མའི་གཡེང་བ་གཞན་གྱིས་བདག་ལ་ཡོན་ཏན་ཅན་དུ་ཡིད་ཆེས་པའི་ཕྱིར་དགེ་བ་ལ་ཞུགས་པས་ཐོག་མ་ནས་དེ་ལས་ཉམས་པ་ལྟ་བུའོ། །གནས་ངན་ལེན་གྱི་གཡེང་བ་དགེ་བ་ལ་ཞུགས་ཚེ་བདེ་བ་ལ་སོགས་པའི་ཚོར་བ་བྱུང་བ་ལ་ང་དང་ང་ཡིར་འཛིན་པས་དགེ་བའི་ཕྱོགས་མི་དགོར་བྱེད་པའོ། །ཡིད་ལ་བྱེད་པའི་གཡེང་བ་ [ཤོག་བུ་༢༧] སྙོམས་འཇུག་གཞན་ལ་ཞུགས་པ་དང་། ཐེག་པ་གཞན་ལ་གནས་པ་ལྟ་བུའི་ཡང་དག་པའི་དོན་ལས་ཉམས་པའོ། །བསྒོམས་པས་དྲུག་གོ །ལས་ནི་འདོད་ཆགས་དང་བྲལ་བའི་བར་དུ་གཅོད་པའོ། །འདི་དག་ཉེ་བའི་ཉོན་མོངས་ཉི་ཤུ་ཞེས་བྱ་སྟེ་རྩ་བའི་ཉོན་མོངས་དང་ཆ་འདྲ་བའི་ཕྱིར་རོ། །གཉིད་ནི་ལུས་སེམས་བཟུང་དུ་མི་བཏུབ་པའོ། །ལས་ནི་བྱ་བ་ཤོར་བའི་རྟེན་བྱེད་དོ། །འགྱོད་པ་ནི་སྔོན་གྱི་བྱ་བ་ལས་སེམས་ཕྱིར་ཕྱོགས་ཏེ་དེ་མ་མི་དགའ་བའོ། །ལས་ནི་སེམས་གནས་པའི་བར་ཆད་བྱེད་དོ། །རྟོག་པ་ནི་དོན་གྱི་ངོ་བོ་ཙམ་འཛིན་པ་སྐྱེ་སེམས་རྩིང་བའོ། །དཔྱོད་པ་ནི་དོན་གྱི་ཁྱད་པར་ལ་དཔྱོད་པ་སྐྱེ་སེམས་ཞིབ་པའོ། །འདི་གཉིས་ཀྱི་བྱེད་ལས་ནི་བདེ་བར་གནས་པ་དང་མི་གནས་པའི་རྟེན་བྱེད་དོ། །ཡང་ཆོས་དགེ་བ་རྣམས་ཀྱི་ལས་ནི་རང་གི་མི་མཐུན་པའི་ཕྱོགས་སྤང་བའོ། །ཉོན་མོངས་དང་ཉེ་ཉོན་གྱི་ལས་ནི་རང་གི་གཉེན་པོས་བར་དུ་གཅོད་པའོ། །འདི་དག་ལ་གཞན་འགྱུར་བཞི་ཞེས་དགེ་མི་དགེ་གཉིས་གར་འགྱུར་དུ་རུང་བས་སོ། །འོ་ན་སེམས་བྱུང་ལྔ་བཅུ་རྩ་གཅིག་ལས་ཚོར་བ་དང་། འདུ་ཤེས་གཉིས་ལོགས་སུ་འཛོག་དགོས་པ་ཅི་ཞེ་ན། མཛོད་ལས། །

རྩོད་པའི་རྩ་བར་གྱུར་ཕྱིར་དང་། །འཁོར་བའི་རྒྱུ་ཕྱིར་རིམ་རྒྱུའི་ཕྱིར། །སེམས་བྱུང་རྣམས་ལས་ཚོར་བ་དང་། །འདུ་ཤེས་ལོགས་ཤིག་ཕུང་པོར་བཞག །ཞེས་རྒྱུ་མཚན་གསུམ་གྱི་[ཤོག་བུ་༢༢]ཕྱིར་བཞག་པའོ། །གཉིས་པ་ལྡན་པ་མ་ཡིན་པའི་འདུ་བྱེད་ནི། མཛོད་ལས། །ཐོབ་དང་མ་ཐོབ་སྐལ་མཉམ་དང་། །འདུ་ཤེས་མེད་སྙོམས་འཇུག་པ་དང་། །སྲོག་དང་མཚན་ཉིད་རྣམས་དང་ནི། །མིང་གི་ཚོགས་ལ་སོགས་པ་ཡང་། །ཞེས་པ་ལྟར། ཐོབ་པ་དང་མ་ཐོབ་པ་དང་། སྐལ་པ་མཉམ་པའམ་རིས་མཐུན་པ་དང་། འདུ་ཤེས་མེད་པ་བ་དང་། དེའི་སྙོམས་འཇུག་དང་། འགོག་པའི་སྙོམས་འཇུག་དང་། སྲོག་གི་དབང་པོ་དང་། སྐྱེ་བ་དང་། གནས་པ་དང་། རྒ་བ་དང་། མི་རྟག་པ་དང་། མིང་དང་ཚིག་དང་། ཡི་གེའི་ཚོགས་ཏེ་བཅུ་བཞི་དང་། ཀུན་བཏུས་ལས། དེ་དག་གི་སྟེང་དུ། འཇུག་པ་དང་། སོ་སོར་ངེས་པ་དང་། སྦྱོར་བ་དང་། མགྱོགས་པ་དང་། གོ་རིམས་དང་། དུས་དང་། ཡུལ་དང་། གྲངས་དང་། ཚོགས་པ་སྟེ་དགུ་བསྣན་ནས་རྣམ་གྲངས་ཉེར་གསུམ་དུ་གསུངས་སོ། །དེ་ལ་ཐོབ་པ་ནི་དགེ་མི་དགེ་ལུང་མ་བསྟན་པའི་ཆོས་གང་ཀླེད་པའོ། །འཕགས་པའི་ཆོས་མ་ཐོབ་པ་ནི་སོ་སོའི་སྐྱེ་བོའོ། །འདུ་ཤེས་མེད་པའི་སྙོམས་འཇུག་ནི། བསམ་གཏན་གསུམ་པའི་འདོད་ཆགས་དང་བྲལ་ཞིང་གོང་མའི་འདོད་ཆགས་དང་མ་བྲལ་བདག་ཚོགས་དྲུག་བཀག་པ་སྟེ་གནས་པའོ། །འགོག་པའི་སྙོམས་འཇུག་ནི་སྲིད་རྩེའི་སེམས་ཐོབ་པའི་འཕགས་པ་དག་ཚོགས་དྲུག་ཉོན་ཡིད་དང་བཅས་པ་འགོག་པའོ། །འདུ་ཤེས་[ཤོག་བུ་༢༣]མེད་པ་ནི། སྙོམས་འཇུག་སྔ་མའི་འབྲས་བུ་ཏེ་འདུ་ཤེས་མེད་པའི་ལྷར་སྐྱེས་པའོ། །སྲོག་གི་དབང་པོ་ནི་མི་ཆེ་གཅིག་ལྟ་བུའི་ཕུང་པོའི་རྒྱུན་གནས་པར་བྱེད་པའོ། །རིས་མཐུན་པ་ནི་སེམས་ཅན་གྱི་རིས་དེ་དང་དེར་ཕན་ཚུན་འདྲ་བའོ། །སྐྱེ་བ་ནི་སེམས་ཅན་གྱི་ཕུང་པོ་གསར་དུ་སྐྱེ་བའོ། །རྒ་བ་ནི་རྒྱུན་གཞན་དུ་འགྱུར་བའོ། །གནས་པ་ནི་རིས་མཐུན་པར་འདུ་བྱེད་རྣམས་ཀྱི་རྒྱུན་གནས་པའོ། །མི་རྟག་པ་ནི་རྒྱུན་དེ་ཉིད་འཇིག་པའོ། །མིང་གི་ཚོགས་ནི་ངོ་བོ་ཉིད་ཀྱི་ཚིག་བླ་དགས་ཏེ་

ལྷ་དང་མི་ཞེས་པ་ལྟ་བུའོ། །ཚིག་གི་ཚོགས་ནི་དེའི་ཁྱད་པར་གྱི་ཚིག་ཏེ་ལྷ་ནི་མཆོག་གི་ཞེས་པ་ལྟ་བུའོ། །ཡི་གེའི་ཚོགས་ནི་དེ་གཉིས་གའི་གནས་འགྱུར་མེད་རྣམས་ཏེ་ཨ་དང་ཨི་ཞེས་པ་ལྟ་བུའོ། །དེ་ལ་ཨ་ཞེས་པ་ལྟ་བུ་དེ་རྣམ་གྲངས་གཞན་གྱིས་འདི་ཞེས་སྟོན་པར་མི་ནུས་པ་ནས་འགྱུར་མེད་ཅེས་བྱའོ། །འཇུག་པ་ནི་རྒྱུ་དང་འབྲས་བུ་རྒྱུན་མི་འཆད་པའོ། །སོ་སོར་ངེས་པ་ནི་རྒྱུ་དང་འབྲས་བུ་ཐ་དད་པར་བལྟའོ། །སྦྱོར་བ་ནི་རྒྱུ་དང་འབྲས་བུ་རྗེས་སུ་མཐུན་པའོ། །དེའང་རྒྱུ་འབྲས་ཐ་དད་དུ་ཟིན་ཀྱང་གང་གི་འབྲས་བུ་གང་འོས་པ་ནི་ངེས་པ་ཡོད་པ་དང་། འགོགས་པ་ནི་རྒྱུ་དང་འབྲས་བུ་མྱུར་བར་འབྱུང་བའོ། །གོ་རིམ་ནི་རྒྱུ་དང་འབྲས་བུ་སྔ་ཕྱིར་འབྱུང་བའོ། །དུས་ནི་རྒྱུ་འབྲས་ཀྱི་དུས་གསུམ་མོ། །[ཤོག་བུ་༢༦]ཡུལ་ནི་རྒྱུ་འབྲས་ཀྱི་ཕྱོགས་བཅུའོ། །གྲངས་ནི་གཉིས་དང་གསུམ་ལ་སོགས་པའོ། །ཚོགས་པ་ནི་རྒྱུ་འབྲས་ཀྱི་རྐྱེན་ཚང་བའོ། །ལྔ་པ་རྣམ་ཤེས་ཕུང་པོ་ལ་འང་། མཚན་ཉིད་དང་དབྱེ་བའོ། །དང་པོ་ནི། །གསལ་ཞིང་རིག་པ་རྣམ་ཤེས་ཀྱི་མཚན་ཉིད་དོ། །གཉིས་པ་ལ། མིག་གི་རྣམ་ཤེས། རྣ་བའི། སྣ་ཡི། ལྕེའི། །ལུས་ཀྱི། ཡིད་ཀྱི་རྣམ་པར་ཤེས་པ་དང་དྲུག་གོ །དེ་རེ་རེ་ལ་དམིགས་པ། རྣམ་པ། གོ་རིམ། བྱེད་ལས། ཤེས་པ་རང་གི་ངོ་བོ་སྟེ་ལྔ་ལྔས་གཏན་ལ་ཕབ་པ་ལས། དམིགས་པ་ནི་རིམ་པ་བཞིན། གཟུགས་དང་། སྒྲ་དང་། དྲི་དང་། རོ་དང་། རེག་བྱ་དང་། ཆོས་རྣམས་སོ། །རྣམ་པ་ནི་མིག་ཤེས་གཟུགས་ཀྱི་རྣམ་པར་སྐྱེ་བ་ནས་ཡིད་ཤེས་ཆོས་ཀྱི་རྣམ་པར་སྐྱེ་བའི་བར་རོ། །གོ་རིམ་ནི་སྐད་ཅིག་དང་པོ་ལ་ཡུལ་དང་དབང་པོ་ཡིད་ལ་བྱེད་པ་གསུམ་འདུས་ནས། གཉིས་པ་ལ་མིག་ཤེས་སྐད་ཅིག་དང་པོ་དང་གསུམ་ལ་ཡིད་ཤེས་སྐད་ཅིག་དང་པོ་སྐྱེས་པ་ལྟ་བུའོ། །དེ་ཡང་སྐད་ཅིག་གི་དབྱེ་བ་དུས་མཐའི་སྐད་ཅིག་ནི་སེ་གོལ་གཅིག་གཏོགས་པའི་ཡུན་ཚད་དྲུག་ཅུར་བགོས་པའི་ཆ་གཅིག་ལྟ་བུའོ། །དེ་ལྟ་བུ་བརྒྱ་དང་ཉི་ཤུ་ལ་དེའི་སྐད་ཅིག་མ་སྟེ་སེ་གོལ་གཉིས་ཀྱི་ཡུན་ནོ། །བྱ་རྫོགས་ཀྱི་སྐད་ཅིག་ནི་རིང་མཐའ་སེམས་བསྐྱེད་ནས་སངས་རྒྱས་པའི་བར་ལྟ་བུ་དང་། ཐུང་མཐའ་སེ་གོལ་གཅིག་གི་ཡུན་ལྟ་བུ་སྟེ་མ

ངེས་སོ། །བྱེད་[ཤོག་བུ་༢༥]ལས་ནི་མཐོང་བར་བྱེད་པ་ནས་ཤེས་པར་བྱེད་པའི་བར་རོ། །ངོ་བོ་ནི་མིག་གི་ཤེས་པ་ནས་ཡིད་ཀྱི་ཤེས་པའི་བར་ཡིན་པའོ། །ཀུན་བཏུས་ལས་ནི། སྔ་མ་དྲུག་གི་སྟེང་དུ་ཀུན་གཞིའི་རྣམ་པར་ཤེས་པ་དང་། ཉོན་ཡིད་ཀྱི་རྣམ་པར་ཤེས་པ་གཉིས་བསྣན་པས་ཚོགས་བརྒྱད་དུ་གསུངས་ཀྱང་དེ་གཉིས་ཀྱི་རྣམ་བཞག་རྒྱས་པར་འོག་ཏུ་ཐེག་ཆེན་སྡོམ་བཞིའི་སྐབས་སུ་འཆད་པར་འགྱུར་བས་འདིར་མི་སྤྲོའོ། །ད་ནི་མཁས་པར་བྱ་བའི་གནས་གཉིས་པ་སྐྱེ་མཆེད་ཀྱི་རྣམ་པར་བཞག་པ་ལ་འང་ངེས་ཚིག་ནི་རྣམ་ཤེས་སྐྱེ་ཞིང་མཆེད་པའི་སྒོར་གྱུར་པས་ན་སྐྱེ་མཆེད་དོ། །དབྱེ་ན་ཕྱིའི་སྐྱེ་མཆེད་དྲུག་དང་། །ནང་གི་སྐྱེ་མཆེད་དྲུག་གོ །དང་པོ་གཟུགས་ཀྱི་སྐྱེ་མཆེད་ནི། མིག་ཤེས་ཀྱི་ཡུལ་ཁ་དོག་དང་དབྱིབས་ཀྱི་གཟུགས་རྣམས་དང་དོན་གཅིག །སྒྲའི་སྐྱེ་མཆེད་ནི། རྣ་ཤེས་ཀྱི་ཡུལ་ཟིན་པ་དང་མ་ཟིན་པའི་སྒྲ་དང་། དྲིའི་སྐྱེ་མཆེད་ནི། སྣ་ཤེས་ཀྱི་ཡུལ་ལྷན་སྐྱེས་དང་སྦྱར་བྱུང་གི་དྲི་དང་། རོའི་སྐྱེ་མཆེད་ནི། ལྕེ་ཤེས་ཀྱི་ཡུལ་མངར་བ་ལ་སོགས་པའི་རོ་དང་། རེག་བྱའི་སྐྱེ་མཆེད་ནི། ལུས་ཤེས་ཀྱི་ཡུལ་འབྱུང་བ་དང་འབྱུང་འགྱུར་གྱི་རེག་བྱ་དང་། ཆོས་ཀྱི་སྐྱེ་མཆེད་ནི། ཡིད་ཤེས་ཀྱི་ཡུལ་ཆོས་རྣམས་དང་དོན་གཅིག་པའོ། །དེ་ཡང་། མཛོད་ལས། །དེ་གསུམ་རྣམ་རིག་བྱེད་མིན་དང་། །འདུས་[ཤོག་བུ་༢༦]མ་བྱས་རྣམས་བཅས་པ་ནི། ཆོས་ཀྱི་སྐྱེ་མཆེད་ཁམས་ཞེས་བྱ། ཞེས་པ་ལྟར། །ཚོར་བ་འདུ་ཤེས་འདུ་བྱེད་གསུམ། །རིག་བྱེད་མ་ཡིན་པའི་གཟུགས། ནམ་མཁའ་འགོག་པ་གཉིས་དང་བདུན་ལ་ཆོས་ཀྱི་སྐྱེ་མཆེད་དང་ཁམས་ཞེས་བྱའོ། །གཉིས་པ་ནང་གི་སྐྱེ་མཆེད་ནི། མིག་གི་སྐྱེ་མཆེད་དང་མིག་དབང་དོན་གཅིག །རྣ་བའི་སྐྱེ་མཆེད་དང་རྣ་དབང་དོན་གཅིག །སྣའི་སྐྱེ་མཆེད་དང་སྣ་དབང་དོན་གཅིག །ལྕེའི་སྐྱེ་མཆེད་དང་ལྕེ་དབང་དོན་གཅིག །ལུས་ཀྱི་སྐྱེ་མཆེད་དང་ལུས་དབང་དོན་གཅིག །ཡིད་ཀྱི་སྐྱེ་མཆེད་དང་རྣམ་ཤེས་ཀྱི་ཕུང་པོས་བསྡུས་པའི་ཚོགས་དྲུག་ཡིད་དབང་དང་བཅས་པ་དོན་གཅིག་གོ །འདི་དག་གི་འཕྲོས་དོན་དབང་པོ་ཉེར་གཉིས་ཀྱི་རྣམ་པར་བཞག་པ་ནི་མིག་གི་དབང་པོ། རྣ་བའི་དབང་པོ།

སྣའི་དབང་པོ། ལྕེའི་དབང་པོ། ལུས་ཀྱི་དབང་པོ། ཡིད་ཀྱི་དབང་པོ། ཕོའི་དབང་པོ། མོའི་དབང་པོ། སྡུག་བསྔལ་གྱི་དབང་པོ། བདེ་བའི་དབང་པོ། ཡིད་བདེ་བའི་དབང་པོ། ཡིད་མི་བདེ་བའི་དབང་པོ། བཏང་སྙོམས་ཀྱི་དབང་པོ། དད་པའི་དབང་པོ། བརྩོན་འགྲུས་ཀྱི་དབང་པོ། དྲན་པའི་དབང་པོ། ཏིང་ངེ་འཛིན་གྱི་དབང་པོ། ཤེས་རབ་ཀྱི་དབང་པོ། ཀུན་ཤེས་བྱེད་པའི་དབང་པོ། ཀུན་ཤེས་པའི་དབང་པོ། ཀུན་ཤེས་པ་དང་ལྡན་པའི་དབང་པོ། སྲོག་གི་དབང་པོ་རྣམས་སོ། །དེ་ལ་མིག་ནས་ལུས་ཀྱི་བར་དབང་པོ་གཟུགས་ཅན་ལྔ་ནི་གོང་དུ་བཤད་ཟིན་ལ། ཡིད་དབང་ནི་༼ཤོག་བུ་༢༧༽རྣམ་པར་ཤེས་པ་དྲུག་འདས་མ་ཐག་པའི་རྟོག་མེད་ཤིན་ཏུ་ཕྲ་བའོ། །ཕོའི་དབང་པོ་ནི་མཐེ་བོང་འདྲ་བའོ། །མོའི་དབང་པོ་ནི་ཧ་ཁོག་འདྲ་བའོ། །སྡུག་བསྔལ་གྱི་དབང་པོ་ནི་རྣམ་པར་ཤེས་པ་དང་དབང་པོར་བཅས་པའི་ལུས་མི་བདེ་བ་མྱོང་བའོ། །བདེ་བའི་དབང་པོ་ནི་དེ་ལ་སིམ་པ་མྱོང་བའོ། །ཡིད་བདེ་བའི་དབང་པོ་ནི་ཡིད་ཀྱི་རྣམ་པར་ཤེས་པ་ལ་དགའ་བ་མྱོང་བའོ། །ཡིད་མི་བདེ་བའི་དབང་པོ་ནི་དེ་ལ་གདུང་བ་སྐྱེས་པའོ། །བཏང་སྙོམས་ཀྱི་དབང་པོ་ནི་ལུས་སེམས་གཉིས་ཀ་ལ་བདེ་སྡུག་གང་ལའང་མ་སྐྱེས་པའོ། །དད་པའི་དབང་པོ་ནི་ལས་འབྲས་དང་བདེན་པ་དང་དཀོན་མཆོག་ལ་ཡོད་པ་དང་ཡོན་ཏན་ཅན་དུ་ཡིད་ཆེས་ཤིང་སེམས་དྭངས་པའོ། །བརྩོན་འགྲུས་ཀྱི་དབང་པོ་ནི་ཉན་པ་དང་། སེམས་པ་དང་། བསྒོམ་པ་ལ་སོགས་པ་སྟེ་དགེ་བའི་ཕྱོགས་རྒྱུན་མི་གཅོད་པའོ། །དྲན་པའི་དབང་པོ་ནི། མཉན་ཞིང་ཐོས་པའི་ཚིག་དང་དོན་བསྙལ་བར་ཡང་མི་བརྗེད་པའོ། །ཏིང་ངེ་འཛིན་གྱི་དབང་པོ་ནི་བསྒོམ་པའི་ཡུལ་ལ་སེམས་རྩེ་གཅིག་ཏུ་གནས་པ་ལས་མི་ཉམས་པའོ། །ཤེས་རབ་ཀྱི་དབང་པོ་ནི་ཆོས་རྣམས་ཀྱི་རང་དང་སྤྱིའི་མཚན་ཉིད་མ་ནོར་བ་ཤེས་པའོ། །ཀུན་ཤེས་བྱེད་པའི་དབང་པོ་ནི། མཐོང་སྤང་སྒོམ་སྤང་བ་ན་དད་པ་ནས་ཤེས་རབ་ཀྱི་བར་ལྔ་དང་། བདེ་བ་དང་། ཡིད་བདེ་བ་དང་། བཏང་སྙོམས་དང་། ཡིད་ཀྱི་དབང་པོ་སྟེ། དགུ་པོ་དེ་དག་གིས་མཐོང་བའི་ལམ་གྱི་༼ཤོག་བུ་༢༨༽སྤང་བྱ་ཀུན་སྦྱོར་ནས་སྔོན་མི་ཤེས་པ་ཀུན་ཤེས་པར་བྱེད་

པའོ། །ཀུན་ཤེས་པའི་དབང་པོ་ནི། བསྒོམ་པས་སྤང་བར་བྱ་བའི་ཉོན་མོངས་པ་སྤངས་པའི་དུས་ན་དབང་པོ་དགུ་པོ་དེ་དག་གི་མི་མཐུན་ཕྱོགས་དང་གཉེན་པོའི་བྱེ་བྲག་ཕྱེད་པའོ། །ཀུན་ཤེས་པ་དང་ལྡན་པའི་དབང་པོ་ནི་དགྲ་བཅོམ་ཐོབ་པའི་དུས་ན་དབང་པོ་དེ་དག་ཐམས་ཅད་ཉིད་ཀྱི་ཁམས་གསུམ་གྱི་ཉོན་མོངས་མ་ལུས་པ་སྤངས་ནས་ཟད་པར་ཤེས་པ་དང་། མི་སྐྱེ་བ་ཤེས་པའི་ཡེ་ཤེས་མངོན་དུ་བྱེད་པའོ། །སྲོག་གི་དབང་པོ་ནི་ཇི་སྲིད་མ་ཤིའི་བར་དུ་ཚེ་དང་སྲོག་འཛིན་པའོ། །དེ་དག་ཀྱང་བསྡུ་ན་ལྔ་སྟེ་སེམས་ཀྱི་རྟེན་དང་། དེར་རྣམ་པར་རྟོག་པ་དང་། ཀུན་ནས་ཉོན་མོངས་པ་དང་། རྣམ་པར་བྱང་བའི་ཚོགས་དང་། རྣམ་པར་བྱང་བའོ། །དེ་ལ་མིག་ནས་ཡིད་ཀྱི་བར་དྲུག་དང་། སྲོག་གི་དབང་པོ་ནི་སེམས་ཀྱི་རྟེན། སྐྱེས་པ་དང་བུད་མེད་ནི་དེར་རྣམ་པར་རྟོག་པ་སྟེ་སྐྱེས་པའོ། །བུད་མེད་དོ་ཞེས་གཞན་གྱིས་ཤེས་པའོ། །བདེ་བ་དང་ཡིད་བདེ་བས་ནི་འདོད་ཆགས་བསྐྱེད། སྡུག་བསྔལ་དང་ཡིད་མི་བདེ་བས་ནི་ཞེ་སྡང་བསྐྱེད། བཏང་སྙོམས་ཀྱིས་ནི་གཏི་མུག་བསྐྱེད་པས་ཀུན་ཉོན་ཕྱོགས་སོ། །དད་པ་ལ་སོགས་པ་ལྔ་ནི་མྱ་ངན་ལས་འདས་པའི་རྒྱུ་ཡིན་པས་རྣམ་པར་བྱང་བའི་ཕྱོགས་སོ། །ཀུན་ཤེས་གསུམ་ནི་རྣམ་པར་བྱང་བའོ། །ད་ནི་མཁས་པར་བྱ་བའི་གནས་གསུམ་པ། ཁམས་ལ་མཁས་པ་ལ་ངེས་ཚིག་ནི་རིགས་ཀྱི་དོན་དང་འབྱུང་ཁུངས་ ༼ཤོག་བུ་༣༩༽ སུ་གྱུར་པས་ན་ཁམས་སོ། །དབྱེ་ན་ཕྱི་ཡུལ་གྱི་ཁམས་དྲུག །ནང་དབང་པོའི་ཁམས་དྲུག །བར་རྣམ་ཤེས་ཀྱི་ཁམས་དྲུག་སྟེ་བཅོ་བརྒྱད་དོ། །དེ་ལ་གཟུགས་ཀྱི་ཁམས་དང་མིག་གི་སྤྱོད་ཡུལ་དུ་གྱུར་བའི་གཟུགས་དོན་གཅིག །སྒྲའི་ཁམས་དང་རྣ་བའི་སྤྱོད་ཡུལ་དུ་གྱུར་པའི་སྒྲ་དོན་གཅིག །དྲིའི་ཁམས་དང་སྣའི་སྤྱོད་ཡུལ་དུ་གྱུར་པའི་དྲི་དོན་གཅིག །རོའི་ཁམས་དང་ལྕེའི་སྤྱོད་ཡུལ་དུ་གྱུར་པའི་རོ་དོན་གཅིག །རེག་བྱའི་ཁམས་དང་ལུས་ཀྱི་སྤྱོད་ཡུལ་དུ་གྱུར་པའི་རེག་བྱ་དོན་གཅིག །ཆོས་ཀྱི་ཁམས་དང་ཡིད་ཀྱི་སྤྱོད་ཡུལ་གྱུར་པའི་ཆོས་རྣམས་དོན་གཅིག་གོ །ཡང་མིག་གི་ཁམས་དང་མིག་དབང་དོན་གཅིག །རྣ་བའི་ཁམས་དང་རྣ་དབང་དོན་གཅིག །སྣའི་ཁམས་དང་སྣ་དབང་དོན་གཅིག །ལྕེའི་

ཁམས་དང་ལྕེ་དབང་དོན་གཅིག །ལུས་ཀྱི་ཁམས་དང་ལུས་དབང་དོན་གཅིག །
ཡིད་ཀྱི་ཁམས་དང་ཡིད་དབང་དོན་གཅིག་གོ །ཡང་མིག་གི་རྣམ་པར་ཤེས་པའི་
ཁམས་དང་མིག་གི་རྣམ་པར་ཤེས་པ་དོན་གཅིག །རྣ་བའི་རྣམ་པར་ཤེས་པའི་ཁམས་
དང་རྣ་བའི་རྣམ་པར་ཤེས་པ་དོན་གཅིག །སྣའི་རྣམ་པར་ཤེས་པའི་ཁམས་དང་སྣའི་
རྣམ་པར་ཤེས་པ་དོན་གཅིག །ལྕེའི་རྣམ་པར་ཤེས་པའི་ཁམས་དང་ལྕེའི་རྣམ་པར་
ཤེས་པ་དོན་གཅིག །ལུས་ཀྱི་རྣམ་པར་ཤེས་པའི་ཁམས་དང་ལུས་ཀྱི་རྣམ་པར་ཤེས་
པ་དོན་གཅིག །ཡིད་ཀྱི་རྣམ་པར་ཤེས་པའི་ཁམས་དང་ཡིད་ཀྱི་རྣམ་པར་ཤེས་པ་
རྣམས་དོན་གཅིག་གོ །ཁམས་(ཤོག་བུ་༣༠)བཅོ་བརྒྱད་པོ་དེ་དག་ཀྱང་བསྟན་དུ་
ཡོད་མེད་ཀྱིས་བསྡུ་ན་མིག་ལ་བསྟན་དུ་ཡོད་པ་ནི་གཟུགས་ཀྱི་ཁམས་གཅིག་པུའོ། །
ལྷག་མ་རྣམས་ནི་མིག་ལ་བསྟན་དུ་མེད་པ་ཡིན་ནོ། །ཐོགས་པ་ཡོད་མེད་ཀྱིས་བསྡུས་
ན། གཟུགས་ཀྱི་ཕུང་པོས་བསྡུས་པའི་ཁམས་བཅུ་པོ་ནི་ཐོགས་པ་དང་བཅས་པ་ཡིན་
ལ། གཞན་བརྒྱད་ནི་ཐོགས་པ་མེད་པའོ། །ཐོགས་པའི་དོན་ནི་རྟགས་པའོ། །
དབྱེ་ན་གསུམ་སྟེ་སྒྲིབ་པ་ལ་ཐོགས་པ། ཡུལ་ལ་ཐོགས་པ། དམིགས་པ་ལ་
ཐོགས་པའོ། །དང་པོ་ནི། རང་གི་ཡུལ་དུ་གཞན་སྐྱེ་བའི་གེགས་བྱེད་པ་སྟེ།
དཔེར་ན་དབྱུག་པ་ལ་ལག་པ་ཐོགས་པ་ལྟ་བུའོ། །གཉིས་པ་ནི། མིག་སོགས་
ཡུལ་ལ་ཐོགས་པ་སྟེ་ཡུལ་གཅིག་མཐོང་བའི་ཚེ་གཞན་སྒྲིབ་པ་ལྟ་བུའོ། །གསུམ་པ་
ནི། སེམས་དང་སེམས་ལས་བྱུང་བ་རྣམས་རང་གིས་དམིགས་པ་ལ་ཐོགས་པ་སྟེ།
དུས་གཅིག་ཏུ་ཡུལ་ཐམས་ཅད་དམིགས་མི་ནུས་པ་ལྟ་བུའོ། །དེ་དག་ལས་འདི་
རྣམས་ནི་སྒྲིབ་པ་ལ་ཐོག་པ་ཡིན་པར་རིག་པར་བྱའོ། །ཡང་འདི་དག་དགེ་མི་དགེ་
ལུང་མ་བསྟན་གསུམ་གྱིས་བསྡུ་ན། ལུང་དུ་མ་བསྟན་པ་ནི། དབང་པོ་ལྔ་དང་དྲི་
རོ་རེག་བྱའི་ཁམས་གསུམ་ཏེ་བརྒྱད་དོ། །གཞན་བཅུ་ནི། དགེ་བ་ལ་སོགས་པ་
གསུམ་ཀ་ཡོད་པར་བལྟའོ། །དེའང་སེམས་ཁམས་བདུན་མ་ཆགས་པ་ལ་སོགས་
དང་མཚུངས་ལྡན་རྣམས་དགེ་བ། ཆགས་པ་སོགས་དང་མཚུངས་པར་ལྡན་པ་དག་
མི་དགེ་བ། གཞན་ནི་ལུང་དུ་མ་བསྟན་པའོ། །ཆོས་ཁམས་ནི་མ་ཆགས་པ་ལ་

སོགས་པའི་ [ཤོག་བུ་༣༧] ངོ་བོ་ཉིད་དང་མཚུངས་པར་ལྡན་པ་དང་། ཀུན་ནས་བསླངས་པ་དང་། སོ་སོར་བརྟག་འགོག་རྣམས་ནི་དགེ་བའོ། །ཆགས་པ་སོགས་ཀྱི་ངོ་བོ་ཉིད་དང་མཚུངས་པར་ལྡན་པ་དང་། ཀུན་ནས་བསླང་བ་ནི་མི་དགེ་བའོ། །གཞན་ནི་ལུང་དུ་མ་བསྟན་པའོ། །གཟུགས་དང་སྒྲའི་ཁམས་ནི་ལུས་ངག་གི་རྣམ་པར་རིག་བྱེད་ཀྱིས་བསྡུས་པ་དགེ་མི་དགེའི་སེམས་ཀྱིས་ཀུན་ནས་བསླང་བ་དག་ནི་དགེ་དང་མི་དགེ་དང་གཞན་ལུང་དུ་མ་བསྟན་པའོ། །ཕུང་པོ་ལ་སོགས་པ་གསུམ་དུ་ངེས་པའི་དགོས་པ་ནི། མཛོད་ལས། །རྨོངས་དབང་འདོད་རྣམས་གསུམ་གྱི་ཕྱིར། །ཕུང་པོ་ལ་སོགས་གསུམ་བསྟན་ཏོ། །ཞེས་པ་ལྟར། ཁ་ཅིག་སེམས་བྱུང་རིལ་པོར་འཛིན་པ་དང་། ལ་ལ་དག་གཟུགས་ལ་རིལ་པོར་འཛིན་པ་དང་། གཞན་དག་གཟུགས་སེམས་གཉིས་ཀ་རིལ་པོར་འཛིན་པའི་རྨོངས་པ་གསུམ་བཟློག་པའི་ཕྱིར་དང་། དབང་པོ་རྣོ་འབྲིང་རྟུལ་གསུམ་གྱི་དབང་དུ་བྱས་པ་དང་། ཚིག་བསྡུས་འབྲིང་རྒྱས་པ་ལ་དགའ་བ་རྣམས་ལ་ཕུང་པོ་ལ་སོགས་པ་གསུམ་དུ་བསྟན་པ་ཡིན་ནོ། །དེ་ལྟར་ན་གཟུགས་ཀྱི་ཕུང་པོ་དང་། ཡིད་ཀྱི་སྐྱེ་མཆེད་དང་། ཆོས་ཁམས་ཏེ་གསུམ་གྱིས་ཤེས་བྱའི་ཆོས་ཐམས་ཅད་བསྡུས་པ་ཡིན་ནོ། །ད་ནི་མཁས་པ་བྱ་བའི་གནས་བཞི་པ་རྟེན་ཅིང་འབྲེལ་འབྱུང་ལ་འང་ངེས་ཚིག་ནི་གང་ལ་རྟེན་ནས་གང་འབྱུང་བས་རྟེན་འབྱུང་ངོ། འདི་ཡོད་པས་འདི་འབྱུང་། འདི་སྐྱེས་པས་འདི་སྐྱེ་ཞེས་གསུངས་པའོ། །དབྱེ་ན་ཀུན་ [ཤོག་བུ་༣༨] ཉོན་ཕྱོགས་དང་རྣམ་བྱང་ཕྱོགས་ཀྱི་རྟེན་འབྲེལ་གཉིས་ལས། དང་པོ་ལ་འང་ཕྱིའི་རྟེན་འབྲེལ་དང་། ནང་གི་རྟེན་འབྲེལ་གཉིས། དང་པོ་ལ་འང་རྒྱུ་དང་འབྲེལ་བ་ཅན་དང་། རྐྱེན་དང་འབྲེལ་བ་ཅན་གཉིས་ལས། དང་པོ་ནི། ས་བོན་ལས་མྱུ་གུ། མྱུར་གུ་ལས་འདབ་མ། འདབ་མ་ལས་སྡོང་པོ། །སྡོང་པོ་ལས་སྦུ་གུ། །སྦུ་གུ་ལས་སྙིང་པོ། །སྙིང་པོ་ལས་མེ་ཏོག །མེ་ཏོག་ལས་འབྲས་བུའོ། །གཉིས་པ་ནི། ཕྱི་རོལ་གྱི་སའི་ཁམས་དང་། །ཆུའི་ཁམས་དང་། མེའི་ཁམས་དང་། རླུང་གི་ཁམས་དང་། ནམ་མཁའི་ཁམས་དང་། དུས་ཀྱི་ཁམས་ཏེ་དྲུག་གོ །གཉིས་པ་ནང་གི་རྟེན

འབྲེལ་ལའང་རྒྱུ་དང་འབྲེལ་བ་ཅན་དང་། རྐྱེན་དང་འབྲེལ་བ་ཅན་གཉིས་ལས།
དང་པོ་ནི། འདི་ལྟ་སྟེ། མ་རིག་པའི་རྐྱེན་གྱིས་འདུ་བྱེད། འདུ་བྱེད་ཀྱི་རྐྱེན་
གྱིས་རྣམ་ཤེས། རྣམ་ཤེས་ཀྱི་རྐྱེན་གྱིས་མིང་གཟུགས། མིང་གཟུགས་ཀྱི་རྐྱེན་
གྱིས་སྐྱེ་མཆེད། སྐྱེ་མཆེད་ཀྱི་རྐྱེན་གྱིས་རེག་པ། །རེག་པའི་རྐྱེན་གྱིས་ཚོར་བ།
ཚོར་བའི་རྐྱེན་གྱིས་སྲེད་པ། སྲེད་པའི་རྐྱེན་གྱིས་ལེན་པ། ལེན་པའི་རྐྱེན་གྱིས་
སྲིད་པ། སྲིད་པའི་རྐྱེན་གྱིས་སྐྱེ་བ། སྐྱེ་བའི་རྐྱེན་གྱིས་རྒ་ཤི་དང་། མྱ་ངན་
དང་། སྨྲེ་སྔགས་འདོན་པ་དང་། །སྡུག་བསྔལ་བ་དང་། ཡིད་མི་བདེ་བ་དང་།
འཁྲུགས་པ་སྟེ་སྡུག་བསྔལ་གྱི་ཕུང་པོ་ཆེན་པོ་འདི་རབ་ཏུ་གྲུབ་བོ། །དེ་དག་གི་ངོས་
འཛིན་ནི། མཛོད་ལས། །མ་རིག་ཉོན་མོངས་སྔོན་གནས་སྐབས། འདུ་བྱེད་
དག་ནི་སྔོན་ལས་ ༼ཤོག་བུ་༣༣༽ ཀྱིའོ། །རྣམ་ཤེས་མཚམས་སྦྱོར་ཕུང་པོ་
ཡིན། །མིང་དང་གཟུགས་ནི་ཕན་ཆད། །སྐྱེ་མཆེད་དྲུག་དོད་ཚུན་ཆད་དོ། །
རེག་པ་བདེ་སྡུག་ལ་སོགས་ཀྱི། །རྒྱུ་ཤེས་ནུས་པ་ཚུན་ཆད་དོ། །ཚོར་འཁྲིག་ཚུན་
ཆད་སྲེད་པ་ནི། །ལོངས་སྤྱོད་འཁྲིག་པ་ཆགས་ཅན་གྱི། །ཉེ་བར་ལེན་པ་ལོངས་
སྤྱོད་རྣམས། །ཐོབ་པར་བྱ་ཕྱིར་ཡོངས་རྒྱུག་པའོ། །དེ་སྲིད་འབྲས་བུ་འབྱུང་འགྱུར་
བའི། །ལས་བྱེད་དེ་ནི་སྲིད་པ་ཡིན། །ཉིང་མཚམས་སྦྱོར་བ་སྐྱེ་བ་ཡིན། །ཚོར་
བའི་བར་ནི་རྒ་ཤི་ཡིན། །ཞེས་པ་ལྟར། མ་རིག་པ་ནི་ཚེ་སྔ་མ་ལ་ཉོན་མོངས་པའི་
གནས་སྐབས་གང་ཡིན་པའོ། །འདུ་བྱེད་ནི་ཚེ་སྔ་མའི་བསོད་ནམས་ལ་སོགས་པའི་
ལས་ཀྱི་གནས་སྐབས་གང་ཡིན་པའོ། །རྣམ་ཤེས་ནི་མའི་མངལ་དུ་ཉིང་མཚམས་
སྦྱོར་བའི་སྐད་ཅིག་མའི་ཕུང་པོ་ལྔའོ། །མིང་དང་གཟུགས་ནི་ཉིང་མཚམས་སྦྱོར་བའི་
སེམས་ཅན་ཕན་ཆད་ནས་ཇི་སྲིད་དུ་སྐྱེ་མཆེད་དྲུག་མ་དོད་ཀྱི་བར་རོ། །སྐྱེ་མཆེད་ནི་
སྐྱེ་མཆེད་དྲུག་དོད་ནས་ཇི་སྲིད་དུ་དབང་པོ་དང་ཡུལ་དང་རྣམ་པར་ཤེས་པ་གསུམ་མ་
འདུས་པ་དེ་སྲིད་སོ། །རེག་པ་ནི། གསུམ་འདུས་ཏེ་དེས་ཚོར་བ་གསུམ་གྱི་རྒྱུ་
ཡོངས་སུ་གཅོད་པར་མ་ནུས་པའི་གནས་སྐབས་སོ། །ཚོར་བ་ནི་འཁྲིག་པའི་འདོད་
ཆགས་ཀུན་ཏུ་སྤྱོད་ནུས་པ་ནས་དེ་མ་སྤྱོད་ཚུན་ཆད་དོ། །སྲེད་པ་ནི་འདོད་པའི་ཡོན་

ཏན་སྐྱི་དང་། འཁྲིག་པའི་འདོད་ཆགས་ཀུན་ཏུ་སྤྱོད་པའི་གནས་སྐབས་སུ་ཧེ་སྲིད་དུ་
ཡུལ་ཡོངས་སུ་ཚོལ་བ་ལ་མ་[ཤོག་བུ་༢༤]ཞུགས་ཚུན་ཆད་དོ། །ལེན་པ་ནི།
གནས་སྐབས་གང་དུ་ཡུལ་ཐོབ་པར་བྱ་བའི་ཕྱིར་ཡོངས་སུ་ཚོལ་བ་ལ་ཞུགས་ནས་ཀུན་
ཏུ་རྒྱུག་པའོ། །སྲིད་པ་ནི། དེ་ལྟར་ཡུལ་ཐོབ་པའི་ཕྱིར་རྒྱུག་པས་ན་སྲིད་པ་ཕྱི་མ་
འགྲུབ་ངེས་སུ་བྱས་པའོ། །སྐྱེ་བ་ནི་ལས་དེས་འདི་ནས་ཤི་འཕོས་ཏེ་ཕྱི་མར་ཉིང་
མཚམས་སྦྱོར་བའོ། །རྒ་ཤི་ནི་སྐྱེ་བ་ཕན་ཆད་ཚོར་བའི་གནས་སྐབས་ཀྱི་བར་
རོ། །འདི་ལ་མིང་གཟུགས་དང་སྐྱེ་མཆེད་དང་། རེག་པ་དང་། །ཚོར་བ་དང་
བཞི་ནི་གཞན་དག་ཏུ་རྒ་ཤིའོ། །འདི་ལ་ཐེག་པ་ཆེན་པོ་པ་དག་གིས་ནི་ངོས་འཛིན་མི་
འདྲ་བ་ཡོད་དོ། །དེ་ལ་མ་རིག་པ་ནི་ལས་དང་ལས་ཀྱི་འབྲས་བུ་དང་། བདེན་པ་
དང་། དཀོན་མཆོག་དང་། ཆོས་རྣམས་ཀྱི་རང་བཞིན་མཐོང་བ་ལ་བསྒྲིབས་པ་སྟེ་
མི་ཤེས་པ་རྨོངས་པའོ། །འདུ་བྱེད་ནི་ཁམས་གསུམ་དུ་ལས་དགེ་མི་དགེ་ལུང་མ་
བསྟན་སྣ་ཚོགས་འདུ་བྱེད་པའོ། །རྣམ་པར་ཤེས་པ་ནི་གཟུགས་སོགས་ཡུལ་ཐ་དད་པ་
སོ་སོར་རིག་ཅིང་ཤེས་པའོ། །མིང་གཟུགས་ནི་མིང་བཞིའི་ཕུང་པོ་དང་གཟུགས་ཀྱི་
ཕུང་པོ་མེར་མེར་པོ་སོགས་གཅིག་ལ་གཅིག་བརྟེན་པས་ན་སྟེ་དཔེར་ན་མདུང་ཁྲིམ་
གཤིབས་པ་ལྟ་བུའོ། །སྐྱེ་མཆེད་ནི་སེམས་དང་སེམས་བྱུང་རྣམས་སྐྱེ་བའི་སྒོ་ལྟ་བུ་
སྟེ་མིག་ལ་སོགས་པ་དབང་པོ་དྲུག་གོ །རེག་པ་ནི་ཡུལ་དང་དབང་པོ་དང་རྣམ་པར་
ཤེས་པ་གསུམ་འདུས་པའོ། །ཚོར་བ་ནི་གསུམ་འདུས་ནས་བདེ་བ་དང་སྡུག་བསྔལ་
[ཤོག་བུ་༢༥]བ་དང་བར་མ་གསུམ་ཉམས་སུ་མྱོང་བའོ། །སྲེད་པ་ནི་སྐོམ་གྱིས་
གདུངས་པ་ལྟར་ཚོར་བ་སྡུག་བསྔལ་དང་བྲལ་བར་འདོད་པ་དང་། བདེ་བ་དང་འཕྲད་
པར་འདོད་པའོ། །ལེན་པ་ནི། འདོད་པ་ཉེ་བར་ལེན་པ་དང་། ལྟ་བ་ཉེ་བར་
ལེན་པ་དང་། ཚུལ་ཁྲིམས་དང་བརྟུལ་ཞུགས་ཉེ་བར་ལེན་པ་དང་། བདག་ཏུ་སྨྲ་
བ་ཉེ་བར་ལེན་པའོ། །སྲིད་པ་ནི་ཁམས་གསུམ་དུ་སྐྱེ་བའི་རྒྱུ་ལས་དང་ཉོན་མོངས་
པའི་བག་ཆགས་བརྟས་ནས་ཚེ་ཕྱི་མར་གྲུབ་པའོ། །སྐྱེ་བ་ནི་ལྷ་དང་མི་ལ་སོགས་པའི་
ལུས་སྔོན་མེད་པ་ལས་གཟོད་བྱུང་བའོ། །རྒ་བ་ནི་སྐྲ་དཀར་དང་གཉེར་མ་ཅན་དུ་གྱུར་

པའོ། །ཤི་བ་ནི། ལུས་ཀྱི་ཕུང་པོ་གནས་པའི་དུས་ཟད་དེ་དྲོད་དང་རྣམ་ཤེས་བཏང་ནས་ཞིག་པའོ། །རྒ་ཤིའི་ཡན་ལག་ཏུ་གྱུར་པའི་མྱ་ངན་ནི་གཉེན་བཤེས་ལོངས་སྤྱོད་སོགས་དང་བྲལ་དུ་དོགས་པའི་གདུང་བའོ། །སྨྲེ་སྔགས་ནི་རྒྱུ་གང་ལས་མྱ་ངན་དུ་གྱུར་པའི་ལོ་རྒྱུས་ཚིག་ཏུ་སྨྲ་བའོ། །སྡུག་བསྔལ་ནི་ལུས་ཉམས་ཤིང་མི་བདེ་བའོ། །ཡིད་མི་བདེ་བ་ནི་སེམས་ཉམས་ཤིང་མི་བདེ་བའོ། །འཁྲུགས་པ་ནི་སྔོན་ཉེས་པ་སྣ་ཚོགས་བྱས་པ་ཀུན་དྲན་ནས་སེམས་སྡུགས་པའོ། །འདི་དག་ཚེ་དུ་ལ་རྫོགས་ཤེ་ན། །དེ་ནི་རྟེན་ཅིང་འབྲེལ་འབྱུང་བའི། །ཡན་ལག་བཅུ་གཉིས་ཆ་གསུམ་མོ། །ཞེས་དང་། སྔོན་ མ་རིག་པ་དང་། འདུ་བྱེད། དང་ཕྱི་ སྐྱེ་བ་དང་། རྒ་ཤི། མཐའི་གཉིས་གཉིས་དང་། བར་དུ་བརྒྱད་ [ཤོག་བུ་༣༦] ཡོངས་རྫོགས་ལྡན་ནོ་ཞེས་པ་ལྟར། ཚེ་གསུམ་གྱིས་རྫོགས་པར་གསུངས་ལ། ཐེག་ཆེན་ལས་ཚེ་གཉིས་ཀྱིས་རྫོགས་པའང་གསུངས་པས་དེ་ལྟར་ན་རྒྱུ་དྲུག ཉོན་མོངས་གསུམ་དང་། ལས་གསུམ་མོ། འབྲས་དྲུག་ཏུ་ སྐྱེ་བར་གཏོགས་པ་རྣམས་སོ། ཤེས་པར་བྱའོ། ། ཡན་ལག་རྣམས་ཀུན་ནས་ཉོན་མོངས་པར་བསྡུ་ན། མ་རིག་པ་གང་ཡིན་པ་དང་། སྲེད་པ་དང་། ཉེ་བར་ལེན་པ་གང་ཡིན་པ་སྟེ་འདི་གསུམ་ནི་ཉོན་མོངས་པའི་ཀུན་ནས་ཉོན་མོངས་པར་བསྡུའོ། །འདུ་བྱེད་དང་། རྣམ་པར་ཤེས་པ་དང་། སྲིད་པ་གང་ཡིན་པ་སྟེ་འདི་གསུམ་ནི་ལས་ཀྱི་ཀུན་ནས་ཉོན་མོངས་པར་བསྡུའོ། །ལྷག་མ་མིང་གཟུགས་དང་། སྐྱེ་མཆེད་དང་། རེག་པ་དང་། ཚོར་བ་དང་། སྐྱེ་བ་དང་། རྒ་ཤི་རྣམས་ནི་སྐྱེ་བའི་ཀུན་ནས་ཉོན་མོངས་པར་བསྡུ་བར་བྱའོ། །དེ་ལ་རྣམ་པར་ཤེས་པ་ལས་ཀྱི་ཀུན་ནས་ཉོན་མོངས་པར་ཅིའི་ཕྱིར་བསྡུ་ཞེ་ན། འདི་ནི་འདུ་བྱེད་ཀྱི་བག་ཆགས་ཀྱིས་རབ་ཏུ་ཕྱེ་བའི་ཕྱིར་རོ། །ཞེས་སློབ་དཔོན་རྒྱལ་སྲས་གསུངས་སོ། །གཞན་ཡང་རྟེན་འབྲེལ་ཡན་ལག་བཅུ་གཉིས་པོ་འདི་དོན་ལྟར་ཡང་འདུ་སྟེ། མ་རིག་པས་ནི་སྲིད་པའི་ཞིང་ས་ལྟ་བུའི་བྱ་བ་བྱེད་དོ། །འདུ་བྱེད་དང་སྲིད་པ་གཉིས་ཀྱིས་ནི་ཞིང་པ་ལྟ་བུའི་བྱ་བ་བྱེད་དོ། །རྣམ་པར་ཤེས་པས་ནི་ས་བོན་ལྟ་བུའི་བྱ་བ་བྱེད་ [ཤོག་བུ་༣༧] དོ། །སྲེད་ལེན་གཉིས་ཀྱིས་ནི་ཆེར་ལྟ་བུའི་བྱ་བ་བྱེད་

དོ། །ལྷག་མ་མིང་གཟུགས་སོགས་དྲུག་གིས་མྱུ་གུ་སྨིན་པ་ལྟ་བུའི་བྱ་བ་བྱེད་པ་ཡིན་
ནོ། །གཉིས་པ་རྐྱེན་དང་འབྲེལ་བ་ནི། ནང་གི་སའི་ཁམས་དང་། ཆུའི་ཁམས་
དང་། མེའི་ཁམས་དང་། རླུང་གི་ཁམས་དང་། ནམ་མཁའི་ཁམས་དང་།
རྣམ་ཤེས་ཀྱི་ཁམས་ཏེ་དྲུག་གོ །གཉིས་པ་རྣམ་བྱང་ཕྱོགས་ཀྱི་རྟེན་འབྲེལ་ལ་ལམ་
དང་འབྲས་བུའི་རྟེན་འབྲེལ་གཉིས་ལས། དང་པོ་ནི། རྒ་ཤི་གང་ལས་བྱུང་
བརྟགས་པས་སྐྱེ་བ་ལས་བྱུང་བ་ནས་འདུ་བྱེད་གང་ལས་བྱུང་བརྟགས་པས་མ་རིག་པ་
ལས་བྱུང་བའི་རྟེན་འབྲེལ་ལུགས་འབྱུང་རྣམས་རྟོགས་ནས་བདག་མེད་རྟོགས་པའི་ཤེས་
རབ་ཀྱིས་སྲིད་པའི་རྩ་བར་གྱུར་པའི་མ་རིག་པ་དྲུང་ནས་ཕྱུང་བས། མ་རིག་པ་
འགགས་པས་འདུ་བྱེད་འགགས་པ་ནས་སྐྱེ་བ་འགགས་པས་རྒ་ཤི་འགགས་པ་སོགས་ཏེ།
རྟེན་འབྲེལ་ལུགས་ལྡོག་གི་ཚུལ་གྱིས་གཏན་ལ་ཕབ་པའོ། །དེའི་ཕྱིར་མ་རིག་པའི་
དངོས་གཉེན་དུ་གྱུར་པའི་ལམ་བདེན་གྱི་གཙོ་བོ་ནི་ཟག་མེད་ཀྱི་ཤེས་རབ་ཉིད་ཡིན་ཏེ།
རྣམ་འགྲེལ་ལས། །བྱམས་སོགས་རྨོངས་དང་འགལ་མེད་ཕྱིར། །ཉེས་པ་ཤིན་ཏུ་
ཚར་གཅོད་མིན། །སྟོང་ཉིད་ལྟ་དང་དེ་འགལ་ཕྱིར། །དེ་ལས་བྱུང་བའི་ཉེས་ཀུན་
དང་། །འགལ་བར་རབ་ཏུ་གྲུབ་པ་ཡིན། །ཞེས་སོ། །དེའི་རྟེན་ནི་ཏིང་ངེ་འཛིན་
གྱི་བསླབ་པ་ཡིན་ཏེ། དེ་མེད་ན་ལྷག་མཐོང་ཡང་རླུང་དཀྱིལ་གྱི་མར་མེ་༼ཤོག་བུ
༣༡༽བཞིན་དུ་གནས་པར་མི་འགྱུར་རོ། །དེའི་རྟེན་ནི་ཚུལ་ཁྲིམས་ཀྱི་བསླབ་པ་ཡིན་
ཏེ་དེ་མེད་ན་འདོད་ཡོན་ལ་ཞེན་ཅིང་ཆགས་པས་ཞི་གནས་འགྲུབ་པའི་སྐབས་མེད་
དོ། །དེའི་ཕྱིར་ལམ་གྱི་ངོ་བོ་བསླབ་པ་གསུམ་དུ་འདུས་པ་ཡང་སློབ་དཔོན་དབྱིག་
གཉེན་གྱིས། ཚུལ་གནས་ཐོས་དང་བསམ་ལྡན་པས། །སྒོམ་པ་ལ་ནི་རབ་ཏུ་
སྦྱོར། །ཞེས་གསུངས་སོ། །གཉིས་པ་ནི། ལམ་གྱིས་མཐོང་སྒོམ་གྱི་སྤང་བྱ་
མཐའ་དག་སྤངས་ཏེ་མཐར་ཐུག་གི་འབྲས་བུ་མངོན་དུ་གྱུར་ནས་རྟག་ཁྱབ་ལྷུན་གྲུབ་ཀྱི་
མཛད་པ་ཆོས་ཀྱི་དབྱིངས་དང་མཉམ་པའོ། །དེ་ཡན་ཆད་ཀྱིས་བདེན་པ་མཐོང་བའི་
སྒོ་བཞི་བཤད་ཟིན་ཏོ། །ད་ནི་ལྔ་པ་གནས་དང་དྲུག་པ་གནས་མ་ཡིན་པ་ལ་མཁས་
པའི་རྣམ་པར་བཞག་པ་ནི། ཉན་ཐོས་ཀྱི་ས་ལས་གནས་དང་གནས་མ་ཡིན་པ་ལ་

མཁས་པ་ནི་རྟེན་ཅིང་འབྲེལ་བར་འབྱུང་བ་ལ་མཁས་པའི་བྱེ་བྲག་ཉིད་ཡིན་པར་རིགས་པར་བྱའོ། །ཁྱད་པར་ནི་འདི་ཡོད་དེ་གནས་དང་གནས་མ་ཡིན་པ་ལ་མཁས་པས་ནི་མི་འདྲ་བའི་རྒྱུ་ཤེས་སོ། །དེ་ཡང་དགེ་བ་དང་མི་དགེ་བའི་ལས་ཀྱི་རྣམ་པར་སྨིན་པའི་འབྲས་བུ་ཡོད་དེ། དགེ་བའི་ལས་རྣམས་ཀྱི་རྣམ་པར་སྨིན་པའི་འབྲས་བུ་འདོད་པ་ཡིན་ནོ། །མི་དགེ་བའི་ལས་རྣམས་ཀྱི་རྣམ་པར་སྨིན་པའི་འབྲས་བུ་ནི་མི་འདོད་པ་ཡིན་ནོ། །ཞེས་གསུངས་པ་ལྟར་ཡིན་པས་འདི་ལ་ལས་རྒྱུ་འབྲས་ཀྱི་རྣམ་བཞག་སྤྱིར་བསྟན་པ་དང་། བདེན་[ཤོག་བུ་༣༩]པ་བཞིའི་རྣམ་བཞག་བྱེ་བྲག་ཏུ་བཤད་པ་གཉིས་ལས་དང་པོ་ལའང་སྤྱིར་ལས་ལ་ལུས་ཀྱི་ལས་དང་། ངག་གི་ལས་དང་། ཡིད་ཀྱི་ལས་དང་གསུམ་མམ། ཡང་ན་བསོད་ནམས་དང་། བསོད་ནམས་མ་ཡིན་པ་དང་། མི་གཡོ་བའི་ལས་དང་གསུམ་མོ། །ཡང་ན་དགེ་བའི་ལས་དང་། མི་དགེ་བའི་ལས་དང་། ལུང་དུ་མ་བསྟན་པའི་ལས་དང་གསུམ་མོ། །དང་པོ་ལའང་། བསོད་ནམས་ཆ་མཐུན་ མངོན་མཐོ་ཐོབ་བྱེད་དེ་དགེ་བཅུ་ལྟ་བུ ཐར་པ་ཆ་མཐུན་ ཐེག་གསུམ་གྱི་ཚོགས་ལམ། ངེས་འབྱེད་ཆ་མཐུན་ ཐེག་པ་གསུམ་གྱི་སྦྱོར་ལམ། ཟག་མེད་ཀྱི་དགེ་བ་དང་བཞིའམ་ ཐེག་པ་གསུམ་གྱི་མཐོང་ལམ་ཡན་ཆད། ཡང་ན་ངོ་བོ་ཉིད་ཀྱི་དགེ་བ་ སེམས་བྱུང་དགེ་བ་བཅུ་གཅིག མཚུངས་ལྡན་གྱི་དགེ་བ་ དད་སོགས་ཀྱི་འཁོར་ཀུན་འགྲོ་ལྟ་བུ། ཀུན་ནས་བསླང་བའི་དགེ་བ་ དད་སོགས་ཀྱིས་བསྐྱེད་པའི་ལུས་ངག་གི་ལས། དོན་དམ་པའི་དགེ་བ་སྟེ་བཞིའོ། མྱ་ངན་ལས་འདས་པའོ། གཉིས་པ་ལའང་། ངོ་བོ་ཉིད་ཀྱིས་མི་དགེ་བ། རྩ་ཉོན་དང་ཉེ་ཉོན། མཚུངས་པར་ལྡན་པའི་མི་དགེ་བའོ། དེ་དག་གི་འཁོར་ཀུན་འགྲོ་ལྟ་བུ། །ཀུན་ནས་བསླང་བའི་མི་དགེ་བ་ ཉོན་མོངས་ཀྱིས་བསྐྱེད་པའི་ལུས་ངག་གི་ལས། དོན་དམ་པའི་མི་དགེ་བ་སྟེ་ འཁོར་བ་མཐའ་དག་གོ བཞིའོ། ། གསུམ་པ་ལའང་། རྣམ་སྨིན་སྐྱེས། སྤྱོད་ལམ་པ། བཟོ་ཡི་གནས། སྤྲུལ་པའི་སེམས་ཏེ་བཞིའོ། །བྱེ་བྲག་ཏུ་རྒྱུ་དང་། རྐྱེན་དང་། འབྲས་[ཤོག་བུ་༤༠]བུ་རྣམ་པར་བཞག་པ་སྟེ་གསུམ་ལས། དང་པོ་ནི། རྒྱུ་དྲུག་ཏེ་བྱེད་རྒྱུ་དང་། ལྷན་ཅིག་འབྱུང་བའི་རྒྱུ་དང་། མཚུངས་པར་ལྡན་པའི་རྒྱུ་དང་། སྐལ་བ་མཉམ་

པའི་རྒྱུ་དང་། ཀུན་ཏུ་འགྲོ་བའི་རྒྱུ་དང་། རྣམ་པར་སྨིན་པའི་རྒྱུའོ། །དེ་ལ་བྱེད་
རྒྱུ་ནི། ཆོས་གང་ཅི་ཡང་རུང་སྟེ་སྐྱེ་བ་ལ་གེགས་མི་བྱེད་པའོ། །དཔེར་ན་མྱུ་གུ་
སྐྱེ་བ་ལ་གཞན་གྱིས་གེགས་མ་བྱས་ན་དེ་ལ་གེགས་མི་བྱེད་པའི་ཕྱིར་བྱེད་རྒྱུ་ཞེས་
བཏགས་སོ། །མྱུ་གུ་ལྟ་བུ་གཅིག་སྐྱེ་བ་ལ་ས་ཆུ་མེ་རླུང་དག་གཅིག་གི་ནང་ནའང་
བཞི་ཆར་ཚང་བར་ཡོད་པས་ཕན་ཚུན་གཅིག་ལ་གཅིག་བརྟེན་ནས་འབྱུང་བས་ལྷན་ཅིག་
འབྱུང་བའི་རྒྱུའོ། །སེམས་དང་སེམས་བྱུང་རེ་རེ་བས་ཡུལ་འཛིན་མི་ནུས་པས་ཕན་
ཚུན་གཅིག་གྲོགས་གཅིག་གིས་བྱས་ནས་འབྱུང་བ་དེ་ལ་མཚུངས་ལྡན་གྱི་རྒྱུ་ཞེས་
བྱའོ། །སེམས་དགེ་བ་ཞིག་སྐྱེས་ན་སེམས་བྱུང་ཡང་དགེ་བ་དང་། སེམས་མི་
དགེ་བ་ཞིག་སྐྱེས་ན་སེམས་བྱུང་ཡང་མི་དགེ་བར་འབྱུང་བ་དེ་ནི་སྐལ་མཉམ་གྱི་
རྒྱུའོ། །འདོད་པ་དང་གཟུགས་དང་གཟུགས་མེད་པའི་ཁམས་གསུམ་དུ་སྔར་སྐྱེས་པ་
ནི་ཕྱིས་ཉོན་མོངས་པ་ཅན་གྱི་ཆོས་སྐྱེ་བར་འགྱུར་བས་ཀུན་ཏུ་འགྲོ་བའི་རྒྱུའོ། །ལས་
དགེ་མི་དགེ་ས་མཐོ་རིས་དང་ངན་སོང་དུ་འཕེན་ཞིང་ལུས་བཟང་ངན་དུ་སྐྱེ་བ་ནི་རྣམ་
སྨིན་གྱི་རྒྱུའོ། །གཉིས་པ་ནི། རྐྱེན་རྣམ་པ་བཞི་སྟེ། རྒྱུའི་རྐྱེན། བདག་
པོའི་རྐྱེན། དེ་མ་ཐག་པའི་རྐྱེན། དམིགས་པའི་རྐྱེན་ནོ། །[ཤོག་བུ་༧༡]དེ་
ལ་ཀུན་གཞིའི་རྣམ་པར་ཤེས་པ་ནི་རྒྱུ་ཡང་བྱེད། རྐྱེན་དུ་ཡང་གྱུར་པས་ན་རྒྱུ་རྐྱེན་
ནོ། །མིག་ལ་སོགས་པའི་དབང་པོ་ལྔ་ནི་རང་རང་གི་རྣམ་པར་ཤེས་པ་སྐྱེ་བའི་བདག་
པོ་བྱེད་པས་བདག་རྐྱེན་ནོ། །དྲུག་པོ་འགགས་མ་ཐག་པ་ནི། ཡིད་ཀྱི་རྣམ་པར་
ཤེས་པའི་དེ་མ་ཐག་རྐྱེན་ཞེས་བྱའོ། །གཟུགས་དང་སྒྲ་ལ་སོགས་པའི་ཡུལ་རྣམས་ནི་
དམིགས་པའི་རྐྱེན་ནོ། །གསུམ་པ་ནི་འབྲས་བུ་ལྔ་སྟེ། རྒྱུ་མཐུན་པའི་འབྲས་བུ།
བདག་པོའི་འབྲས་བུ། སྐྱེས་བུ་བྱེད་པའི་འབྲས་བུ། རྣམ་པར་སྨིན་པའི་འབྲས་བུ།
བྲལ་བའི་འབྲས་བུ་རྣམས་སོ། །དེ་ལ་སྔོན་དགེ་བ་བྱེད་པ་རྣམས་ཚེ་འདིར་ཡང་དགེ་
བ་བྱེད་འདོད་པ་དང་། སྔོན་མི་དགེ་བ་བྱེད་པ་ནི་ཚེ་འདི་ལ་ཡང་མི་དགེ་བ་བྱེད་པ་སྟེ་
རྒྱུ་མཐུན་པའི་འབྲས་བུའོ། །ཚེ་རབས་སྔ་མ་ལ་མི་དགེ་བ་བྱེད་པ་ནི་ཚེ་འདིར་ཡང་
ཡུལ་ཁམས་ངན་པར་སྐྱེས་པ་དང་། དགེ་བ་བྱས་པས་ཡུལ་བཟང་པོར་སྐྱེས་ཏེ་ཡུལ་

བཟང་ངན་གྱི་བདག་པོར་བྱེད་པ་ནི་བདག་པོའི་འབྲས་བུའོ། །ཞིང་ལ་སོ་ནམ་བྱས་
པས་ནས་མང་དུ་འཕེལ་བ་ལྟར་ལས་བྱས་པའི་འབྲས་བུ་གོང་ནས་གོང་དུ་འཕེལ་བ་ནི་
སྐྱེས་བུ་བྱེད་པའི་འབྲས་བུ་ཞེས་བྱའོ། །སྦྱིན་པས་ལོངས་སྤྱོད་ཐོབ་པ་དང་། སྲོག་
བཅད་པས་ཚེ་ཐུང་བ་སོགས་ནི་རྣམ་པར་སྨིན་པའི་འབྲས་བུའོ། །འཕགས་པའི་ལམ་
བསྒོམས་ནས་ཉོན་མོངས་པ་སྤང་པ་ནི་བྲལ་བའི་འབྲས་བུ་ཞེས་བྱའོ། །གཉིས་པ་
བདེན་བཞི་བྱེ་བྲག་ཏུ་༼ཤོག་བུ་༦༢༽བཤད་ལའང་དང་པོ་ངེས་ཚིག་ནི། བསྟན་པ་
དང་མི་མཐུན་པ་མེད་པས་ན་བདེན་པའོ། །དབྱེ་ན། རྒྱུད་བླ་མ་ལས། །ནད་ནི་
ཤེས་བྱ་ནད་ཀྱི་རྒྱུ་ནི་སྤང་བྱ་ལ། །བདེ་གནས་ཐོབ་ཕྱིར་སྨན་ནི་བརྟེན་པར་བྱེད་པ་
ལྟར། །སྡུག་བསྔལ་རྒྱུ་དང་དེ་འགོག་པ་དང་དེ་བཞིན་ལམ། །ཤེས་བྱ་སྤང་བྱ་
རེག་པར་བྱ་ཞིང་བརྟེན་པར་བྱ། །ཞེས་པ་ལྟར་བཞི་ལས། དང་པོ་སྡུག་བསྔལ་
ལའང་དབྱེ་ན། གང་དུ་སྨིན་པ་སྡུག་བསྔལ་གྱི་གནས། །གང་ལ་སྨིན་པ་སྡུག་
བསྔལ་བའི་སེམས་ཅན། གང་ཞིག་སྨིན་པ་སྡུག་བསྔལ་གྱི་རྣམ་གྲངས། ཇི་ལྟར་
སྨིན་པ་སྡུག་བསྔལ་གྱི་འཇུག་རིམ་དང་བཞིའོ། །རྣམ་པའང་བཞི་སྟེ་སྐད་ཅིག་མ་རེ་
རེ་བཞིན་སྐྱེ་ཞིང་འཆི་བའི་ཆོས་ཅན་ཡིན་པས་མི་རྟག་པ། སྡུག་བསྔལ་གསུམ་དང་
བརྒྱད་ཀྱིས་རྒྱུན་མི་འཆད་པར་འཚེ་བས་ན་སྡུག་བསྔལ་བ། ཕུང་པོ་ལྔའི་ནང་ན་མུ་
སྟེགས་ཀྱིས་བརྟགས་པའི་བདག་རྟག་པ་མེད་པས་ན་སྟོང་པ། །ཕུང་པོ་ལྔ་པོ་ཉིད་ཀྱང་
མུ་སྟེགས་ཀྱིས་བརྟགས་པའི་བདག་མ་ཡིན་པས་བདག་མེད་པའོ། །གཉིས་པ་ཀུན་
འབྱུང་ལ་དབྱེ་ན་ལས་ཀྱི་ཀུན་འབྱུང་དང་ཉོན་མོངས་པའི་ཀུན་འབྱུང་གཉིས་སོ། །
དེའི་རྣམ་པ་ནི་བཞི་སྟེ་འདོད་ཆགས་ལ་སོགས་པའི་ཉོན་མོངས་པ་རྣམས་དང་། དེས་
བསྐྱེད་པའི་དགེ་བ་དང་མི་དགེ་བ་རྣམས་ནི་སྲིད་པའི་རྒྱུར་གྱུར་པས་ན་རྒྱུ། དེའི་བག་
ཆགས་སེམས་ཀྱི་རྒྱུད་ལ་སོགས་ཏེ་ཁམས་གསུམ་པའི་སྐྱེ་༼ཤོག་བུ་༦༣༽བའི་ས་
བོན་དུ་གནས་པ་ནི་ཀུན་འབྱུང་། ཕྱི་མའི་ལས་དགེ་བས་ནི་དགེ་བའི་བག་ཆགས་
བརྟས་ཤིང་འབྲས་བུ་བདེ་བ་དང་མི་དགེ་བས་ནི་མི་དགེ་བའི་བག་ཆགས་བརྟས་ཤིང་
འབྲས་བུ་སྡུག་བསྔལ་སྨིན་པར་བྱེད་པས་ན་རྐྱེན། དེ་ལྟར་རྒྱུ་རྐྱེན་གཉིས་ཚོགས་ཏེ་

བག་ཆགས་སོ་སོར་བརྟས་ནས་གནས་རིས་མཐོ་དམན་དུ་སྡུག་བསྔལ་གྱི་ཕུང་པོ་མངོན་པར་གྲུབ་པ་ནི་རབ་སྐྱེའོ། །གསུམ་པ་འགོག་པ་ལ་དབྱེ་ན་སོ་སོར་བརྟག་པའི་འགོག་པ་དང་། སོ་སོར་བརྟག་པ་མ་ཡིན་པའི་འགོག་པ་གཉིས་སོ། །རྣམ་པ་བཞི་སྟེ། འདོད་ཆགས་ལ་སོགས་པའི་ཉོན་མོངས་པ་དང་སྲོག་གཅོད་སོགས་སྡིག་པའི་ལས་རྣམས་སྤངས་ཏེ་སླར་མི་འབྱུང་བ་ནི་འགོག་པ། ལས་དང་ཉོན་མོངས་པས་བསྐྱེད་པའི་འབྲས་བུ་སྡུག་བསྔལ་ཅི་ཡང་མི་འབྱུང་བས་ན་ཞི་བ། གཏན་བདེ་འགྱུར་བ་མེད་པའི་གནས་ཐོབ་པས་གྱ་ནོམ་པ། ཁམས་གསུམ་དེ་ཙོན་ར་དང་འདྲ་བ་ལས་ཐར་ཟིན་ཅིང་མྱང་འདས་ཀྱི་བདེ་བ་ཐོབ་ཟིན་པས་ན་ངེས་པར་འབྱུང་བའོ། །བཞི་པ་ལམ་ལའང་དབྱེ་ན་ལམ་གང་གིས་སྡུག་བསྔལ་ཡོངས་སུ་ཤེས་པ་དང་། ཀུན་འབྱུང་སྤོང་བ་དང་། འགོག་པ་མངོན་དུ་བྱེད་པ་དང་། ལམ་བསྒོམ་པ་སྟེ་བཞིའམ། ཡང་ན་ཚོགས་ཀྱི་ལམ་དང་། སྦྱོར་བའི་ལམ་དང་། མཐོང་བའི་ལམ་དང་། བསྒོམ་པའི་ལམ་དང་། མཐར་ཕྱིན་པའི་ལམ་མོ། །རྣམ་པ་ནི་བཞི་སྟེ། སོ་སོའི་སྐྱེ་བོའི་ས་ནས་ [ཤོག་བུ་༤༤] འཕགས་པའི་གནས་སུ་འགྲོ་བས་ན་ལམ། མ་རིག་པ་དང་། ཉོན་མོངས་པ་སྤང་བའི་གཉེན་པོར་གྱུར་པས་ན་རིགས་པ། སེམས་ཕྱིན་ཅི་ལོག་སྤངས་ཏེ་ཕྱིན་ཅི་མ་ལོག་པར་སྦྱོར་བས་ན་སྒྲུབ་པ། འཁོར་བའི་ཉེས་པ་དང་གཏན་ནས་བྲལ་ཞིང་མྱ་ངན་ལས་འདས་པའི་གནས་སུ་ཕྱིན་པར་བྱེད་པས་ན་ངེས་པར་འབྱིན་པའོ། །གཞན་ཡང་རིགས་པ་བཞིའི་ཆོས་རྣམས་ཀྱི་ངོ་བོ་ཕྱིན་ཅི་མ་ལོག་པར་གཏན་ལ་ཕབ་པའང་ལམ་བདེན་དུ་འདུའོ། །དེ་ལ་རིགས་པ་བཞི་ནི་ལྟོས་པའི་རིགས་པ། བྱ་བ་བྱེད་པའི་རིགས་པ། འཐད་པ་བསྒྲུབ་པའི་རིགས་པ། ཆོས་ཉིད་ཀྱི་རིགས་པའོ། །དེ་ཡང་མིག་གི་རྣམ་པར་ཤེས་པ་སྐྱེ་བ་ལ་མིག་གི་དབང་པོ་དང་ཡུལ་གཟུགས་གཉིས་ལ་ལྟོས་ནས་འབྱུང་བ་རིགས་པ་དེ་བཞིན་དུ་གཞན་ལའང་སྦྱར་ཏེ། མྱུ་གུ་ནི་ས་བོན་ལ་ལྟོས་ནས་འབྱུང་བ་དང་། མ་རིག་པ་ལ་ལྟོས་ནས་འདུ་བྱེད་འབྱུང་བ་ལ་སོགས་པ་ནི་ལྟོས་པའི་རིགས་པའོ། །མིག་གི་རྣམ་པར་ཤེས་པ་དེ་བྱུང་ནས་གཟུགས་ལ་ལྟ་བའི་བྱ་བ་བྱེད་ཀྱི། སྒྲ་ལ་ནི་ཉན་པར་མི་བྱེད་དོ། །མིག་

གི་དབང་པོས་ཀྱང་མིག་ཤེས་བསྐྱེད་ཀྱི། རྣ་བ་ལ་སོགས་པའི་ཤེས་པ་གཞན་ནི་མི་བསྐྱེད་དོ། །དེ་བཞིན་དུ་ཀུན་ལ་སྦྱར་ཏེ་ནས་ཀྱི་ས་བོན་གྱིས་ནས་ཉིད་བསྐྱེད་ཀྱི། བྲ་སྨན་ལྟ་བུ་གཞན་མི་བསྐྱེད་པ་དག་ནི་བྱ་བ་བྱེད་པའི་རིགས་པའོ། །འཐད་སྒྲུབ་ལ་གསུམ་ལས་རྗེས་སུ་དཔག་པ་ནི། དུ་བ་ལས་མེར་ཤེས་པ་དང་། ཆུ་བྱ་ལས་[ཤོག་བུ་༥༥]ཆུར་ཤེས་པ་ལྟ་བུའོ། །མངོན་སུམ་ནི་རྣམ་པར་ཤེས་པ་དྲུག་གིས་མ་འཁྲུལ་བར་མཐོང་བ་དང་། རྣལ་འབྱོར་པའི་སེམས་ཀྱིས་མཐོང་བ་དག་གོ །ལུང་ནི་མི་བསླུ་བའི་ཚིག་སངས་རྒྱས་ཀྱི་ཞལ་ནས་གསུངས་པ་རྣམས་ཏེ། མདོ་ལས། །ལུང་ནི་ཡིད་ཆེས་ཚིག་ཡིན་ཏེ། །ཉེས་པ་ཟད་པས་རྫུན་གྱི་ཚིག །སྨྲ་བར་མི་འགྱུར་རྒྱུ་མེད་ཕྱིར། །ཉེས་ཟད་ལུང་དུ་ཤེས་པར་བྱ། །ཞེས་པ་ལྟར་རོ། །དེ་དག་ནི་ཚད་མའམ་འཐད་སྒྲུབ་ཀྱི་རིགས་པའོ། །ས་སྲ་བ་དང་། ཆུ་གཤེར་བ་སོགས་དང་། ཆོས་རྣམས་སྟོང་པ་དང་། བདག་མེད་པ་དང་། ལས་ཀྱི་འབྲས་བུ་བསླུ་བ་མེད་པ་ལ་སོགས་པ་སྤྱི་སྤྱི་དང་རང་གི་མཚན་ཉིད་ཡེ་ནས་དེ་ལྟར་གནས་པ་དག་ནི་ཆོས་ཉིད་ཀྱི་རིགས་པའོ། །བདེན་པ་འདི་དག་ལ་འཕགས་པའི་བདེན་པ་ཞེས་པའི་རྒྱུ་མཚན་ཡང་། མདོ་ལས། །ལག་མཐིལ་སྤྱུ་ཉག་གཅིག་བཞག་པ། །མི་རྣམས་ཀྱིས་ནི་མི་རྟོགས་ལ། །མིག་ཏུ་ཡོང་ན་དེ་ཉིད་ཀྱིས། །མི་བདེ་བ་དང་གནོད་བསྐྱེད་བཞིན། །བྱིས་པ་དག་ནི་ལག་མཐིལ་འདྲ། །འདུ་བྱེད་སྡུག་བསྔལ་སྤྱུ་མི་རྟོགས། །མཁས་པ་རྣམས་ནི་མིག་དང་འདྲ། །དེ་ཡིས་ཤིན་ཏུ་ཡིད་ཀྱང་འབྱུང་། ཞེས་གསུངས་པ་ལྟར་བདེན་པ་བཞིའི་རང་བཞིན་ཇི་ལྟ་བ་བཞིན་དུ་མཁྱེན་པ་ནི་འཕགས་པ་རྣམས་ཡིན་པས་ན་དེ་སྐད་ཅེས་བྱའོ། །དེ་དག་ཀྱང་བསྡུ་ན་ཀུན་ཉོན་ཕྱོགས་ཀྱི་རྒྱུ་འབྲས་དང་། རྣམ་བྱང་ཕྱོགས་ཀྱི་རྒྱུ་འབྲས་གཉིས་སམ[ཤོག་བུ་༥༦]ཡང་ན་ཀུན་རྫོབ་ཀྱི་བདེན་པ་དང་། དོན་དམ་པའི་བདེན་པ་གཉིས་སུ་འདུ་སྟེ། མདོ་ལས། །འཇིག་རྟེན་མཁྱེན་པས་བདེན་པ་འདི་གཉིས་ནི། །ཁྱོད་ཀྱི་གཞན་ལས་མ་གསན་རང་གིས་རིག །འཇིག་རྟེན་ཀུན་རྫོབ་དེ་བཞིན་དོན་དམ་སྟེ། །བདེན་པ་གསུམ་པ་གང་ཡང་མ་མཆིས་སོ། །ཞེས་གསུངས་པས་སོ། །

དེ་བས་ཀྱང་བསྡུ་ན། མདོ་ལས། །སྐྱེ་བ་མེད་པ་བདེན་པ་གཅིག་ཉིད་ལ། །དེ་
ལ་ཁ་ཅིག་བདེན་པ་བཞི་ཞེས་འཛེར། །བྱང་ཆུབ་སྙིང་པོར་ཞུགས་ན་བདེན་གཅིག་
ཀྱང་། །གྲུབ་པ་མེད་ན་བཞི་ལྟ་ག་ལ་ཡོད། །ཞེས་གསུངས་པ་ལྟར་ཆོས་ཉིད་དོན་
དམ་པའི་བདེན་པ་གཅིག་པུ་རུ་འདུ་བ་ཡིན་ནོ། །རྩ་བའི་ས་བཅད་གཉིས་པ་ཐེག་ཆེན་
ཆོས་ཀྱི་སྡོམ་བཞི་བཤད་པ་ལ། །སྤྱིར་ཐེག་པ་ཆེ་ཆུང་གི་ཁྱད་པར་དང་། །ཁྱད་
པར་དེ་ལྡན་གྱི་ཐེག་ཆེན་བཤད་པ་གཉིས་ལས། དང་པོ་ནི། མདོ་སྡེ་རྒྱན་
ལས། །དམིགས་པ་ཆེ་བ་ཉིད་དང་ནི། །དེ་བཞིན་སྒྲུབ་པ་གཉིས་དག་དང་། །
ཡེ་ཤེས་བརྩོན་འགྲུས་རྩོམ་པ་དང་། །ཐབས་ལ་མཁས་པར་གྱུར་པ་དང་། །ཡན་
ལག་གྲུབ་པ་ཆེན་པོ་དང་། །སངས་རྒྱས་ཕྲིན་ལས་ཆེན་པོ་སྟེ། །ཆེན་པོ་འདི་དང་
ལྡན་པའི་ཕྱིར། །ཐེག་ཆེན་ཞེས་ནི་ངེས་པར་བརྗོད། །ཞེས་པ་ལྟར། མདོ་ལ་
སོགས་པའི་ཆོས་རྒྱ་ཆེན་པོ་དཔག་ཏུ་མེད་པ་ལ་དམིགས་པ་དང་། རང་གཞན་གྱི་དོན་
གཉིས་བསྒྲུབ་པ་དང་། ཆོས་དང་གང་ཟག་གི་བདག་མེད་པ་རྟོགས་པའི་ཡེ་ཤེས་དང་།
བསྐལ་པ་གྲངས་མེད་གསུམ་དུ་གུས་རྟག་གི་ ༼ཤོག་བུ་༨༢༽ བརྩོན་འགྲུས་བརྩམས་
པ་དང་། འཁོར་བ་ཡོངས་སུ་མི་གཏོང་ཞིང་ཀུན་ནས་ཉོན་མོངས་པ་མེད་པའི་ཐབས་
མཁས་པ་དང་། སྟོབས་དང་མི་འཇིགས་པ་དང་། ཆོས་མ་འདྲེས་པ་བཅོ་བརྒྱད་
རྣམས་འགྲུབ་པ་དང་། ཡང་དང་དུ་མངོན་པར་རྫོགས་པར་བྱང་ཆུབ་པ་དང་། མྱ་
ངན་ལས་འདས་པ་ཆེན་པོ་ཀུན་དུ་སྟོན་པ་སྟེ། འདི་དག་ནི་ཐེག་པ་ཆེན་པོ་པ་རྣམས་ལ་
ཡོད་ཀྱི་དམན་པ་རྣམས་ལ་ནི་མ་ཡིན་ནོ། །གཉིས་པ་ལ་དོན་རྣམ་པ་བཅུའི་སྒོ་ནས་
ཐེག་ཆེན་གཏན་ལ་དབབ་པ་དང་། དེ་ཉིད་བཞི་རུ་བསྡུ་བ་སྟེ་གཉིས་ལས། དང་པོ་
ནི། ཐེག་བསྡུས་ལས། །ཤེས་བྱའི་གནས་དང་མཚན་ཉིད་དེར་འཇུག་དང་། །
དེ་ཡི་རྒྱུ་འབྲས་དེ་རབ་དབྱེ་བ་དང་། །བསླབ་པ་གསུམ་དང་དེ་འབྲས་སྤངས་པ་
དང་། །ཡེ་ཤེས་ཐེག་པ་མཆོག་གྱུར་ཁྱད་པར་འཕགས། །བསྟན་འདི་འདི་ལྟར་
གཞན་ན་མ་མཐོང་ལ། །འདི་དག་བྱང་ཆུབ་མཆོག་གི་རྒྱུར་མཐོང་བས། །གནས་
བཅུ་བསྟན་པས་ཁྱད་ཞུགས་གང་ཡིན་པ། །ཐེག་པ་ཆེན་པོ་སངས་རྒྱས་བཀར་འདོད་

དོ། །ཞེས་གསུངས་པ་ལྟར་ལས། ཤེས་བྱའི་གནས་ནི། ཤེས་བྱའི་མཚན་ཉིད་ངོ་བོ་ཉིད་གསུམ་གྱི་རྒྱུའི་གནས་ཏེ་ཀུན་གཞི་དང་། ཤེས་བྱའི་མཚན་ཉིད་ནི་ཤེས་བྱའི་ངོ་བོ་ཞེས་པའི་དོན་ཏེ་ངོ་བོ་ཉིད་གསུམ་མོ། །ཤེས་བྱའི་མཚན་ཉིད་དེ་ལ་གང་གིས་འཇུག་པར་འགྱུར་བ་ནི་རྣམ་པར་ཤེས་པ་ཙམ་དང་། འཇུག་པ་དེའི་ [ཤོག་བུ ༩༨] རྒྱུའང་འབྲས་བུ་ནི་རྣམ་པར་ཤེས་པ་ཙམ་ལ་འཇུག་པ་ནི་འཇིག་རྟེན་པའི་སྦྱིན་པ་ལ་སོགས་པ་ཕ་རོལ་ཏུ་ཕྱིན་པ་ལ་ཞུགས་པ་ནི་རྒྱུའོ། །དེ་ཉིད་མངོན་དུ་གྱུར་ཅིང་འཇིག་རྟེན་ལས་འདས་པར་གྱུར་པ་ནི་འབྲས་བུའོ། །དེའི་རྒྱུ་དང་འབྲས་བུ་སྒོམ་པས་རབ་ཏུ་དབྱེ་བ་ནི་སྒོམ་པ་གོམས་པ་སྐྱེ་སའི་ཁྱད་པར་ས་བཅུ་རྣམས་དང་། དེའི་ཚེ་ན་ལྷག་པ་ཚུལ་ཁྲིམས་དང་། ཏིང་ངེ་འཛིན་དང་། ཤེས་རབ་ཀྱི་བསླབ་པ་ཡོངས་སུ་དག་པ་དང་། སོ་སོ་རང་གི་རིག་པ་ཉན་ཐོས་ཀྱི་སྒྲིབ་པ་སྤང་བའི་མི་གནས་པའི་མྱ་ངན་ལས་འདས་པ་ནི་དེའི་འབྲས་བུ་སྤངས་པ་དང་། སྐུ་གསུམ་ནི་དེའི་འབྲས་བུ་ཡེ་ཤེས་ཏེ་དེ་ལྟར་ན་གནས་བཅུ་པོ་འདི་དག་གིས་ཐེག་པ་ཆེན་པོ་མཐའ་དག་བསྡུས་པ་ཡིན་ནོ། །དེ་ལ་ཐོག་མར་ཀུན་གཞིའི་རྣམ་པར་ཤེས་པ་ནི། ཤེས་བྱའི་གནས་སོ་ཞེས་གསུངས་པ་ལ་སྒྲུབ་བྱེད་ལུང་དང་རིགས་པ་གཉིས་ལས། དང་པོ་ནི། བཅོམ་ལྡན་འདས་ཀྱིས་ཆོས་མངོན་པའི་མདོ་ལས། །ཐོག་མ་མེད་པའི་དུས་ཀྱི་དབྱིངས། །ཆོས་རྣམས་ཀུན་གྱི་གནས་ཡིན་ཏེ། །དེ་ཡོད་པས་ནི་འགྲོ་བ་དང་། །མྱ་ངན་འདས་པའང་ཐོབ་པར་འགྱུར། །ཞེས་དང་། །ཆོས་ཀུན་ས་བོན་ཐམས་ཅད་པའི། །རྣམ་པར་ཤེས་པ་ཀུན་གཞི་སྟེ། །དེ་བས་ཀུན་གཞིའི་རྣམ་ཤེས་དེ། །དམ་པ་དག་ལ་ངས་བཤད་དོ། །ཞེས་དང་། དགོངས་པ་ངེས་འགྲེལ་ལས། །ལེན་པའི་རྣམ་པར་ཤེས་པ་ཟབ་ཅིང་ཕྲ། །ས་ [ཤོག་བུ ༩༩] བོན་ཐམས་ཅད་ཆུ་བོའི་རྒྱུན་བཞིན་འབབས། …དེར་ས་བོན་ཐམས་ཅད་སྐད་ཅིག་མའི་རིམ་གྱིས་འཇུག །བདག་ཏུ་རྟོག་པར་གྱུར་ན་མི་རུང་ཞེས། །འདི་ནི་བྱིས་པ་རྣམས་ལ་ངས་མ་བསྟན། །ཞེས་ཇི་སྐད་གསུངས་པ་ལྟ་བུའོ། །དེར་ཡང་དབང་པོ་ཐམས་ཅད་ཀྱི་གནས་པའི་རྒྱུ་ཡིན་པ་དང་། ལུས་ཐམས་ཅད་ཉེ་བར་ལེན་པའི་གནས་སུ་འགྱུར་བའི་ཕྱིར་ལེན་པའི་རྣམ་པར་ཤེས་པ་ཞེས་

བྱིའོ། །གཉིས་པ་ནི། རྣམ་པར་གཏན་ལ་དབབ་པ་བསྡུ་བ་ལས། །ལེན་དང་དང་པོ་གསལ་བ་དང་། །ས་བོན་ལས་དང་ལུས་ཚོར་དང་། །སེམས་མེད་སྙོམས་པར་འཇུག་པ་དང་། །དེ་བཞིན་འཆི་འཕོ་མི་རུང་འགྱུར། །ཞེས་གསུངས་པ་ལྟར། །གལ་ཏེ་ཀུན་གཞིའི་རྣམ་པར་ཤེས་པ་མེད་ན། གནས་ལེན་པ་མི་སྲིད་པ་དང་། དང་པོ་འཇུག་པ་མི་སྲིད་པ་དང་། གསལ་བར་འཇུག་པ་མི་སྲིད་པ་དང་། ས་བོན་ཉིད་མི་སྲིད་པ་དང་། ལས་མི་སྲིད་པ་དང་། ལུས་ཀྱི་ཚོར་བ་མི་སྲིད་པ་དང་། སེམས་མེད་པའི་སྙོམས་པར་འཇུག་པ་མི་སྲིད་པ་དང་། རྣམ་པར་ཤེས་པའི་འཆི་འཕོ་མི་སྲིད་པའི་སྐྱོན་དང་། སྐྱོན་རྣམ་པ་བརྒྱད་དུ་འགྱུར་རོ། །དང་པོ་ལའང་། ལུས་ལེན་པ་ལ་ནི་སྔོན་གྱི་ལས་ཀྱིས་འཇུག་པའི་རྣམ་སྨིན་རྒྱུན་བརྟན་པ་ཞིག་དགོས་པས་ཀུན་གཞིའི་རྣམ་པར་ཤེས་པ་ནི་སྔོན་གྱི་ལས་ལས་འབྱུང་བ་ཡིན་ལ། འཇུག་ཤེས་དྲུག་ནི་ད་ལྟར་གྱི་རྐྱེན་སྣ་ཚོགས་ལས་འབྱུང་ [ཤོག་བུ་༥༠] བ་དང་། ཡང་རྣམ་ཤེས་དྲུག་ནི། ལུང་དུ་མ་བསྟན་པ་རྣམ་པར་སྨིན་པ་ནི་མེད་ལ་དགེ་བ་དང་མི་དགེ་བར་སྣང་བ་དང་། ཡང་ཚོགས་དྲུག་གི་ཤེས་པ་ནི་གནས་ངེས་པ་ལས་བྱུང་བས་རང་གི་གནས་ཀྱིས་ཟིན་ཀྱང་། ལྷག་མ་རྣམས་ཀྱིས་མ་ཟིན་པ་དང་། ལན་འགའ་འབྱུང་ལ་ལན་འགའ་མི་འབྱུང་བས། ཡང་ཡང་གནས་ལེན་པའི་སྐྱོན་དུ་འགྱུར་བ་རྣམས་སོ། །གཉིས་པ་ནི། གལ་ཏེ་དེ་ལྟར་ན་རྣམ་ཤེས་གཉིས་གཅིག་ཆར་འབྱུང་བར་འགྱུར་བས་ཏེ་རྣམ་པར་ཤེས་པ་གནས་ཀྱི་དུས་ན་ཀུན་གཞི་རྒྱུན་མི་འཆད་པས་སོ་ཞེ་ན། དེ་ནི་འདོད་པ་ཡིན་ཏེ། ཀུན་གཞིའི་རྣམ་པར་ཤེས་པ་ནི། མིག་ལ་སོགས་པའི་རྣམ་ཤེས་པ་གཞན་དང་ལྷན་ཅིག་ཏུ་འབྱུང་བ་པོ་ན་སྟེ། དེ་མེད་ན་འགའ་ཞིག་གིས་ལྟ་བར་འདོད་པ་ནས་རྣམ་པར་ཤེས་པའི་བར་འདོད་པ་ལ། དང་པོ་རྣམ་པར་ཤེས་པ་གང་ཡང་རུང་བ་གཅིག་འཇུག་པར་མི་རུང་སྟེ། དྲུག་པོའི་ཡིད་ལ་བྱེད་པ་དང་དབང་པོ་དང་ཡུལ་མངོན་དུ་གྱུར་པར་བྱེ་བྲག་མེད་པའི་ཕྱིར་རོ། །གསུམ་པ་ནི། ཡིད་ཤེས་དེ་འདས་པའི་དུས་ན་ཉམས་སུ་མྱོང་བའི་ཡུལ་དྲན་པའི་ཚེ་ནི་མི་གསལ་བའི་ཚུལ་གྱིས་འཇུག་པ་ཡིན་ལ། ད་ལྟ་བའི་ཡུལ་ལ་ནི་དབང་ཤེས་དང་ལྷན་

ཅིག་ཡིད་ཀྱི་འཇུག་པ་གསལ་བས་དེ་ན་ཅིག་ཆར་འབྱུང་བ་མེད་ན་ཡིད་ཤེས་གསལ་བའང་ཡོད་པ་མ་ཡིན་ནོ། །བཞི་པ་ནི། ཚོགས་དྲུག་པོ་དག་གཅིག [ཤོག་བུ ༥༧] གིས་བོན་དུ་གཅིག་འགྱུར་བ་མི་རུང་སྟེ། འདི་ལྟར་དགེ་བའི་སེམས་ཀྱི་འཇུག་ཐོགས་སུ་མི་དགེ་བ་དང་། མི་དགེ་བའི་མཇུག་ཐོགས་སུ་དགེ་བ་དང་གཉིས་ཀའི་མཇུག་ཐོགས་སུ་ལུང་དུ་མ་བསྟན་པ་སོགས་ཕན་ཚུན་མི་མཐུན་པ་ཉིད་དང་། སེམས་ཀྱི་རྒྱུན་འགགས་ཏེ་ཡུན་རིང་པོར་ལོན་པ་ན་སླར་འབྱུང་བར་མི་རུང་བས་སོ། །ལྔ་པ་ནི། འདི་ལྟར་གནས་དང་། དོན་དང་། ལུས་སུ་སྣང་བའི་རྣམ་པར་རིག་པ་དག་ནི། ཅིག་ཆར་དུ་འབྱུང་བར་སྣང་བས། ལྷན་ཅིག་འབྱུང་བ་མེད་པར་གྱུར་ན། རྣམ་པར་ཤེས་པ་གཅིག་དུས་སྐད་ཅིག་གཅིག་ལ་ལས་སྣ་ཚོགས་སོགས་པ་ནི་མེད་པ་ཁོ་ནའོ། །དྲུག་པ་ནི། སེམས་ཀྱིས་རྟོག་དཔྱོད་ཚུལ་བཞིན་དུའམ། །ཚུལ་བཞིན་མ་ཡིན་པར་བྱེད་པ་དང་། ཡང་ན་སེམས་མཉམ་པར་བཞག་ཀྱང་རུང་སྟེ། དེའི་ལུས་ལ་ཚོར་བ་སྣ་ཚོགས་སུ་འབྱུང་བའང་རུང་བ་མ་ཡིན་ཏེ་ཡིད་ཤེས་ཀྱིས་ནི་ཚུལ་བཞིན་དུ་སེམས་པ་སོགས་ཡིན་ལ་ཀུན་གཞི་མེད་པས་ཚོར་བ་མང་པོའི་རྒྱུ་ཡོད་པ་མ་ཡིན་ནོ། །བདུན་པ་ནི། འདི་ལྟར་འདུ་ཤེས་མེད་པ་ལ་སྙོམས་པར་ཞུགས་པའམ། འགོག་པ་ལ་ཞུགས་པའི་ཚེ་དེའི་རྣམ་པར་ཤེས་པ་ལུས་དང་བྲལ་བས་ཤི་བར་འགྱུར་རོ། །བརྒྱད་པ་ནི། འདི་ལྟར་འཆི་འཕོ་བའི་ཚེ་ལུས་ཀྱི་སྟོད་དམ་སྨད་དུ་དྲོད་ཡལ་བ་ནི་རྟག་ཏུ་འཕེལ་འགྲིབ་བརྟན་པ་ལུས་ལེན་པར་བྱེད་པའི་ཀུན་གཞིའི་རྣམ་པར་ཤེས་པ་ཁོ་ན་དང་བྲལ་བས་ཡིན་གྱི་མི་བརྟན་པ་ཡིད་ཀྱི་རྣམ་པར་ [ཤོག་བུ ༥༨] ཤེས་པ་དང་བྲལ་བས་ནི་མ་ཡིན་ནོ། །གཉིས་པ་ཤེས་བྱའི་མཚན་ཉིད་ལ་གསུམ་ལས། ཀུན་བརྟགས་ནི། མདོ་སྡེ་རྒྱན་ལས། མིང་དང་དོན་ནི་ཇི་ལྟ་བ། །དོན་དང་མིང་དུ་སྣང་བ་གང་། །ཡང་དག་མིན་རྟོག་རྒྱུ་མཚན་ནི། །ཀུན་བརྟགས་པ་ཡི་མཚན་ཉིད་དོ། །ཞེས་གསུངས་པས་མིང་ཇི་ལྟར་བར་དོན་དུ་སྣང་བ་དང་། དོན་ཇི་ལྟ་བར་མིང་དུ་སྣང་བ་ཡང་དག་བ་མ་ཡིན་པའི་ཀུན་དུ་རྟོག་པའི་དམིགས་པ་གང་ཡིན་པའོ། །གཉིས་པ་གཞན་གྱི་དབང་ནི། དེ་ཉིད་ལས། །རྣམ་གསུམ་རྣམ་གསུམ་

སྣང་བ་ཅན། །གཟུང་དང་འཛིན་པའི་མཚན་ཉིད་དེ། །ཡང་དག་མ་ཡིན་ཀུན་རྟོག
ནི། །གཞན་གྱི་དབང་གི་མཚན་ཉིད་དོ། །ཞེས་པས་དེ་ལ་རྣམ་པ་གསུམ་གནས་སུ་
སྣང་བ་དང་། དོན་དུ་སྣང་བ་དང་། ལུས་སུ་སྣང་བའོ། །ཡང་གསུམ་ནི་ཉོན་
མོངས་བ་ཅན་གྱི་ཡིད་དང་། འཛིན་པ་སྒོ་ལྔའི་ཤེས་པ་དང་། རྟོག་པ་ཡིད་ཀྱི་རྣམ་
པར་ཤེས་པ་རྣམས་སོ། །དེ་དག་ལས་སྤྱི་མ་གསུམ་གཟུང་བའི་མཚན་ཉིད་དང་།
ཕྱི་མ་གསུམ་འཛིན་པའི་མཚན་ཉིད་དོ། །གསུམ་པ་ཡོངས་སུ་གྲུབ་བ་ནི། སྤྱི་མ་
ལས། །མེད་དང་ཡོད་ཉིད་གང་ཡིན་དང་། །ཡོད་དང་མེད་པ་མཉམ་ཉིད་
དང་། །མ་ཞི་ཞི་དང་རྣམ་མི་རྟོག །ཡོངས་སུ་གྲུབ་པའི་མཚན་ཉིད་དོ། །ཞེས་
པ་ལྟར། །དེ་བཞིན་ཉིད་ལ་ཀུན་བརྟགས་པའི་ཆོས་རྣམས་ནི་མེད་པ་དང་། དེའི་
མེད་པ་ཉིད་ནི་ཡོད་པའི་ཕྱིར་དང་། ཡོད་མེད་དེ་དག་གཉིས་སུ་མེད་པས་མཉམ་པ་
ཉིད་དང་། ཐེ་༼ཤོག་བུ་༤༢༽མ་གློ་བུར་བ་རྣམས་ཀྱིས་མ་ཞི་བ་དང་། ངོ་བོ་ཉིད་
ཀྱིས་ཞི་བའི་བདག་ཉིད་ཅན་དང་། སྤྲོས་པ་མེད་པས་རྣམ་པར་རྟོག་པའི་སྤྱོད་ཡུལ་མ་
ཡིན་པ་རྣམས་སོ། །གསུམ་པ་དེ་ལ་ཇི་ལྟར་འཇུག་པ་ལ། །གང་འཇུག་ན་བྱང་
ཆུབ་སེམས་དཔའ་རྣམས་འཇུག །གང་དུ་འཇུག་ན་ཐེག་པ་ཆེན་པོ་ལ་མོས་པས་སྤྱོད་
པའི་ས་དང་། མཐོང་བའི་ལམ་དང་། བསྒོམ་པའི་ལམ་དང་། མཐར་ཕྱིན་
པའི་ལམ་དག་ལ་འཇུག་གོ །ཚུལ་ཇི་ལྟར་འཇུག་ན། དགེ་བའི་སྟོབས་བསྐྱེད་པ་
དང་། རྣམ་པ་གསུམ་གྱིས་སེམས་སྦྱོང་བ་དང་། གནས་བཞི་སྤངས་པ་དང་།
ཆོས་དང་དོན་ལ་དམིགས་པའི་ཞི་གནས་དང་ལྷག་མཐོང་བསྒོམ་པ་ལ་གུས་པས་སྦྱོར་བ་
དང་། རྟག་ཏུ་སྦྱོར་བའི་བརྩོན་འགྲུས་དང་བཅས་པས་འཇུག་གོ །དེ་ལས་སེམས་
སྦྱོང་བ་གསུམ་ནི། འདི་ལྟར་འཇིག་རྟེན་གྱི་ཁམས་རྣམས་སུ་མིར་གྱུར་པའི་སེམས་
ཅན་དཔག་ཏུ་མེད་པ་དག་སྐད་ཅིག་རེ་རེ་ལ་ཡང་མངོན་པར་རྫོགས་པར་འཚང་རྒྱའོ་
སྙམས་ནས་ཞུམ་པ་མི་བྱ་བ་དང་། བསམ་པ་གང་གིས་སྦྱིན་པ་ལ་སོགས་པའི་ཕ་
རོལ་ཏུ་ཕྱིན་པ་ཀུན་ཏུ་སྤྱོད་པའི་བསམ་པ་དེ་བདག་གིས་ཐོབ་པས་བདག་གིས་ཚེགས་
ཆུང་ངུས་ཕ་རོལ་ཏུ་ཕྱིན་པ་ཡོངས་སུ་རྫོགས་པར་འགྱུར་རོ་སྙམ་པ་དང་། དགེ་བ་

ཟག་པ་དང་བཅས་པའི་འབྲས་བུ་ཡང་ཤི་མ་ཐག་མཐོ་རིས་སུ་ཇི་ལྟར་འདོད་པའི་ལུས་ཐོབ་ན། བདག་ནི་དགེ་བ་ཟག་པ་མེད་པ་དང་ལྡན་པས་ཕུན་སུམ་ཚོགས་པ་ཡིད་ལ་མི་བྱེད་པ་དང་ ཤོག་བུ་༥༤ ཆོས་རྣམས་ཅིའི་ཕྱིར་མི་ཐོབ་སྙམ་པ་རྣམས་ཡིན་ནོ། །གནས་བཞི་སྤྱང་བ་ཡང་འདི་ལྟར་སྟེ། ཡིད་ལ་བྱེད་པ་སྤྱངས་པས་ཉན་ཐོས་དང་རང་སངས་རྒྱས་ཀྱི་ཐེག་པ་ཡིད་ལ་མི་བྱེད་པ་དང་། ཡིད་གཉིས་དང་སོམ་ཉི་སྤྱང་བས་ཐེག་པ་ཆེན་པོ་ལ་ཐེ་ཚོམ་མི་ཟ་བ་དང་། ཆོས་ལ་མངོན་པར་ཞེན་པ་སྤྱང་བས་ཐོས་པ་དང་བསམ་པའི་ཆོས་ལ་ང་དང་ང་ཡིར་མི་འཛིན་པ་དང་། རྣམ་པར་རྟོག་པ་སྤྱངས་པས་མདུན་ན་གནས་པ་དང་། བཞག་པའི་མཚན་མ་ཐམས་ཅད་ཡིད་ལ་མི་བྱེད་ཅིང་རྣམ་པར་མི་རྟོག་པ་རྣམས་སོ། །གཞན་ནི་གོ་སླའོ། །བཞི་པ་དེའི་རྒྱུ་དང་འབྲས་བུ་བསྟན་པ་ནི། འདི་ལ་བྱང་ཆུབ་སེམས་དཔའ་ལོངས་སྤྱོད་རྣམས་ལ་ཀུན་ཏུ་མ་ཆགས་པ་དང་། ཚུལ་ཁྲིམས་ལ་ལྟུང་བ་མེད་པ་དང་། སྡུག་བསྔལ་རྣམས་ལ་འཁྲུགས་པ་མེད་པ་དང་། བསྒོམ་པ་ལེ་ལོ་མེད་པ་དང་། རྣམ་པར་གཡེང་བའི་རྒྱུ་རྣམས་ལ་མི་འཇུག་པ་དང་། སེམས་རྩེ་གཅིག་ཏུ་བྱས་ནས་ཚུལ་བཞིན་དུ་ཆོས་རྣམས་རབ་ཏུ་འབྱེད་པའི་ཕ་རོལ་ཏུ་ཕྱིན་པ་དྲུག་ལ་རྣམ་པར་རིག་པ་ཙམ་ཉིད་ལ་འཇུག་གོ །དེ་ལྟར་ཞུགས་པའི་བྱང་ཆུབ་སེམས་དཔའ་ནི་ལྷག་པའི་བསམ་པ་དག་པས་ཡོངས་སུ་ཟིན་པའི་ཕ་རོལ་ཏུ་ཕྱིན་པ་དྲུག་པོ་དག་འཐོབ་སྟེ། ཐེག་པ་ཆེན་པོ་མདོ་སྡེའི་རྒྱན་ལས། །བྱང་ཆུབ་སེམས་དཔའ་སྦྱིན་པ་ནི། །མ་ཆགས་…ལོངས་སྤྱོད་ལ། མི་ཆགས་…ཕྱི་བཤོལ་ལ། ཆགས་པ་མེད།…ཚིག་ཤེས་ལ། ཆགས་པ་…ལན་ལ། ཉིད་ཀྱང་མ་ཡིན་ལ། །མ་ཆགས་…རྣམ་སྨིན་ལ། ཤོག་བུ་༥༥ མི་ཆགས་…སེར་སྣ་དང་ཐྲ་བ་ལ། ཆགས་པ་མེད་…རྣམ་གཡེང་ལ། ཞེས་གསུངས་པ་ལྟར་ཆགས་བདུན་སྤྱང་བའི་ཕྱིན་དྲུག་གི་ལམ་ལ་བསླབ་ནུས་པ་ཡིན་ནོ། །ལྔ་པ་བསྒོམ་པའི་རབ་ཏུ་དབྱེ་བ་ནི། །བྱང་ཆུབ་སེམས་དཔའ་རྣམས་ཀྱི་ས་བཅུའོ། །དེ་ཡང་། །ཐེག་པ་ཆེན་པོ་བསྡུས་པ་ལས། །ཆོས་ཀྱི་དབྱིངས་ལ་མ་རིག་པ། །ཉོན་མོངས་ཅན་མིན་སྒྲིབ་པ་བཅུ། །ས་བཅུའི་མི་མཐུན་ཕྱོགས་རྣམས་ཀྱི། །གཉེན་པོ་དག་ནི་ས་ཡིན་ནོ། །ཞེས

གསུངས་པ་ལྟར་མི་མཐུན་པའི་ཕྱོགས་མ་རིག་པ་བཅུའི་གཉེན་པོ་ཞེས་བྱ་ཆོས་ཀྱི་དབྱིངས་བཅུ་མངོན་དུ་གྱུར་པ་ལ་ས་ཞེས་བྱའོ། །དེ་ལ། ས་དང་པོར་རབ་ཏུ་དགའ་བ་ནི། བྱང་ཆུབ་སེམས་དཔའ་དེའི་ཐོག་མར་ཁོ་ནར་བདག་དང་གཞན་གྱི་དོན་བསྒྲུབ་ནུས་པ་ཐོབ་པས་དགའ་བ་ཁྱད་པར་ཅན་གྱི་གནས་ཡིན་པའི་ཕྱིར་རོ། །གཉིས་པ་དྲི་མ་མེད་པ་ནི། འཆལ་བའི་ཚུལ་ཁྲིམས་ཀྱི་དྲི་མ་ཐག་བསྲིང་བའི་ཕྱིར་རོ། །གསུམ་པ་འོད་བྱེད་པ་ནི། ཏིང་ངེ་འཛིན་དང་སྙོམས་འཇུག་ཉམས་པ་མེད་པའི་གནས་ཡིན་པས་ཆོས་ཀྱི་སྣང་བ་ཆེན་པོའི་གནས་སུ་གྱུར་པའི་ཕྱིར་རོ། །བཞི་པ་འོད་འཕྲོ་བ་ནི། བྱང་ཆུབ་ཕྱོགས་ཀྱི་ཆོས་འོད་ལྟ་བུས་སྒྲིབ་གཉིས་ཀྱི་དྲི་མ་ཐམས་ཅད་སྲེག་པའི་ཕྱིར་རོ། །ལྔ་པ་སྦྱངས་དཀའ་བ་ནི། ཏིང་ངེ་འཛིན་ལས་མི་ཉམས་ཤིང་སེམས་ཅན་ཡོངས་སུ་སྨིན་པ་འང་རྒྱུན་མི་གཙོད་པས་དེ་ལྟར་བྱ་དཀའ་བའི་གནས་རྟག་ཏུ་གནས་པའི་ཕྱིར་རོ། ⌈ཤོག་བུ་༥༧⌉ དྲུག་པ་མངོན་དུ་གྱུར་པ་ནི། རྟེན་ཅིང་འབྲེལ་བར་འབྱུང་བ་ཤེས་པའི་གནས་ཡིན་པས་ཤེས་རབ་ཀྱི་ཕ་རོལ་ཏུ་ཕྱིན་པ་མངོན་དུ་གྱུར་པའི་ཕྱིར་རོ། །བདུན་པ་རིང་དུ་སོང་བ་ནི། མཚན་མ་ཐམས་ཅད་ཀྱི་མཐར་ཕྱིན་པའི་ཕྱིར་རོ། །བརྒྱད་པ་མི་གཡོ་བ་ནི། མཚན་མ་དང་མངོན་པར་འདུ་བྱེད་པ་ཐམས་ཅད་ཀྱིས་མི་བསྐྱོད་པའི་ཕྱིར་རོ། །དགུ་པ་ལེགས་པའི་བློ་གྲོས་ནི། ཆོས་སོ་སོ་ཡང་དག་པར་རིག་པ་དང་། དོན་སོ་སོ་ཡང་དག་པར་རིག་པ་དང་། ངེས་པའི་ཚིག་སོ་སོ་ཡང་དག་པར་རིག་པ་དང་། སྤོབས་པ་སོ་སོ་ཡང་དག་པར་རིག་པ་བཞི་དང་ལྡན་པའི་ཕྱིར་རོ། །བཅུ་པ་ཆོས་ཀྱི་སྤྲིན་ནི། གཟུངས་དང་ཏིང་ངེ་འཛིན་གྱི་སྒོ་ཐམས་ཅད་ཁོང་དུ་ཆུད་པ་དང་ཆོས་ཀྱི་སྐུ་ཡོངས་སུ་རྫོགས་པའི་ཕྱིར་རོ། དེ་ཡང་གྲངས་མེད་གསུམ་གྱི་དབང་དུ་བྱས་ན་མོས་སྤྱོད་དུ་གྲངས་མེད་དང་པོ་དང་། བདུན་པ་མན་ཆད་ཀྱིས་གྲངས་མེད་གཉིས་པ་དང་། དེ་ཡན་ཆད་རྣམས་གྲངས་མེད་གསུམ་པ་ལ་སྒོམ་པ་ཡོངས་སུ་རྫོགས་པར་འགྱུར་རོ། །དྲུག་པ་ལྷག་པའི་ཚུལ་ཁྲིམས་ནི། ཉེས་སྤྱོད་སྡོམ་པའི་ཚུལ་ཁྲིམས་མི་མཐུན་པའི་ཕྱོགས་རྣམས་བསྡམས་པ་སྟེ་སྡོམ་པ་ཉི་ཤུ་པ་ལས་ཇི་སྐད་གསུངས་པ་ལྟ་བུ་དང་། དགེ་བ་ཆོས་སྡུད་ཀྱི་ཚུལ་ཁྲིམས་ཕ་རོལ་

དུ་ཕྱིན་པ་རྣམས་དང་། སེམས་ཅན་དོན་བྱེད་ཀྱི་ཚུལ་ཁྲིམས་བསྡུ་བའི་དངོས་པོ་བཞིས་འགྲོ་བའི་དོན་ལ་བརྩོན་པ་རྣམས་སོ། །དེ་ལ་བསྡུ་དངོས་བཞི་ནི། སྦྱིན་པས་འཁོར་དུ་བསྡུ་བ་[ཤོག་བུ་༥༧]དང་། དེ་ལ་དམ་ཆོས་སྨན་པར་སྨྲ་བ་དང་། བསླབ་པ་གསུམ་གྱི་དོན་ལ་སྤྱོད་དུ་འཇུག་པ་དང་། བདག་ཀྱང་དོན་དེ་དང་མཐུན་པར་འཇུག་པ་རྣམས་ཡིན་ནོ། །བདུན་པ་ལྷག་པ་སེམས་ཀྱི་བསླབ་པ་ནི། དབྱེ་བ་རྣམ་པ་དྲུག་གིས་ཤེས་པར་བྱ་སྟེ། དམིགས་པས་རབ་ཏུ་དབྱེ་བ་ནི། ཐེག་པ་ཆེན་པོའི་ཆོས་ཁོ་ན་ལ་དམིགས་པའོ། །སྣ་ཚོགས་ཉིད་ཀྱིས་རབ་ཏུ་དབྱེ་བ་ནི། གང་ལ་སྙོམས་པར་ཞུགས་ན་ཐེག་ཆེན་གྱི་ཆོས་མཐའ་དག་སྣང་བའི་ཏིང་ངེ་འཛིན་དང་། གང་ལ་ཞུགས་ན་ཕྱོགས་བཅུའི་དེ་བཞིན་གཤེགས་པ་རྣམས་མངོན་སུམ་དུ་མཐོང་བར་འགྱུར་བ་ཏིང་ངེ་འཛིན་གྱི་རྒྱལ་པོ་བཟང་སྐྱོང་དང་། གང་ལ་ཞུགས་ནས་བདུད་ཀྱི་ཚོགས་ཐམས་ཅད་འཇོམས་ནུས་པ་དཔའ་བར་འགྲོ་བ་ལ་སོགས་པ་རྣམས་སོ། །གཉེན་པོའི་རབ་ཏུ་དབྱེ་བ་ནི། ཆོས་ཐམས་ཅད་འདྲེས་པ་ལ་དམིགས་པའི་ཡེ་ཤེས་ཀྱི་ཁྱེའུའི་ཁྱེའུ་དབྱུང་བའི་ཚུལ་དུ་ཀུན་གཞིའི་རྣམ་པར་ཤེས་པ་ལ་སྦྲིབ་པའི་གནས་ངན་ལེན་ཡོད་པ་ཐམས་ཅད་འབྱིན་པའི་ཕྱིར་རོ། །ལས་སུ་རུང་བ་ཉིད་ཀྱིས་རབ་ཏུ་དབྱེ་བ་ནི། བསམ་གཏན་གྱི་བདེ་བ་དག་གིས་གནས་གང་ནས་གང་དུ་འདོད་པར་སྐྱེ་བ་ཡོངས་སུ་འཛིན་པས་ཏེ་ཏིང་ངེ་འཛིན་ལས་སུ་རུང་བའི་ཕྱིར་རོ། །མངོན་པར་སྒྲུབ་པས་རབ་ཏུ་དབྱེ་བ་ནི། ཏིང་ངེ་འཛིན་གྱི་ཡོན་ཏན་གྱི་འཇིག་རྟེན་གྱི་ཁམས་དཔག་ཏུ་མེད་པ་རྣམས་སུ་ཐོགས་པ་མེད་པའི་མངོན་པར་ཤེས་པ་བསྐྱེད་དོ། །དེ་ལ་གཡོ་བ་ལ་སོགས་[ཤོག་བུ་༥༨]པའི་རྣམ་པར་འཕྲུལ་པ་འབྱུང་སྟེ། གཡོ་བར་བྱེད་པ་དང་། འབར་བར་བྱེད་པ་དང་། ཁྱབ་པར་བྱེད་པ་དང་། སྟོན་པ་དང་། གཞན་གྱི་དངོས་པོར་བསྒྱུར་བ་དང་། འགྲོ་བ་དང་། འོང་བ་དང་། སྡུད་པ་དང་། རྒྱས་པར་བྱེད་པ་དང་། གཟུགས་ཀྱི་ལུས་ཐམས་ཅད་འཇོག་པ་དང་། སྐལ་པ་མཉམ་པས་འགྲོ་བ་དང་། སྣང་བར་བྱེད་ཅིང་མི་སྣང་བར་ཡང་བྱེད་པ་དང་། དབང་ཉིད་དུ་བྱེད་པ་དང་། གཞན་གྱི་རྫུ་འཕྲུལ་རབ་ཏུ་འཇོག་པ་དང་། སྤོབས་པ་

དང་། དྲན་པ་དང་། བདེ་བ་སྦྱིན་པ་དང་། འོད་ཟེར་གཏོང་བའི་རྫུ་འཕྲུལ་ཆེན་པོ་མངོན་པར་སྒྲུབ་པ་དང་། དགའ་བ་སྐྱེད་པ་ཐམས་ཅད་བསྡུས་པ་རྣམ་པ་བཅུ་མངོན་པར་སྒྲུབ་པའི་ཕྱིར་རོ། །དགའ་བ་སྐྱེད་པ་རྣམ་པ་བཅུ་ནི་འདི་ལྟ་སྟེ། ཁས་བླང་བ་དགའ་བ་སྐྱེད་པ་ནི། བྱང་ཆུབ་ཆེན་པོར་སྨོན་ལམ་འདེབས་པ་ཁས་ལེན་པའི་ཕྱིར་རོ། །མི་ལྡོག་པར་དགའ་བ་སྐྱེད་པ་ནི། འཁོར་བའི་སྡུག་བསྔལ་རྣམས་ཀྱིས་མི་ཟློག་པའི་ཕྱིར་རོ། །ཕྱིར་མི་ཕྱོགས་འར་དགའ་བ་སྐྱེད་པ་ནི། སེམས་ཅན་གྱི་ལོག་སྒྲུབ་རྣམས་ཀྱིས་དེ་ལས་ཕྱིར་མི་ཕྱོགས་པའོ། །མངོན་སུ་ཕྱོགས་པར་དགའ་བ་སྐྱེད་པ་ནི། གནོད་པར་བྱེད་པའི་སེམས་ཅན་རྣམས་ཀྱི་དོན་ཐམས་ཅད་བྱ་བ་ལ་མངོན་སུ་ཕྱོགས་པའི་ཕྱིར་རོ། །མི་གོས་པར་དགའ་བ་སྐྱེད་པ་ནི། འཇིག་རྟེན་དུ་སྐྱེས་ཀྱང་འཇིག་རྟེན་པའི་ཆོས་ཀྱིས་མི་གོས་པའི་ཕྱིར་རོ། །མོས་པ་དགའ་བ་སྐྱེད་པ་ནི། རྟོག་པ་མེད་པའང་ཐེག་[ཤོག་བུ་༥༩]པ་ཆེན་པོ་ལ་རྒྱ་ཆེ་བ་ཉིད་དང་། ཟབ་པ་ཉིད་ཐམས་ཅད་ལ་མོས་པའི་ཕྱིར་རོ། །རྟོག་པར་དགའ་བ་སྐྱེད་པ་ནི། གང་ཟག་དང་ཆོས་ལ་བདག་མེད་པ་རྟོགས་པའི་ཕྱིར་རོ། །ཁོང་དུ་ཆུད་པར་དགའ་བ་སྐྱེད་ནི། དེ་བཞིན་གཤེགས་པ་རྣམས་ཀྱིས་དགོངས་ཏེ་གསུང་བ་ཟབ་མོ་ཁོང་དུ་ཆུད་པའི་ཕྱིར་རོ། །མི་འབྱེད་པ་ཀུན་ནས་ཉོན་མོངས་མེད་པར་དགའ་བ་སྐྱེད་པ་ནི། འཁོར་བ་ཡོངས་སུ་མི་གཏོང་ཡང་དེས་ཀུན་ནས་ཉོན་མོངས་པ་མེད་པའི་ཕྱིར་རོ། །སྦྱོར་བ་དགའ་བ་སྐྱེད་པ་ནི། སྒྲིབ་པ་ཐམས་ཅད་ལས་རྣམ་པར་གྲོལ་བ་ལ་བཞུགས་པའི་སངས་རྒྱས་རྣམས་འཁོར་བའི་མཐའ་ཡི་བར་དུ་ལྷུན་གྱིས་གྲུབ་པར་སེམས་ཅན་རྣམས་ཀྱི་དོན་ཐམས་ཅད་མཛད་པ་དག་ལ་སྦྱོར་བའི་ཕྱིར་རོ། །ལས་ཀྱིས་རབ་ཏུ་དབྱེ་བ་ནི། ཕ་རོལ་ཏུ་ཕྱིན་པ་བསྒོམ་པ་དང་། སེམས་ཅན་ཡོངས་སུ་སྨིན་པར་བྱ་བ་དང་། སངས་རྒྱས་ཀྱི་ཞིང་ཡོངས་སུ་དག་པར་བྱ་བ་དང་། སངས་རྒྱས་ཀྱི་ཆོས་ཐམས་ཅད་སྒྲུབ་པའི་ཕྱིར་བྱང་ཆུབ་སེམས་དཔའི་ཏིང་ངེ་འཛིན་རྣམས་ནི་ལས་ཀྱིས་རབ་ཏུ་དབྱེ་བར་བལྟའོ། །བརྒྱད་པ་ལྷག་པའི་ཤེས་རབ་ཀྱི་བསླབ་པ་ལ། རྣམ་པར་མི་རྟོག་པའི་ཡེ་ཤེས་ནི་ཤེས་རབ་དངོས་ཡིན་པས་དེ་སྒྲུབ་པའི་ཐབས་མ་ནོར་བ་ནི་ཐེག་པ་ཆེན་པོའི་

མདོའི་དོན་ཁོང་དུ་ཆུད་པ་ཉིད་ཡིན་ལ། འདིར་དེ་ཉིད་གཏན་ལ་འབེབས་དགོས་པས། དེའང་ཐེག་པ་ཆེན་པོའི་མདོ་སྡེ་རྒྱན་ལས། གཞུག་པ་ལྡེམ་པོར་དགོངས་པ་དང་། །མཚན་ཉིད་ལྡེམ་པོར་དགོངས་[ཤོག་བུ་༦༠]པ་དང་། །གཉེན་པོ་ལྡེམ་པོར་དགོངས་པ་དང་། །བསྒྱུར་བ་ལྡེམ་པོར་དགོངས་པ་སྟེ། །ཞེས་པ་བཞིན་སངས་རྒྱས་ཀྱི་གསུང་ལ་ལྡེམ་པོར་དགོངས་པ་ནི་བཞི་རུ་རིག་པ་བྱའོ། །འདི་དག་གི་དགོངས་གཞི་དང་དགོས་པ་ནི། དེ་ཉིད་ལས། ཉན་ཐོས་དང་ནི་ངོ་བོ་ཉིད། །དེ་བཞིན་ཉེས་པ་འདུལ་བ་དང་། །བརྗོད་པ་ཟབ་པ་ཉིད་ལ་ནི། །ལྡེམ་པོར་དགོངས་པ་རྣམ་པ་བཞི། །ཞེས་པ་ལྟར་ཉན་ཐོས་རྣམས་ཐེག་པ་ཆེན་པོའི་བསྟན་པ་ལ་འཇུག་པའི་དོན་དུ་མི་སྐྲག་པར་བྱ་བའི་ཕྱིར་གཟུགས་ལ་སོགས་པ་ཡོད་པར་བསྟན་པ་ནི་གཞུག་པ་ལྡེམ་པོར་དགོངས་པའོ། །ཀུན་བརྟགས་ལ་མཚན་ཉིད་ངོ་བོ་ཉིད་མེད་པ་དང་། གཞན་དབང་ལ་སྐྱེ་བ་ངོ་བོ་ཉིད་མེད་པ་དང་། ཡོངས་གྲུབ་ལ་དོན་དམ་པར་ངོ་བོ་ཉིད་མེད་པ་ལ་དགོངས་ནས་ཆོས་ཐམས་ཅད་ངོ་བོ་ཉིད་མེད་པ་དང་། མ་སྐྱེས་པ་ལ་སོགས་པར་བསྟན་པ་ནི་མཚན་ཉིད་ལྡེམ་པོར་དགོངས་པའོ། །སྒྲིབ་པ་བརྒྱད་ཀྱི་གཉེན་པོར་ཐེག་པ་ཆེན་པོ་གསུངས་པ་ནི་གཉེན་པོ་ལ་ལྡེམ་པོར་དགོངས་པའོ། ། དེའང་འདི་ལྟར་སངས་རྒྱས་ལ་བརྙས་པའི་སྒྲིབ་པའི་གཉེན་པོར་ང་ཉིད་དེའི་ཚེ་ན་ཡང་དག་པར་རྫོགས་པའི་སངས་རྒྱས་རྣམ་པར་གཟིགས་སུ་གྱུར་ཏོ་ཞེས་གསུངས་པ་ལྟ་བུའོ། །ཆོས་ལ་བརྙས་པའི་སྒྲིབ་པའི་གཉེན་པོར་གངྒཱའི་ཀླུང་གི་བྱེ་མ་སྙེད་དང་མཉམ་པའི་སངས་རྒྱས་ལ་བསྙེན་བཀུར་བྱས་ན་ད་གདོད་ཐེག་ཆེན་གྱི་རྟོགས་པ་སྐྱེའོ་ཞེས་གསུངས་པ་ལྟ་བུའོ། །ལེ་ལོའི་སྒྲིབ་པའི་གཉེན་པོར་དེ་བཞིན་གཤེགས་པ་བཟླ་འོད་དྲི་མེད་ཀྱི་མཚན་སྨོས་པ་ཙམ་གྱིས་བླ་ན་མེད་པའི་བྱང་ཆུབ་ཏུ་ངེས་[ཤོག་བུ་༦༡]པ་ཡིན་ནོ་ཞེས་གསུངས་པ་ལྟ་བུའོ། །ཅུང་ཟད་ཙམ་གྱིས་ཆོག་ཤེས་པར་འཛིན་པའི་སྒྲིབ་པའི་གཉེན་པོར་བཅོམ་ལྡན་འདས་ཀྱིས་ལ་ལར་སྦྱིན་པ་ལ་སོགས་པ་སྨད་ལ་གཞན་དུ་ནི་བསྔགས་པ་ལྟ་བུའོ། །འདོད་ཆགས་ལ་སྤྱོད་པའི་སྒྲིབ་པའི་གཉེན་པོར་བཅོམ་ལྡན་འདས་ཀྱིས་སངས་རྒྱས་ཀྱི་ཞིང་གི་འབྱོར་བ་ལ་བསྔགས་ལྟ་བུའོ། །ང་རྒྱལ་ལ་སྤྱོད

པའི་སྨིན་པའི་གཉེན་པོར་བཅོམ་ལྡན་འདས་ཀྱིས་སངས་རྒྱས་ལ་ལའི་ཕུན་སུམ་ཚོགས་པ་ལྷག་པར་བསྔགས་པ་ལྟ་བུའོ། །འགྱོད་པའི་སྨིན་པའི་གཉེན་པོར་གང་དག་སངས་རྒྱས་དང་བྱང་ཆུབ་སེམས་དཔའ་རྣམས་ལ་གནོད་པར་བྱེད་པ་དེ་དག་ནི་མཐོ་རིས་སུ་འགྲོ་བར་འགྱུར་རོ། །ཞེས་གསུངས་པར་ལྟ་བུའོ། །རིགས་མ་ངེས་པ་ཐེག་དམན་དུ་ལྡོག་པའི་སྨིན་བའི་གཉེན་པོར་ཉན་ཐོས་ཆེན་པོ་རྣམས་སངས་རྒྱས་སུ་ལུང་བསྟན་པ་དང་། མཐར་ཐུག་ཐེག་པ་གཅིག་ཏུ་གསུངས་པ་ལྟ་བུའོ། །བརྗོད་པ་ཟབ་མོ་ལ་ལྡོས་ཏེ་གསུངས་པ་ནི་བསྒྱུར་བ་ལྡེམ་པོར་དགོངས་པའོ། །དེ་ཡང་འདི་ལྟར་མདོ་སྡེ་དག་ལས། །ཕ་དང་མ་ཡང་གསད་བྱ་ཞིང་། །རྒྱལ་པོ་གཙང་སྦྲ་ཅན་གཉིས་དང་། །ཡུལ་འཁོར་འཁོར་དང་བཅས་བཅོམ་ན། །མི་དེ་དག་པ་འགྱུར་བ་ཡིན། ཞེས་གསུངས་པ་ལྟར་ལུས་བསྐྱེད་པའི་ཕ་མ་གཉིས་དང་། སྐྱོང་བར་བྱེད་པའི་རྒྱལ་པོ་དང་། སྦྱིན་གནས་ཀྱི་བྲམ་ཟེ་གཙང་སྦྲ་ཅན་དང་། ཡུལ་འཁོར་རྟ་དང་བ་ལང་ཛ་མོ་སོགས་འཁོར་ [ཤོག་བུ་༥༢] དང་བཅས་པ་རྣམས་སོ། །འདི་དག་ཡང་དག་པའི་དོན་དུ་བསྒྱུར་བ་ནི་གོ་རིམ་བཞིན་དུ། སྲེད་ལེན་གཉིས་དང་ལྟ་བ་མཆོག་འཛིན་དང་། ཚུལ་ཁྲིམས་དང་བརྟུལ་ཞུགས་མཆོག་འཛིན་དང་། སྐྱེ་མཆེད་དྲུག་ཡུལ་དང་བཅས་པའི་དབང་དུ་བྱས་ནས་རིག་པར་བྱའོ། །ཡང་ཡིད་མི་ཆེས་དང་བྱས་མི་གཟོ། །མི་གང་ཁྱིམ་འཕིགས་བྱེད་པ་དང་། །གོ་སྐབས་བཅོམ་དང་སྐྱུག་པ་ཟ། །དེ་ནི་སྐྱེས་བུ་མཆོག་ཡིན་ནོ། །ཞེས་འཇིག་རྟེན་ཕ་རོལ་ཡོད་པ་ལ་ཡིད་མི་ཆེས་པ་དང་། བྱས་པ་དྲིན་དུ་མི་གཟོ་བ་དང་། ཁྱིམ་འཕིགས་བའི་རྐུན་པོ་བྱེད་པ་དང་། གོ་སྐབས་བཅོམ་པའི་ངག་ཏེ་རྫུན་སྨྲ་བ་དང་། ཁྱི་དང་བྱ་བཞིན་སྐྱུགས་པ་ཟ་བ་དང་རྣམས་སོ། །འདི་དག་མཆོག་གི་དོན་དུ་བསྒྱུར་བ་ནི། འདི་དག་དགྲ་བཅོམ་པ་སྟེ་གོ་རིམ་བཞིན་རྣམ་པར་གྲོལ་བའི་ཡེ་ཤེས་མཐོང་བ་དང་ལྡན་པས་རང་གི་ཡིད་ཆེས་པའི་ཕྱིར་དང་། འདུས་མ་བྱས་པའི་མྱ་ངན་ལས་འདས་པ་ཤེས་པའི་ཕྱིར་དང་། ཡང་སྲིད་ཉེ་བར་ལེན་པའི་རྒྱུ་སྤངས་པའི་ཕྱིར་དང་། འགྲོ་བ་གང་དུའང་སྡུག་བསྔལ་མངོན་པར་མི་འགྲུབ་པའི་ཕྱིར་དང་། མཐོང་བའི་ཆོས་ལ་ཡོ་བྱད་ཀྱི་

ལུས་འཛིན་ཡང་སྲོག་དང་ལོངས་སྤྱོད་ལ་རེ་བ་མེད་པ་རྣམས་སུ་ལྟ་བར་བྱའོ། །ཡང་སྙིང་པོ་མེད་ལ་སྙིང་པོར་ཤེས། །ཕྱིན་ཅི་ལོག་ལ་ཞེན་ཏུ་གནས། །ཉོན་མོངས་ཀུན་ནས་རབ་ཉོན་མོངས། །བྱུང་བ་དམ་པ་ཐོབ་པར་འགྱུར། །ཞེས་པ་ཡང་འདི་ལྟར་སྙིང་པོ་ནི་སེམས་ཀྱི་རྣམ་པར་གཡེང་བའོ། །[ཤོག་བུ་༧༣]དེ་མེད་པ་ལ་སྙིང་པོར་འཛིན་པ་དང་། ཕྱིན་ཅི་ལོག་ནི་གཙང་བ་དང་། བདེ་བ་དང་། བདག་དང་། རྟག་པ་རྣམས་ལས་ལོག་པའི་མི་གཙང་བ་དང་། སྡུག་བསྔལ་བ་དང་། བདག་མེད་པ་དང་། མི་རྟག་པ་རྣམས་ལ་གནས་པའོ། །ཉོན་མོངས་ནི་ཡུན་རིང་དུ་དཀའ་བ་སྤྱོད་པའི་ངལ་དུབ་ཀྱི་གདུང་བའོ། །དེ་ལ་སོགས་པ་དཔག་ཏུ་མེད་དོ། །དེ་ནི་དགོངས་པ་རྣམ་པ་བཞི་ཡང་སྡུ་མ་ལས། མཉམ་པ་ཉིད་དང་དོན་གཞན་དང་། །དེ་བཞིན་དུ་ནི་དུས་གཞན་དང་། །གང་ཟག་གི་ནི་བསམ་པ་ལ། །དགོངས་པ་རྣམ་བཞིར་ཤེས་པར་བྱ། ཞེས་པ་ལྟར་བཞི་ལས། །མཉམ་པ་ཉིད་ལ་དགོངས་པ་ནི། ང་ཉིད་དེའི་ཚེ་ཡང་དག་པར་རྫོགས་པའི་སངས་རྒྱས་རྣམ་པར་གཟིགས་སུ་གྱུར་ཏོ་ཞེས་པ་ལྟ་བུ་སྟེ་ཆོས་ཀྱི་སྐུ་མཉམ་པ་ཉིད་ལ་དགོངས་སོ། །དོན་གཞན་ལ་དགོངས་པ་ནི། ཆོས་ཐམས་ཅད་ངོ་བོ་ཉིད་མེད་པ། མ་སྐྱེས་པ་ཞེས་པ་ལྟ་བུ་སྟེ། དོན་ལ་སྒྲ་ཇི་ལྟ་བ་བཞིན་མ་ཡིན་པས་སོ། །དུས་གཞན་ལ་དགོངས་པ་ནི། དེ་བཞིན་གཤེགས་པ་ཟླ་འོད་དྲི་མེད་ཀྱི་མཚན་སྨོས་པས་བྱང་ཆུབ་ཏུ་ངེས་པའང་དུས་རིང་མོ་ཞིག་ལ་དགོངས་པས་སོ། །གང་ཟག་གི་བསམ་པ་ལ་དགོངས་པ་ནི། །སྦྱིན་པ་ལྟ་བུའང་འགའ་ལ་བསྔགས་ཤིང་ཆུང་དུའི་ཚོག་ཤེས་པ་པ་ཁ་ཅིག་ལ་ནི་སྨད་པ་སྟེ་མཆོག་འཛིན་ལྡོག་པ་ལ་དགོངས་པས་སོ། །འདི་དག་ནི་མི་རྟོག་ཡེ་ཤེས་ཀྱི་རྒྱུའོ། །མི་རྟོག་པ་དངོས་ནི། ཐེག་བསྡུས་ལས། [ཤོག་བུ་༧༨]བྱང་ཆུབ་སེམས་དཔའ་རྣམས་ཀྱི་ཤེས། །རྣམ་རྟོག་མེད་པའི་དམིགས་པ་ནི། །ཆོས་རྣམས་བརྗོད་དུ་མེད་པ་ཉིད།...ཡིན་ཏེ་བརྗོད་པ་ནི་ཀུན་བརྟགས་ཡིན་པས་སོ། བདག་མེད་དེ་བཞིན་ཉིད་ཀྱང་དེ།...རྣམ་གྲངས་ཡིན་ནོ། །ཞེས་པ་ལྟར་ཡིན་ནོ། །དགུ་པ་སྒྲུབ་པའི་ཁྱད་པར་ནི། བྱང་ཆུབ་སེམས་དཔའི་སྦྱོང་བ་ནི་འཇིག་རྟེན་པ་དང་ཉན་ཐོས་ལྟར་

འཁོར་བ་དང་མྱ་ངན་ལས་འདས་པའི་མཐའ་ལ་མི་གནས་པས་ན་མི་གནས་པའི་མྱ་ངན་ལས་འདས་པ་ཞེས་བྱ་སྟེ། །འདི་ནི་ཀུན་ནས་ཉོན་མོངས་པའི་གནས་ཡོངས་སུ་བཏང་བ་ཡིན་ཀྱང་སྙིང་རྗེས་གཞན་དབང་གིས་འཁོར་བ་མ་སྟོངས་བར་དུ་འགྲོ་བའི་དོན་བྱེད་པའི་མཐུས་ཉམས་པ་མེད་པ་ཡིན་ནོ། །བཅུ་པ་ཡེ་ཤེས་ཀྱི་ཁྱད་པར་ནི། ངོ་བོ་ཉིད་ཀྱི་སྐུ་དང་། ལོངས་སྤྱོད་རྫོགས་པའི་སྐུ་དང་། སྤྲུལ་པའི་སྐུའི་ཡེ་ཤེས་ཀྱི་ཁྱད་པར་རྣམས་སོ། །དེ་ལ་ངོ་བོ་ཉིད་ཀྱི་སྐུ་ནི། དེ་བཞིན་གཤེགས་པ་རྣམས་ཀྱི་ཆོས་ཀྱི་སྐུ་སྟེ། སངས་རྒྱས་ཀྱི་སའི་ཡོན་ཏན་ཐམས་ཅད་ཀྱི་གནས་ཡིན་པས་སོ། ། ལོངས་སྤྱོད་རྫོགས་སྐུ་ནི། ཆོས་ཐེག་པ་ཆེན་པོ་ལ་ལོངས་སྤྱོད་པའི་སྐུ་སྟེ། ས་ར་གནས་ཀྱི་བྱང་ཆུབ་སེམས་དཔའ་རྣམས་ཀྱི་དོན་བྱེད་པ། ཆོས་ཀྱི་སྐུ་ལ་བརྟེན་ནས་བྱུང་བར་བལྟའོ། །སྤྲུལ་པའི་སྐུ་ནི། གང་ཆོས་ཀྱི་སྐུ་ལ་བརྟེན་པ་ཉིད་དེ། དགའ་ལྡན་གྱི་གནས་ན་བཞུགས་པ་ནས་མཛད་པ་ཡོངས་སུ་རྫོགས་པར་སྟོན་པ་སྟེ། རྒྱུད་བླ་མ་ལས། །དགའ་ལྡན་གནས་ནས་འཕོ་བ་དང་། །ལྷུམས་སུ་[ཤོག་བུ་༨༥]འཇུག་དང་བལྟམས་པ་དང་། །བཟོ་ཡི་གནས་ལ་མཁས་པ་དང་། །བཙུན་མོའི་འཁོར་དགྱེས་རོལ་པ་དང་། །ངེས་འབྱུང་དཀའ་བ་སྤྱོད་པ་དང་། །བྱང་ཆུབ་སྙིང་པོར་གཤེགས་པ་དང་། །བདུད་སྡེ་འཇོམས་དང་རྫོགས་པར་ནི། །བྱང་ཆུབ་ཆོས་ཀྱི་འཁོར་ལོ་དང་། །མྱ་ངན་འདས་པར་གཤེགས་མཛད་རྣམས། །ཡོངས་སུ་མ་དག་ཞིང་རྣམས་སུ། །སྲིད་པ་ཇི་སྲིད་གནས་པར་སྟོན། །ཞེས་གསུངས་པ་ལྟ་བུའོ། །གཉིས་པ་དེ་ཉིད་བཞི་རུ་བསྡུ་བ་ནི། ལང་ཀར་གཤེགས་པ་ལས། ། ཆོས་ལྔ་དང་ནི་རང་བཞིན་གསུམ། །རྣམ་ཤེས་བརྒྱད་པོ་ཉིད་དག་གང་། །བདག་མེད་གཉིས་ཀྱི་དངོས་པོར་ནི། །ཐེག་ཆེན་ཐམས་ཅད་བསྡུས་པ་ཡིན། ཞེས་པ་ལྟར་བཞི་ལས། དང་པོ་ཆོས་ལྔ་ནི། །མིང་དང་། མཚན་མ་དང་། རྣམ་པར་རྟོག་པ་དང་། དེ་བཞིན་ཉིད་དང་། རྣམ་པར་མི་རྟོག་པའི་ཡེ་ཤེས་སོ། །དེ་ལ་རྣམ་པར་ཤེས་པའི་སྤྱོད་ཡུལ་དུ་མི་སྣང་ཞིང་བརྗོད་དུ་མེད་ཀྱང་མིང་གིས་བཏགས་ཏེ་མཚོན་པའི་ཕྱིར་མིང་ངོ་། །རྣམ་པར་ཤེས་པ་བདུན་དང་ཀུན་གཞིའི་རྣམ་པར་ཤེས་པ

པན་ཚུན་རྒྱུ་དང་འབྲས་བུའི་ཚུལ་དུ་གནས་པ་ནི་མཚན་མའོ། །རྣམ་ཤེས་བརྒྱད་ཀྱི་
ཆོས་རྣམས་ཀྱི་རང་དང་སྤྱིའི་མཚན་ཉིད་ལ་ལྟོས་པས་ན་རྣམ་པར་རྟོག་པའོ། །ཆོས་
ཐམས་ཅད་དངོས་པོར་མ་གྲུབ་པས་ནི་དེ་བཞིན་ཉིད་དོ། །ཕྱིན་ཅི་མ་ལོག་པར་ཡོངས་
སུ་གྲུབ་པའི་ཡེ་ཤེས་ནི་རྣམ་པར་མི་ [ཤོག་བུ་༨༨] རྟོག་པའི་ཡེ་ཤེས་སོ། །གཉིས་
པ་རང་བཞིན་གསུམ་ནི། རྒྱས་པར་གོང་དུ་བསྟན་ཟིན་ལ། མདོར་བསྡུ་ན།
བསྟན་བཅོས་དབུས་དང་མཐའ་རྣམ་པར་འབྱེད་པ་ལས། ཡང་དག་མ་ཡིན་ཀུན་རྟོག
གཞན་དབང་དུ་གཏོགས་པའི་ཁམས་གསུམ་གྱི་སེམས་སེམས་བྱུང་ཡོད། །དེ་ལ་གཉིས་པོ་
གཟུང་འཛིན ཡོད་མ་ཡིན། །སྟོང་པ་ ཡོངས་གྲུབ ཉིད་ནི་ སྟོང་གཞི་གཞན་དབང
འདི་ལ་ཡོད། དེ་ལ་ སྟོང་ཉིད ཡང་ནི་དེ་ སྟོང་གཞི་ཡོད་དོ། ཞེས་གསུངས་པ་
ལྟར་རོ། །གསུམ་པ་རྣམ་ཤེས་བརྒྱད་ནི། མིག་ནས་ཡིད་ཀྱི་ཤེས་པའི་བར་འཇུག
ཤེས་དྲུག་གོང་དུ་སྨོས་པ་དག་དང་ཀུན་གཞིའི་རྣམ་པར་ཤེས་པ་དང་། ཉོན་མོངས་པ
ཅན་གྱི་ཡིད་དེ་བརྒྱད་དོ། །དེ་ཡང་ཀུན་གཞི་ནི། སུམ་ཅུ་པ་ལས། །དེ་ལ་ཀུན
གཞིའི་རྣམ་ཤེས་ནི། །རྣམ་སྨིན་ས་བོན་ཐམས་ཅད་པ། །དེ་ནི་མ་སྒྲིབ་ལུང་མ་
བསྟན། །རེག་ལ་སོགས་པའང་དེ་བཞིན་ནོ། །ཞེས་པ་ལྟར། རྣམ་པར་སྨིན
པའི་རྣམ་པར་ཤེས་པ་བག་ཆགས་ཐམས་ཅད་ཀྱི་བསྒོ་གཞི་ངོ་བོ་ལུང་དུ་མ་བསྟན་པ
འཁོར་ཀུན་ཏུ་འགྲོ་བ་རྣམས་དང་མཚུངས་པར་ལྡན་པ་ཞིག་ཡིན་ནོ། ཡང་། རང་
བཞིན་མཚན་ཉིད་དམིགས་རྣམ་འཁོར། འཇུག་པའི་ཚུལ་དང་ལྡོག་པའི་དུས། །
དབྱེ་བ་རྣམ་གྲངས་སྒྲ་བཤད་དོན། །ཚད་མ་དག་གིས་ཤེས་པར་བྱ། ཞེས་པ་ལྟར།
རང་བཞིན་ལུང་མ་བསྟན། མཚན་ཉིད་སྣ་ཚོགས་སུ་སྣང་བ། དམིགས་པ་སྣོད་
བཅུད་རྒྱ [ཤོག་བུ་༨༩] ཆེན་པོ། རྣམ་པ་ཡུལ་གྱི་སྤྱི་རིས་མི་འབྱེད་པ། འཁོར་
ཀུན་འགྲོ་ལྔ་དང་བཅས་པ། འཇུག་ཚུལ་རྒྱུད་གང་ལ་འཇུག་ན་སྤྱིར་སེམས་ཅན
ཐམས་ཅད་ཀྱི་རྒྱུད་ལ་དང་། ཁྱད་པར་ཉན་རང་ཕུང་པོ་ལྷག་མེད་དུ་མ་འདས་ཀྱི་བར་
དང་། བྱང་སེམས་རྒྱུན་མཐའི་བར་དུ་འཇུག་གོ །རྣམ་ཤེས་གང་དང་ལྷན་ཅིག་ཏུ་
འཇུག་ན། འདུ་ཤེས་པ་མེད་པ་དང་། དེའི་སྙོམས་འཇུག་དང་། གཉིད་འཐུག

པོ་དང་བརྒྱལ་བའི་སྐབས་རྣམས་སུ་ཉོན་མོངས་པ་ཅན་གྱི་ཡིད་གཅིག་པུ་དང་ངོ། །གཟུགས་མེད་པ་ན་ཉོན་མོངས་པ་ཅན་གྱི་ཡིད་དང་ཡིད་ཀྱི་ཤེས་པ་གཉིས་དང་ངོ། །གཟུགས་སུ་སྣ་ལྕེའི་ཤེས་པ་མེད་པས་གཞན་ལྔ་དང་ངོ། །འདོད་པར་ཚོགས་བདུན་ཀ་ཡོད་པས་དེ་དག་དང་ལྷན་ཅིག་འཇུག་པའང་འགོག་པའི་སྙོམས་འཇུག་གི་སྐབས་སེམས་གཞན་གྱི་ཟླ་མེད་པར་འཇུག་གོ །བཟློག་པའི་དུས་ནི། །ཉན་རང་ལྷག་མེད་དུ་འདའ་བ་དང་། བྱང་སེམས་མངོན་པར་སངས་རྒྱས་པ་ན་བཟློག་གོ །དབྱེ་ན་ས་བོན་གྱི་ཆ་དང་རྣམ་པར་སྨིན་པའི་ཆ་སྟེ་གཉིས་སོ། །མིང་གི་རྣམ་གྲངས་ནི། །ལེན་པའི་རྣམ་པར་ཤེས་པ་དང་། ས་བོན་ཐམས་ཅད་པའི་རྣམ་པར་ཤེས་པ་དང་། ཀུན་གཞིའི་རྣམ་པར་ཤེས་པ་དང་། རྣམ་པར་སྨིན་པའི་རྣམ་པར་ཤེས་པ་ཞེས་བྱའོ། །སྒྲ་བཤད་ནི། ལུས་ཡང་ཡང་ལེན་པའི་རྒྱུར་གྱུར་པས ༼ཤོག་བུ ༥༨༽ ལེན་པའི་རྣམ་པར་ཤེས་པ་དང་། བག་ཆགས་ཐམས་ཅད་ཀྱི་གཞིར་གྱུར་པས་ས་བོན་ཐམས་ཅད་པའི་རྣམ་པར་ཤེས་པ་དང་། དེ་དག་པ་དང་མ་དག་པའི་དབང་གིས་འཁོར་འདས་ཐམས་ཅད་འབྱུང་བས་ཀུན་གཞིའི་རྣམ་པར་ཤེས་པ་དང་། སྔོན་གྱི་ལས་ལས་བྱུང་བས་རྣམ་པར་སྨིན་པའི་རྣམ་པར་ཤེས་པ་ཞེས་བྱའོ། །ཀུན་གཞི་མེད་པའི་སྐྱོན་སོགས་སྒྲུབ་བྱེད་ཀྱི་ཚད་མ་དག་གིས་ཀྱང་འགྲུབ་པ་ཡིན་ནོ། །ཉོན་ཡིད་ནི། ཀུན་གཞི་ལ་ཁ་ནང་དུ་ལྟ་བ། བདག་ཏུ་ལྟ་བ་དང་། བདག་ཏུ་ང་རྒྱལ་བ་དང་། བདག་ལ་ཆགས་པ་དང་། བདག་ཏུ་རྨོངས་པ་སྟེ་བཞི་དང་། ཀུན་འགྲོ་ལྔ་སྟེ་འཁོར་དགུ་དང་། རྟག་ཏུ་མཚུངས་པར་ལྡན་པའོ། །འདི་ནི་རྣམ་པར་ཤེས་པ་ཀུན་ནས་ཉོན་མོངས་པའི་གནས་ཡིན་ཏེ། །གཅིག་གིས་ནི་རྣམ་པར་ཤེས་པ་བསྐྱེད་ལ། གཉིས་པས་ནི་ཉོན་མོངས་པ་ཅན་དུ་བྱེད་དོ། །དང་པོ་ནི་དེ་མ་ཐག་རྐྱེན་གྱི་ཡིད་དང་། གཉིས་པ་ནི་ངར་འཛིན་པའི་ཡིད་དོ། །གལ་ཏེ་ཉོན་མོངས་པ་ཅན་གྱི་ཡིད་མེད་ན་སྐྱོན་ལྔ་ལས། དང་པོ་མ་འདྲེས་པའི་མ་རིག་པ་མེད་པའི་སྐྱོན་ནི། མ་རིག་པ་དེ་ནི་དེ་ཁོ་ན་ལ་ཤེས་པ་སྐྱེ་བའི་གེགས་བྱེད་པ་གཏི་མུག་གི་རང་བཞིན་ཏེ། དེ་ནི་རྣམ་པར་ཤེས་པ་ལྔ་དང་། ཉོན་མོངས་ཅན་མ་ཡིན་པའི་ཡིད་ཤེས་ལ་མེད་པས

དང་། ཉོན་མོངས་པ་ཅན་ལ་ཡང་མ་ཡིན་ཏེ། དེ་ལས་གཞན་དུ་མི་འགྲུབ་པའི་ [ཤོག་བུ་༦༩] ཕྱིར་རོ། །དེ་ལ་མ་འདྲེས་པ་ཞེས་པ་ནི་རང་དབང་ཅན་གྱི་མ་རིག་པ་ཞེས་པའི་དོན་ཏོ། གཉིས་པ་ལྔ་པོ་དག་དང་། འདྲ་བ་མེད་པའི་སྐྱོན་ནི་མིག་ལ་སོགས་པའི་རྣམ་ཤེས་ལྔ་དང་། ཡིད་ཀྱི་རྣམ་པར་ཤེས་པ་ལྷན་ཅིག་སྐྱེ་བའི་གནས་ཐུན་མོང་བ་མེད་པར་ཕྱིར་ཏེ། རྣམ་ཤེས་ལྔ་མིག་སོགས་ལས་སྐྱེ་ལ་ཡིད་ཤེས་ལ་བདག་རྐྱེན་མེད་པས་སོ། དེའི་ཕྱིར་ཡིད་ཀྱི་རྣམ་པར་ཤེས་པ་ཞེས་པའི་མིང་ཡང་བརྗོད་དུ་མི་འགྱུར་རོ། །གསུམ་པ་སྙོམས་འཇུག་གཉིས་ལ་བྱེ་བྲག་མེད་པའི་སྐྱོན་ནི། ཉོན་མོངས་པ་ཅན་གྱི་ཡིད་མེད་པའི་འདུ་ཤེས་མེད་པའི་སྙོམས་པར་འཇུག་པ་ལ་ནི་ཉོན་མོངས་པ་ཅན་གྱི་ཡིད་ཡོད་པས་མ་ཞི་ལ། འགོག་པའི་སྙོམས་འཇུག་ལ་ནི་མེད་པས་ཞི་བ་ཉིད་དོ་ཞེས་ཁྱད་པར་དབྱེར་མེད་པར་འགྱུར་བའི་ཕྱིར་རོ། །བཞི་པ་ངེས་ཚིག་མེད་པའི་སྐྱོན་ནི། ངར་འཛིན་པའི་ཕྱིར་ཡོད་དོ་ཞེས་པའང་རྣམ་པར་ཤེས་པ་དྲུག་ལ་ནི་མེད་དེ་རྟག་པར་ངར་འཛིན་པ་མེད་པའི་ཕྱིར་རོ། ལྔ་པ་འདུ་ཤེས་མེད་པར་སྐྱེ་བའི་རྒྱུན་ལ་ངར་འཛིན་མེད་པའི་སྐྱོན་ནི། འདུ་ཤེས་མེད་པའི་ལྷ་རྣམས་ཀྱི་ནང་དུ་སེམས་དང་སེམས་ལས་བྱུང་བ་འགགས་པས་ཚེ་དེའི་ཚེ་ངར་འཛིན་པའང་མེད་པར་འགྱུར་རོ། བཞི་པ་བདག་མེད་པ་རྣམ་པ་གཉིས་ནི། གང་ཟག་གི་བདག་མེད་དང་། ཆོས་ཀྱི་བདག་མེད་པའོ། དང་པོ་ནི། གཟུགས་བདག་མ་ཡིན། བདག་གཟུགས་དང་ལྡན་པ་མ་ཡིན། གཟུགས་བདག་གི་མ་ཡིན། [ཤོག་བུ་༧༠] གཟུགས་ལ་བདག་གནས་པ་མ་ཡིན་པ་ནས་རྣམ་པར་ཤེས་པ་ལ་བདག་གནས་པ་མ་ཡིན་པའི་བར་ཏེ་འཇིག་ལྟ་ཉི་ཤུའི་གཉེན་པོར་བསྒོམ་པའོ། གཉིས་པ་ནི། ཐེག་བསྡུས་ལས། །གཟུང་བ་མེད་པ་རབ་རྟོགས་བྱེད། །དེའི་ཕྱིར་འཛིན་པ་མེད་རྟོགས་ཀྱིས། །དེས་ན་དམིགས་པ་མེད་ལ་རེག །ཞེས་པ་ལྟར་ཐོག་མར་གཟུང་བ་མེད་པར་གཏན་ལ་འབེབས་དགོས་པས་དེའང་སྡུ་མ་ལས། །ཡི་དྭགས་དུད་འགྲོ་མི་རྣམས་དང་། །ལྷ་རྣམས་ཇི་ལྟར་རིགས་རིགས་སུ། །དངོས་གཅིག་ཡིད་ནི་ཐ་དད་ཕྱིར། །དོན་མ་གྲུབ་པར་འདོད་པ་ཡིན། ཞེས་པས། ཡི་དྭགས་དང་། དུད་འགྲོ་དང་། མི་

དང་ལྷ་རྣམས་ཀྱིས་དངོས་པོ་གཅིག་ལ་རྣམ་པར་རིག་པ་ཐ་དད་པར་མཐོང་བས་འདི་དག་ནི་ཀུན་ཏུ་བརྟགས་པ་ཡིན་པས་དོན་ལ་མེད་པར་བལྟའོ། དེ་བཞིན་དུ་གཟུང་བ་མེད་ན་དེར་འཛིན་མེད། ཅེས་གཟུང་བརྫུ་ན་བཞིན་དུ་དེ་འཛིན་པའི་སེམས་བདེན་པ་ཞིག་མི་སྲིད་པ་གསུངས་པས་གཉིས་ཀས་སྟོང་ངོ་། དེས་ན་གཟུང་འཛིན་གཉིས་སྟོང་གི་ཤེས་པ་རང་རིག་རང་གསལ་ཙམ་ཞིག་ནི་མེད་པའང་མ་ཡིན་ཏེ། ཐེག་བསྡུས་ལས། །གཞན་གྱི་དབང་དང་ཡོངས་སུ་གྲུབ། །རྣམ་པ་ཀུན་ཏུ་ཡོད་མིན་ན། །ཀུན་ནས་ཉོན་མོངས་རྣམ་པར་དག །དུས་ཀུན་དུ་ནི་མེད་པར་འགྱུར། །ཞེས་དང་། ལང་ཀར་གཤེགས་པ་ལས། །ཆོས་རྣམས་ངོ་བོ་ཉིད་མེད་ཆོས་རྣམས་མ་སྐྱེས་དང་། །ཆོས་རྣམས་མ་འགག་ཆོས་རྣམས་གཟོད་ནས་ཞི་བ་དང་། །ཆོས་རྣམས་ཐམས་[ཤོག་བུ་༢༧]ཅད་རང་བཞིན་མྱ་ངན་འདས་པ་ནི། །དགོངས་པ་མེད་པར་མཁས་པ་སུ་ཞིག་སྨྲ་བར་བྱེད། །མཚན་ཉིད་ངོ་བོ་ཉིད་མེད་སྐྱེ་བ་ངོ་བོ་མེད། །དོན་དམ་ངོ་བོ་ཉིད་མེད་དོ་ཞེས་ངེས་བཤད་དོ། །འདི་ལ་མཁས་པ་ཁང་ཞིག་དགོངས་པ་ཤེས་པ་ནི། །རབ་ཏུ་ཉམས་པར་འགྱུར་བའི་ལམ་དུ་དེ་མི་འགྲོ། ཞེས་གསུངས་པ་ལྟར་རོ། །དེ་ཡན་ཆད་ཀྱིས་འཕགས་པ་ཐོགས་མེད་སྐུ་མཆེད་ཀྱི་གཞུང་གི་གཅེས་གཅེས་རྣམས་ཕྱོགས་གཅིག་ཏུ་བསྡུས་ཏེ་བསྟན་ནས། ད་ནི་དུས་གསུམ་གྱི་རྒྱལ་བ་ཐམས་ཅད་ཀྱི་ཐུགས་ཀྱི་གསང་བ་རྒྱལ་སྲས་བྱང་ཆུབ་སེམས་དཔའ་རྣམས་ཀྱི་དོན་དུ་གཉེར་བྱ་བླ་ན་མེད་པ་ཆོས་ཐམས་ཅད་ཀྱི་གནས་ལུགས་མ་ནོར་བ་གཏན་ལ་འབེབས་པ་རྩ་བའི་ས་བཅད་གསུམ་པ་མཐའ་བྲལ་དབུ་མའི་ལམ་ལ་ཇི་ལྟར་འཇུག་པའི་ཚུལ་བཤད་པ་ལ་གསུམ། འཇུག་ཡུལ་དབུ་མའི་རང་བཞིན་ངོས་བཟུང་བ། དེ་ལ་ཇི་ལྟར་འཇུག་པའི་ཚུལ། དེ་ལྟར་ཞུགས་པའི་འབྲས་བུའོ། །དང་པོ་ནི། མཐའ་དང་བྲལ་བས་དབུ་མ་སྟེ། ཡབ་རྗེ་དཔལ་མགོན་འཕགས་པ་ཀླུ་སྒྲུབ་ཀྱི་ཞལ་སྔ་ནས། །རྟེན་ཅིང་འབྲེལ་བར་འབྱུང་བ་གང་། །དེ་ནི་སྟོང་པ་ཉིད་དུ་བཤད། །དེ་ནི་བརྟེན་ནས་གདགས་པ་སྟེ། །དེ་ཉིད་དབུ་མའི་ལམ་ཡིན་ནོ། །ཞེས་དང་། རྗེ་བཙུན་འཕགས་པ་ལྷས། །ཡོད་མིན་མེད་མིན་ཡོད་མེད་མིན། །གཉིས་ཀའི་

བདག་ཉིད་ཀྱང་མིན་པ། །མཐའ་བཞི་ལས་གྲོལ་༼ཤོག་བུ་༤༢༽དབུ་མ་བ། །མཁས་པ་རྣམས་ཀྱི་དེ་ཁོ་ན། ཞེས་གསུངས་པས། རྟེན་འབྱུང་གི་ངོ་བོ་སྟོང་པ་དང་སྟོང་པའི་ངོ་བོ་སྤྲོས་པའི་མཐའ་ཐམས་ཅད་དང་བྲལ་བར་གཏན་ལ་དབབ་པ་ནི་དོན་དམ་པ་སྟེ་དེ་ཉིད་ལ་མཐའ་དང་བྲལ་བས་ན་དབུ་མ་ཞེས་བརྗོད་པ་ཡིན་ནོ། །གཉིས་པ་ནི། བསྟན་བཅོས་ཆེན་པོ་རྣམས་ལ་བརྟེན་ནས་དེ་ལ་འཇུག་དགོས་པས། སློབ་དཔོན་གྱི་ཞལ་སྔ་ནས། དབུ་མའི་བསྟན་བཅོས་ཐམས་ཅད་ཀྱི་གཞུང་ཕྱི་མོ་དང་ལུས་ལྟ་བུའི་རྩ་བ་ཤེས་རབ་དང་། དེ་ལས་འཕྲོས་པ་ཡན་ལག་ལྟ་བུའི་རྩོད་བཟློག་པ་དང་། སྟོང་པ་ཉིད་བདུན་ཅུ་པ་གཉིས་དང་། མུ་སྟེགས་རིགས་པ་ཅན་གྱི་འདོད་པ་རྟོག་གེའི་ཚིག་དོན་བཅུ་དྲུག་འགོག་བྱེད་དུ་ཞིབ་མོ་རྣམ་པར་འཐག་པ་དང་། ཡང་རང་སྡེའི་གྲུབ་མཐའ་འོག་མའི་ལོག་རྟོག་འགོག་པ་གཙོ་བོར་བྱས་ཏེ་གསུངས་པའི་རིགས་པ་དྲུག་ཅུ་པ་དང་བཅས་པ་རིགས་ཚོགས་ལྔར་བཤད་དེ། དེ་སྐད་དུ་ཡང་། དབུ་མ་རིན་ཆེན་སྒྲོན་མེ་ལས། །དབུ་མ་རྩ་བ་རྩོད་པ་བཟློག །སྟོང་ཉིད་བདུན་ཅུ་རིགས་དྲུག་ཅུ། །རྣམ་པར་འཐག་པ་ཞེས་བྱ་བས། །དངོས་རྣམས་སྐྱེ་མེད་གཏན་ལ་དབབ། །ཞེས་གསུངས་པ་ལྟར་རོ། །གཞན་ཡང་དབུ་མའི་ཕྱོགས་ཀྱི་བསྟན་བཅོས་དུ་མར་གསུངས་པ་རྣམས་ལ་དགོངས་པ་འགྲེལ་ཚུལ་གྱིས་ཐལ་རང་གཉིས་དང་ནང་གསེས་མང་བས་དབུ་མ་པ་ལ་ཡང་མཆོག་དམན་སྣ་ཚོགས་སུ་མཆིས་ཀྱང་འདིར་ཐལ་འགྱུར་བའི་སློབ་དཔོན་ཀུན་གྱི་གཙུག་གི་ནོར་བུ་ལྟ་བུར་གྱུར་པ་དཔལ་༼ཤོག་བུ་༤༣༽ལྡན་ཟླ་བ་གྲགས་པས་ནི། མགོན་པོ་ཀླུ་སྒྲུབ་ཀྱི་དགོངས་པ་འགྲེལ་བའི་བསྟན་བཅོས་དཔག་ཏུ་མེད་པ་སྤྱི་དང་ཁྱད་པར་དུ་དབུ་མ་རྩ་བའི་ཚིག་གི་འགྲེལ་པ་ལ་ཚིག་གསལ་བ་དང་། དོན་གྱི་འགྲེལ་པ་ལ་འཇུག་པ་རྩ་འགྲེལ་གཉིས་དང་། རིགས་པ་དྲུག་ཅུ་དང་འཕགས་པ་ལྷའི་བཞི་བརྒྱ་བའི་འགྲེལ་ཆེན་ཏེ་ཐར་པ་འདོད་པ་རྣམས་ལ་འཛམ་གླིང་གི་ནོར་ལས་ཀྱང་རིན་ཐང་ཆེ་བའི་ལེགས་བཤད་ཟླ་ན་མེད་པ་རྣམས་མཛད་པ་དག་ལ་བརྟེན་ནས་འཇུག་པར་བྱ་སྟེ། ཀུན་མཁྱེན་ཕྱི་མས། །འདི་ནི་འོག་མའི་རྣམ་པ་ཐམས་ཅད་དང་། །བརྩད་ཅིང་བརྟག་པས་གོང་མར་ནོར་མི་འགྱུར། །

གཞན་དབང་དངོས་པོར་འདོད་ལྟའི་ཀུན་རྫོབ་ཀྱང་། །དེ་ཡི་གྲུབ་པའི་མཐའ་རུ་ཁས་མ་བླང་། །དེ་ནི་ཐལ་འགྱུར་ཤིང་རྟའི་སྲོལ་འབྱེད་ཆེ། །མཁས་དབང་ཟླ་བ་གྲགས་པའི་ཁྱད་ཆོས་ཡིན། ཅེས་གསུངས་པ་ལྟ་བུའོ། །གཞན་ཡང་སློབ་དཔོན་བི་མ་ལ་དང་རྒྱལ་སྲས་ཞི་བ་ལྷ་མཁས་མཆོག་སངས་རྒྱས་བསྐྱངས་ལ་སོགས་པ་འཕགས་ཡུལ་གྱི་པཎྜི་ཏ་རྣམས་ཀྱིས་མཛད་པའི་གཞུང་ལུགས་དྲི་མ་མེད་པ་རྣམས་ནི་ཡིད་རྟོན་དུ་རུང་བའི་གནས་སོ། །གསུམ་པ་ནི། གནས་སྐབས་སུ་རང་དོན་དུ་འཁོར་བའི་འཁྲུལ་སྣང་ལ་བདེན་འཛིན་གྱི་བློ་མི་འབྱུང་བ་དང་། གཞན་དོན་དུ་བསམ་བཞིན་འགྲོ་བའི་དོན་དུ་བསྐལ་པ་ཇི་སྲིད་དུ་གནས་ནུས་པ་ཡིན་ཏེ། འཕགས་པ་ལྷས། །བསོད་ནམས་ཆུང་དུས་ཆོས་འདི་ལ། །ཐེ་ཚོམ་ཟ་བར་ཡང་མི་འགྱུར། །ཐེ་[ཤོག་བུ་༧༨]ཚོམ་ཟ་བ་ཙམ་ཞིག་གིས། །སྲིད་པ་རུལ་པོར་བྱས་པར་འགྱུར། ཞེས་དང་། སྤྱོད་འཇུག་ལས། །སྟོངས་པས་སྡུག་བསྔལ་ཅན་དོན་དུ། །ཆགས་དང་འཇིགས་མཐའ་ལས་གྲོལ་བས། །འཁོར་བ་གནས་པ་གྲུབ་འགྱུར། །འདི་ནི་སྟོང་ཉིད་འབྲས་བུ་ཡིན། ཞེས་གསུངས་པ་ལྟར་རོ། །མཐར་ཐུག་གི་འབྲས་བུ་ནི་རྫོགས་པའི་བྱང་ཆུབ་ཀྱི་གོ་འཕང་དམ་པ་མངོན་དུ་གྱུར་པ་ཡིན་ནོ། །རྩ་བའི་ས་བཅད་བཞི་པ་འོད་གསལ་རྫོགས་པ་ཆེན་པོ་ཇི་ལྟར་བསྒོམ་པའི་ཚུལ་ནི། རོང་ཟོམ་མི་ཡི་སེང་གེའི་ཞལ་སྔ་ནས། སྤྱིར་རྫོགས་ཆེན་ལ་སྡེ་ཆེན་པོ་གསུམ། ཀློང་ཆེན་པོ་དགུ། བམ་པོ་ཉི་ཁྲི་ཆིག་སྟོང་། རྒྱུད་སྡེ་ཁྲི་ཕྲག་གཅིག །འཁྲིད་ཆེན་པོ་བརྒྱད་ཅུ། གཟེར་བུ་ལྔ་བརྒྱ་དང་བརྒྱད་ཅུ། གནད་ཀྱི་མན་ངག་ཁྲི་དྲུག་སྟོང་། ངོ་སྤྲོད་སྟོང་དང་དགུ་བརྒྱ། ལ་བཟླ་བའི་གདམས་ངག་ཁྲི་ཕྲག་གསུམ། ཤན་འབྱེད་ཀྱི་གདམས་ངག་སྟོང་ཕྲག་དགུ། ཤོ་ལོ་ཀ་འབུམ་ཕྲག་དྲུག་ཅུ་རྩ་བཞི་དང་བཅས་ཡོད་པར་གསུངས་ལ། བསྟན་པ་འཛིན་པའི་སྐྱེས་བུ་འང་འཕགས་པའི་ས་ལ་གནས་པའི་མཁས་གྲུབ་རིམ་པར་བྱོན་པ་ལས་སླིགས་མའི་དུས་འདིར། སྒྲ་ཐལ་འགྱུར་རྩ་བའི་རྒྱུད་ལས། །དེ་ནས་སྒྲ་མཁས་དཔལ་འཛིན་གྱིས། ཞེས་པ་ཀུན་མཁྱེན་ཆེན་པོ་ཡིན་ཞེས་ལྷ་བཙུན་གྱིས་བཞེད་ལ། བདག་ཅག

གི་འདྲེན་པ་ཆོས་ཀྱི་རྗེ་དཔལ་ལྡན་བླ་མ་དམ་པ་ནི། །དེ་འོག ༼ཤོག་བུ་༢༥༽ དགེ་སློང་དཔལ་དང་ལྡན། །ཞེས་པ་རིག་འཛིན་ཀུ་མཱ་རཱ་ཛ་དང་། །དེ་ནས་བློ་གྲོས་མཆོག་གིས་འཛིན། ཞེས་པ་ཀུན་མཁྱེན་བླ་མ་ཡིན་གསུངས་ལ་གང་ལྟར་རྒྱལ་བ་རྡོ་རྗེ་འཆང་རང་ཉིད་ཀྱིས་རྫོགས་པ་ཆེན་པོའི་བསྟན་པའི་བདག་པོར་ལུང་བསྟན་པ་ལྟར་ཀུན་མཁྱེན་ངག་གི་དབང་པོ་ཀློང་ཆེན་རབ་འབྱམས་པའི་མཛོད་ཆེན་བདུན་སྙིང་ཐིག་བཞི་ངལ་གསོ་གསུམ་སོགས་སུ་རྫོགས་ཆེན་གྱི་རྒྱུད་སྡེ་མཐའ་དག་གི་དོན་བསྡུས་ཏེ་ཡེ་ཤེས་ཆེན་པོའི་ཚིག་དོན་བྱིན་གྱིས་བརླབས་པས་སྐལ་བ་ཅན་ལ་དགོངས་བརྒྱུད་སྨྱུར་དུ་འཕོ་བ་མོས་གུས་ཅན་རྣམས་མན་ངག་དང་འཕྲད་པ་ཙམ་གྱིས་ལྡན་སྐྱེས་ཀྱི་ཡེ་ཤེས་རང་ངོ་འཕྲོད་པ། རིག་འཛིན་བརྒྱུད་པའི་ཕ་ཕོག །ལས་འཕྲོ་ཅན་གྱི་སྤྱོད་ཡུལ། སངས་རྒྱས་ལག་བསྐྱངས་གི་གདམས་ངག །ཆོས་རང་བཞིན་རྫོགས་པ་ཆེན་པོ་ཀུན་མཁྱེན་ཆོས་ཀྱི་རྒྱལ་པོ་ཡབ་སྲས་ཀྱི་གཞུང་ལ་བརྟེན་ནས་ཆོས་སྐུ་རང་མལ་ནས་རྐྱེད་པས་གུད་ཡངས་ཤེང་བློ་བདེ་བ་འདི་འདྲ་ཞིག་ཅི་ནས་ཀྱང་དོན་དུ་གཉེར་བྱ་ཡིན་ནོ། །

འདིར་སྨྲས་པ། །བློ་ཆེན་འཕགས་པའི་སྐྱེ་བོ་བརྒྱ་ཕྲག་གིས། །ཐེག་གསུམ་ཆོས་ཀྱི་སྒོ་འཕར་ཕྱེས་མོད་ཀྱི། །མ་སྨིན་བློ་གྲོས་གསར་བུའི་ཚོང་ཟོང་གིས། །རྣམ་མཁྱེན་རིན་ཆེན་རྐྱེད་པར་ནུས་མ་ཡིན། །སྨོན་བྱིན་དམ་པ་སྟོང་གི་ལེགས་བཤད་དང་། །གྲུབ་བརྙེས་རིག་པ་འཛིན་པའི་ཞལ་གྱི་ལུང་། །ད་ལྟའི་བྱིས་པ་རྣམས་ལ་མཛའ་མིན ༼ཤོག་བུ་༢༦༽ ན། །རྒྱ་ཆེན་གཞུང་གི་སྦྱོས་པས་ཅི་ཞིག་བྱ། །རྒྱལ་དང་རྒྱལ་བའི་སྲས་པོ་ཧཱི་སྐྱེད་ཀྱིས། །ཐུགས་བསྐྱེད་སྨོན་པའི་ཡུལ་དུ་འདོར་མིན་ཡང་། །སྙིགས་མའི་རྒྱུད་པས་གདུང་བའི་སྐྱེ་བོ་ཀུན། །རང་རང་ལས་ཀྱི་བགོ་སྐལ་ལ་སྤྱོད་དོ། །དེ་ཕྱིར་བདག་འདྲའི་བྱིས་པའི་བསམ་སྤྱོད་ཀྱིས། །འགྲོ་ཁམས་ཕན་བདེའི་ལམ་ལ་འགོད་མིན་ཡང་། །སྨྲ་བའི་ཉི་མ་རྒྱལ་སྲས་ཆོས་ཀྱི་རྗེའི། །ཐུགས་ཀྱི་དགོངས་པ་རྫོགས་སྣང་ངས་འདི་བྲིས། །འདི་ལ་མ་རྟོགས་ལོག་པར་རྟོག་པའི་སྐྱོན། །ཇི་སྙེད་མཆིས་ཀུན་མཁས་པའི་ཚོགས་ལ་འཆགས། །དམ་ཆོས་ཚུལ་ལ་ཚད་མར་གྱུར་པ་ནི། །འཕགས་པའི་ཚོགས་ལས་གཞན་དུ་ཡོངས་མ་

མཆིས། །དགེ་བ་འདི་དང་དགེ་བའི་རྩ་བ་གཞན། །བདག་དང་གཞན་གྱིས་ལེགས་པར་སྤྱད་པ་རྣམས། །གཅིག་ཏུ་བསྡོམས་ཏེ་རྒྱལ་བསྟེན་རིན་པོ་ཆེ། །མི་ཉམས་ཡུན་དུ་གནས་པའི་རྒྱུ་རུ་བསྔོ། །ཞེས་པ་འདི་ནི་ཐོས་བསམ་ལ་གསར་དུ་ཞུགས་པ་དག་གི་བློ་གྲོས་ཀྱི་སྣོ་འབྱེད་བྱེད་དུ་མཁས་པ་ཆེན་པོ་ཨོ་རྒྱན་བསྟན་འཛིན་ནོར་བུའི་ཞབས་རྡུལ་སྤྱི་བོས་རིག་པའི་བཙུན་པ་གཞན་ཕན་སྣང་བས་སྦྱར་བ་དགེ་ལེགས་སུ་གྱུར་ཅིག། །།རྒྱལ་བསྟན་རིན་ཆེན་ཁྲིད་ནས་ལེགས་བླངས་པ། །མཁས་པར་བྱ་བའི་གནས་དྲུག་འཇིག་རྟེན་ན། །ཉི་མ་བཞིན་དུ་གསལ་བའི་ལེགས་བཤད་ནི། །སྨྲ་བའི་དབང་ཕྱུག་མཆོག་གི་ཞལ་ནས་སྤྲོས། །རྨོངས་པའི་མུན་པ་རབ་སེལ་ཤེས་བྱ་ཡི། །རང་སྤྱིའི་མཚན་ཉིད་བདེ་བླག་གཏོགས་པ་ལ། །ཁྱད་འཕགས་བློ་མིག་ཉིད་དུ་མཐོང་འདི་ཀོ། །བདེན་གསུང་རང་གཤིས་ལས་ནི་ [ཤོག་བུ་༢༢] གཞན་ཡོད་མིན། །ཤེས་བྱ་ཤེས་ནས་ཆོས་ཉིད་ཟབ་མོའི་དོན། །ཉམས་སུ་སྐྱོང་དགོས་དེ་ཕྱིར་ཀུན་མཁྱེན་ལམ། །འདི་དང་འདི་འདྲའི་དབྱིངས་ནས་མ་ཚོལ་ན། །ཐབས་ལ་མཁས་པ་གཞན་གྱིས་ཅི་བྱར་ཡོད། །དེ་ཕྱིར་དྲི་མེད་བློ་གྲོས་བློ་གསལ་གྱི། །སྐྱེ་བོའི་ཚོགས་ལ་ངེས་པར་གསལ་སླད་དུ། །བརྟན་པའི་འཁོར་ལོ་མིང་ཚིག་བརྗོད་པ་ཡི། །ཡི་གེའི་གཟུགས་སུ་མངོན་སུམ་བཀྲུས་པ་བཞིན། །འགྲོ་རྒྱུད་ཤེས་བྱས་བདེ་བར་བསིལ་སླད་དུ། །ཆོས་སྣོ་རྒྱ་མཚོ་འཕེལ་བའི་འཕྲུལ་ཆེན་འདི། །སྙིང་པོའི་ཉམས་ལེན་ཡར་ཟླ་ལྟར་འཕེལ་བའི། །ཁྱུང་རམ་ལྷུམ་ཆུང་རིགས་བཟང་ལྡན་དེས་བསྐྲུན། །ཉུང་ངུའི་ངག་ལ་བརྗོད་བྱ་རྒྱ་ཆེ་བས། །འཁོར་འདས་ཆོས་ལ་དབང་བསྒྱུར་འདོད་པ་རྣམས། །གཞུང་འདི་ཐོས་དང་བསམ་པས་བརྟེན་མཛོད་དང་། །རིང་པོར་མི་ཐོགས་མཁས་པའི་ཡང་རྩེར་འགྲོ། །འདིར་འབད་དགེ་ཚོགས་གང་མཆིས་འཁོར་གསུམ་ནི། །དམིགས་མཐའ་བྲལ་བའི་རྒྱུར་བསྔོ་འགྲོ་འདི་དག །ཇི་ལྟ་ཇི་སྙེད་སོ་སོར་རྟོགས་པ་ཡི། །གོ་འཕང་ལ་ནི་བདེ་བླག་འགོད་གྱུར་ཅིག །ཅེས་པའང་འཇམ་དབྱངས་ཆོས་ཀྱི་རྒྱལ་མཚན་ནས་ཤར་མར་སྨྲས་པ་དགེ་ཞིང་བཀྲ་ཤིས།། །།

Index

A Complete Summation of Determinations 65, 97
A Marvellous Garland of Rare Gems vii
A Teaching on the Six Topics in which One is to Become Expert . . . . iii, v, xiv, xxii
abandonment of the four places 70
abbot . . . . vii, viii, x, xi
Abhidharma . . xii, xv, xvi, 24, 62, 64, 97-100
abode of the knowable . . . 62, 63
about key terms iii, xxii, 10, 37, 38
about the author . . . . iii, vi
about the text . . . . iii, xiv
actuality 89, 101, 108
adventitious 69, 101
adventitious stains 69
afflicted mental consciousness 82, 84
affliction . . xxi, 18, 19, 23, 24, 27, 28, 31, 39, 40, 44-48, 53, 56, 59, 62, 72, 75, 78, 80, 84, 101, 104, 120
Agaru 14
aggregate . . xxiii-xxvi, 10, 17, 19-21, 34, 38, 41, 43, 45, 47
aggregate of consciousness . . . . xxvi, 10
aggregate of feeling . . . . . xxiv, 10
aggregate of form xxiii, xxv, 10, 21
aggregate of formatives . . xxv, 10
aggregate of perception . . xxiv, 10
aggregates . . . . xii, xvi, xxiii, xxv, xxvi, 9, 22, 27, 31, 33, 43, 45-47, 56, 83
aggregates or heaps xii
ālaya . . . . xiii, 63, 110
alertness 24, 29, 102
All-knowing One 91, 102
annotations . . . . xxviii, 3, 12
appropriation 45-47, 49, 64, 78, 102
Āryadeva 90-92, 98
Asaṅga . . xiv-xvi, 87, 97, 99, 100
Ati . . . . xv, xx, 25, 102, 103
Ati vehicle . . . . xv, 102
authoritative statement . . 58, 103
awareness . . . xxvi, 26, 31, 35, 36, 35, 36, 39, 66, 74, 79, 86, 103, 105, 110, 121
awareness of superficies xxvi
āyatanas . . . xii, xvi-xviii, xxvii, 40
āyatanas are restrained . . xvi, xviii

bases or elements xii
basic constituents . . . . xvii, 40
Become Manifest . 39, 63, 66, 72
becoming . 21, 26, 28, 32, 45-49, 56, 70, 78, 80, 92, 96, 103, 106
bliss 56, 57, 103, 120
bodhisatva . ix, xxii, 3, 70-72, 76, 77, 79, 80, 83, 89, 92, 97, 103, 104, 107, 117
bodhisatvas 3, 70, 71, 76, 77, 79, 80, 83, 89, 97
body faculty 11, 38, 41
buddha type of existence . . . xviii
Buddhapalita 92
burning house of saṃsāra . . xviii
causal form 10
cause and effect . . xii, xix, xxi, 28, 34, 51, 52, 81, 122
Chandabhadra . . . . xv, 17
Chandrakīrti . . . . xi, 91, 97
chapter four iv
chapter one iii
chapter three iii
chapter two . . . . iii, 111
characteristic and divisions . . 10, 17, 20, 21, 34
characteristics of the knowable 63, 67, 68
Chokyi Nangwa . . iii, vi, viii, ix, 4
Citraka 15
Clear Words 97
clinging . 20, 28, 29, 50, 70, 104
Cloud of Dharma 73
Compendium of Abhidharma . . xvi
complete buddhahood . xiv, 7, 77
complete purification 18, 19, 39, 40, 44, 49, 59, 86, 104, 120
completion in three lives 48
completion in two lives 48
completion stage with signs . . xii
concept tokens . . . xxv, 20, 21, 70, 72, 73, 81, 104
conceptual process . xxiv, xxv, 106
confusion 104, 118
conquerors 5, 89, 95
conquerors of the three times 89
Conquerors' Son Zhanphen Thaye vi
conquerors' sons 5, 89, 95
consciousness only 63
Consequence . . . . xi, 91
Consequence and Autonomy . 91
covert intents 76
death and transference 46, 65, 67
definition of formative xxv
Descent into Laṅka 81, 86, 97
development stage xii
dharma dhātu 41-43
dharma igniter 37
dharmadhātu . . . xxvii, xxviii, 38, 51, 72, 105
dharmakāya . 51, 73, 80, 94, 105, 112, 113
dharmatā . . . xxi, 57, 58, 60, 106
dhātu . . . xxvii, xxviii, 38, 40-43, 51, 64, 72, 105
dhātus of inner faculties 40
dhātus of intervening consciousness 40
dhātus of outer objects 40
dhyāna 17, 32, 74, 106
diacritical marks . . . . ii, xxviii
Difficult Training 72
Direct Crossing . . . . viii, 106
direct perception xxv, 58, 74, 108
discursive thought . . 69, 79, 106
divisions of cessation 56
divisions of source 56
divisions of the truth of unsatisfactoriness 55

Dodrupchen . . . . vii, viii
duḥkha 103, 120
Dzogchen Monastery . . v-viii, xi, xiv, xv, xxx
Dzogchen Rinpoche . . . . . viii, x
ear faculty 11, 38, 41
earth, water, fire, and wind 10, 53
East Tibet . . . . xi, xiv
eight analogies of illusion xi
eight visual form shapes 12
eighteen dhātus . . . . xviii, 41, 51
elaboration 6, 29, 69, 90, 106, 107
electronic editions 126
electronic texts 126, 127
engaging consciousnesses . 65, 82
English translations . . . . xxiv, 122
enlightenment mind . . ix, 36, 71, 95, 103, 107
Entering into the Bodhisatvas' Conduct 92, 97
entity . 16, 33, 35, 36, 63, 82, 90, 107, 119
epilogue . . . . iv, xiv, 95
equilibrium . . 21, 30, 32, 33, 67, 74, 83, 84
equivalence . xxv, 20, 22, 42, 52-54, 82, 84
etymological definition . . xxiii, 9, 37, 40, 43, 55, 85
etymological definition of āyatana 37
etymological definition of skandha . . . . xxiii, 9
exaggeration 108
experience of contact 17
external interdependent origination 44
eye faculty 11, 22, 38, 41, 57
fact . . . xv, xix, xxiv, 6, 25, 30, 31, 59, 63, 69, 79, 81, 85, 104, 105, 108-114, 117, 118
facts 6, 5, 6, 66, 85, 118
feeling . . xxiv, 10, 17, 23, 24, 28, 31, 32, 45-48, 65
fictional . . . 59, 91, 108, 109, 121
fictional truth 59, 109
fictional truth and superfactual truth 59
fifth Dzogchen Rinpoche x
fifty-one mental events 24, 31, 112
Finely Woven Sūtra 90, 98
five aggregates 27, 46, 56
five faculties 10, 11, 38, 42
five fruitions 54
five mutual equivalences of minds and mental events 22
five objects 10, 11
five omnipresent ones . 24, 83, 84
Followers of Sūtra . xv, xvi, 11, 58
foremost instruction 109
foremost oral instructions . . . viii
formative unsatisfactoriness . . 59
fortunate ones 5, 94
fortunate person 109
forty-six mental events 24
foundation teachings xii
four dharma summaries . . . iii, 61
Four Hundred 91, 93, 98
four individual right cognitions 3
four major schools of Buddhist philosophy xv
four name aggregates 47
Four Quintessences 94, 98
four types of condition 54
fourth aggregate . . . . xxv, 19
fourth Dzogchen Rinpoche . . viii
freedom from elaboration . 6, 107
full-ripening . . . xix, 52-55, 65, 82
fundament . . . . xii, xiii, 6, 36, 54, 63-67, 74, 81-84, 86, 100, 104,

110, 115, 122
fundament consciousness . . . . xiii, 6, 36, 54, 64-66, 74, 81, 82
Gone Far 72
Good Intellect 73
grammar texts 33, 124
grasped-grasping . . . 69, 82, 110
great aggregates of unsatisfactoriness 45
Great Completion . . . . iv, vi-viii, xiii-xv, xxii, 3, 7, 93, 94, 98-100, 103, 106, 107, 110, 111, 113, 115, 124
great elements 13, 16
Great Vehicle . . . iii, v-vii, xii-xvi, xix, xxi, 5, 7, 36, 47, 48, 61-64, 70, 71, 74-77, 80, 81, 92, 99, 100, 107, 111-113, 119, 121
groups of names, phrases, and letters 32, 33
Gyalsay Zhanphen Thaye . . . . vi, vii, 49
heap . . . . xxiii, 9
heaps . . . . xii, xviii, xxii
higher training of discipline . 50
higher training of mind 74
higher training of prajñā 76
higher training of samādhi . . . 74
higher trainings . . 50, 62, 63, 73, 119
higher vehicles xii
igniter 37, 38, 43, 45, 46, 48
igniters . . . . xii, xvii, xviii, xxvi, 9, 10, 21, 37, 43, 45-47, 78
Illuminator Tibetan-English Dictionary 120, 124, 127
immediates xx
impedance 41, 42
Indian Buddhism xiv
Indian science of sound 13
individualized beings 18, 57
inference 58
inner igniters 37
instant of conception 46
intent 64, 76, 77, 79, 86, 91, 100, 111
intentional conduct . 70, 73, 112
interdependent origination . . xii, xix, 9, 43, 44, 48, 49, 51, 68, 72, 102
internal interdependent 44
Jewelled lamp of the Middle Way 90, 98
Jigmey Gyalway Nyugu . . . vi, vii
Jigmey Lingpa . . . . vi, xxii
Jigmey Trinley Ozer vii
Kama, Terma, and Dagnang traditions vii
karmic cause and effect . . xii, xix, xxi, 52
karmic seeds xix
Kāśhyapa xx
kāya . 51, 53, 64, 73, 80, 94, 105, 112, 113
Knower of the World 59
knowledgeability 4, 73
Kumārāja 94
latencies 47, 56, 82, 83
latency 49, 113
learned and accomplished masters . . . . vii, viii
Lesser Vehicle . . . xii, xiii, xv-16, 45, 51, 60-62, 77, 100, 111, 113, 119
levels of familiarization 63
Lhatsun Namkha Jigmey 94
liberation in this life 5
Light Maker 72
limited type of awareness . . . xxvi, 105

Longchen Rabjam 91, 94, 98-100
Longchenpa . . . . vi, 94, 102
luminosity . . . iv, xv, xxi, 6, 7, 35, 93, 113
Luminosity Great Completion . . . . iv, xv, 7, 93
Madhyamaka . . . . xv, 98
Mahāmudrā . . 107, 110, 113, 115
māra 74, 80, 114
mental events . . . . xxii, 22-25, 31, 32, 35, 36, 42, 43, 47, 52-54, 82, 85, 112, 114
Middle Way . . . . iii, xi, xiii-xv, 7, 89-92, 98, 107, 110
Middle Way Consequence . . . xi
migrator 64, 78, 114
Mind Only . . . . xiii-xvi, 5, 14, 32, 63, 67, 68, 97-100, 110, 116
minds and mental events . 22, 42
Mingyur Namkhay Dorje . . . viii
Mipham . . . . . viii, 100, 125, 126
monastic colleges xi
motivated occurrence 16, 42
Myrobalan 15
Nāgārjuna 89-91, 97-99
name and form 45-49
nine types of beings 4
nirmāṇakāya 53, 80, 112, 113
noble one . . . viii, xix, 13, 87, 89, 93, 109, 115
Noble One, Sutra of the Store of the Tathāgata xix
noble ones . . . xx, 13, 14, 32, 57, 59, 95, 96
non-abiding nirvāṇa 63
non-dualistic types of awareness 31
non-revelatory . . . 10-12, 16, 17, 37, 38
non-revelatory form 11, 10, 12, 16
non-self of persons 85
non-self of phenomena 85
nose faculty 11, 38, 41
no-thought wisdom 79
Nyoshul Khenpo 97
Oceanic Single Understanding Prayer of the Bardo xxii
official lineage holder vi
one truth 60
one-pointedness of mind 25, 71, 102, 118
Orgyan Tenzin Norbu . . vi-x, 94, 96
outer igniters 37
outflow 70, 115
outflowed 17, 115, 120
Padma Namgyal xi
Padmasambhava 98, 111, 117
pāramitā . . . . . . xii, 63, 70-73, 75
Particularist . . . . . . xv, xvi, 11, 99
peak of becoming 21, 32
perception . . xvii, xviii, xxiv, xxv, xxvii, 10, 20, 21, 23, 24, 28, 31-33, 40, 58, 67, 74, 83, 85, 104, 108
perceptual process . . . . . xvi, xvii
personal emancipation . . xxii, 111
pervasive unsatisfactoriness of the formatives 18
phrase linker 34
prajñā . . . . xii, 26, 38, 39, 49, 50, 63, 72, 76, 97-99, 115, 119
Prajñāpāramitā . . . . xii, 72
pratītyasamutpāda xii
pratyekabuddha . . . xx, 51, 70, 83
preliminary, main, and concluding section xiv
presentation of the four truths 52
preserve 116
primary colours 12

process of samsaric perception . . . . xvii, xxvii, 40
prologue . . . . iii, xii, xiv, 3
psycho-physical makeup . . . . xvi, xvii, xxiii
Quintessence Great Completion . . . . vi, xv, 98
Radiant Light 72
rational mind . . . 6, 92, 104, 116
realization . vii, 77, 103, 116, 117
reference . . . xvii, 16, 22, 24, 27, 33, 35, 41, 42, 51, 61, 74, 82, 104, 116, 117, 124, 127
referencing . . 22, 74, 79, 85, 116, 117
Refutation of Objections . . . 90, 98
renunciation . . . . . . ix, 57, 59, 80
resultant form 10
revelatory 10-12, 16, 17, 37, 38, 42, 66
Richard Barron 97
Rongzom 93
root causes of samsaric existence xviii
roots of virtue 28
saṃbhogakāya 80, 112, 113
saṃsāra . . xvi, xviii, 5, 18, 28, 31, 32, 53, 57, 62, 64, 75, 80, 83, 92, 103, 105, 109, 110, 112, 114, 116, 118, 121
samsaric being . . . . xvii, xxvi
samsaric perceptions xvii
samsaric unsatisfactoriness . . 18
Sanskrit . xiii, xv, xvii, xxii-xxviii, 9-12, 15, 33, 34, 48, 97, 101, 103, 105, 106, 109, 110, 112-115, 117, 118, 120, 121
Sanskrit terms . . . . . xxii, 10, 117
satva . . . . ix, 104, 117
Sautrāntika xv
second Chandrakīrti xi
second Nālandā viii
secondary colours 12
self of the sort thought of by the Tīrthikas 56
Seven Great Treasuries 94
Seventy Verses on Emptiness 90, 98
shapes 12
six causes 48, 53
six inner igniters 37
six root afflictions 28
Six Topics . . . 2, i, iii, v, vi, xii-xvi, xix, xxii, xxvi, xxvii, 1, 5, 7, 9, 20
Six Topics in which One is to Become Expert . . . iii, v, xiii, xiv, xxii, 5, 7
six ways of being consciousness 35
Sixty Verses on Reasoning 90, 91, 98
skandhas . . . . . . xii, xvi, xxii, xxvi, xxvii, 32, 114
smells 11, 14, 15, 37
Sound Breakthrough 93, 98
sounds 11-13, 37, 58
sources . . . . . . ix, xii, xiv, xvii, 40
sources or igniters . . . . . . xii, xvii
special deity 3
Stainless 72, 92
study and translation of Tibetan texts 126
study program 125
suffering . . . . xviii, 39, 45, 47, 55, 78, 95, 120, 121
superfact . . . 30, 53, 86, 108, 109, 118, 121
superfactual . . 53, 59, 60, 76, 90, 109, 118, 119, 121
superfactual truth 59, 60, 118, 119
superfice . . . . xxvi, 12, 16, 22, 35, 36, 82, 83, 85, 105, 119
superficies . . . . xxvi, 68, 69, 105, 106, 119

svabhāvakikāya 80
sūtra . . . vii, ix, x, xii, xv, xvi, xviii, 9, 11, 17, 24, 43-45, 58, 59, 61, 64, 68, 71, 73, 76, 77, 90, 97-101, 107, 119, 125
Sūtra of the Recollection of the Noble Three Jewels . . . . . xvi, 100, 125
Tai Situ xi
Taking Joy in Others 5
Tastes 11, 15, 37
tathāgatas 74, 75, 80
ten levels of the bodhisatvas . 71
ten meanings 62
ten non-virtuous actions xx
Tīrthika . . . . . xx, 14, 56, 90, 120
the acts of complete enlightenment 80
the aggregate of consciousness . . . . xxvi, 10
the aggregate of feeling xxiv
the aggregate of formatives . . xxv, 10
the aggregate of perception . . . . xxiv, 10
the eight consciousnesses . 81, 82
the five dharmas 81, 99, 100
the five object ascertainers . . . 26
the five omnipresent ones . . . 24, 83, 84
the Fivefold Collection of Reasonings 90
the four covert intents 76
the four extremes 90
the four individual authentic knowledges 73
the four things of magnetizing 73
the four truths 26, 52, 59
The Highest Continuum . 55, 80, 99
the levels . . . 3, 63, 72, 73, 80, 97
The Ornament of the Great Vehicle Sūtra Section 71, 99
The Ornament of the Sūtra Section 61, 76, 99
the other-powered . . . 76, 80, 82, 86, 91
The Root Prajna 90, 99
the six root afflictions 28
the superfactual . . 60, 76, 90, 121
The Sūtra of the Recollection of the Noble Three Jewels 100, 125
the ten levels 63, 71
the ten types of hardship 75
The Thirty Verses 33, 82, 99
the three characteristics . . . 67, 68
the three natures 82
the three types of mind training 70
the wholly-existent 76, 81
thirteen great texts . . . . x, xi
Thorough Cut . . . . viii, 106
three and eight unsatisfactorinesses 56
three countless great æons . . . 73
three epithets of the Buddha . xvi
three higher trainings . . . 50, 62, 63, 73, 119
three kinds of unsatisfactoriness 18
three types of impedance 41
three vehicles . . . 52, 95, 111, 119
Tibet . . . . ii, iv-vii, x, xi, xiii-xvi, xxiii-xxx, 4, 9, 11, 14, 15, 33-35, 42, 47, 97-100, 102-106, 110-114, 116-118, 120, 121, 123-127, 129
Tibetan Buddhism . . vii, 99, 106, 125
Tibetan grammar 33, 34, 124
Tibetan text . iv, xxviii, xxix, 126, 129

Tibetan texts x, 118, 124, 126, 127
Tibetan translator Vairochana
 . . . . vi, vii
Tibetan word "khams" xxvii
tongue faculty 11, 38, 41
topics and non-topics . . . . xix, 51
total affliction . . . . xxi, 18, 19, 27, 39, 40, 44, 48, 59, 62, 75, 78, 80, 84, 104, 120
total affliction and complete purification . . . 18, 19, 44, 120
total thought . 68, 69, 76, 79, 82
touches 11, 15, 37, 96
Treasury of Abhidharma . . . xv, 62
Trilogy of Resting up 94, 100
truth of unsatisfactoriness . . . 55
Tuṣhita 80
twelve limbs of interdependent origination 48
twelve links 20, 43, 45, 48-50, 102
two types of non-self 85
two types of perseverance . . . 62
śhamatha 27, 50, 70, 102, 118, 121
śhamatha and vipaśhyanā 70
Śhāntarakṣhita vii
Śhāntideva 92, 97
śhrāvakas 51, 76, 77, 80, 83
Śhrī Singha . . . v, vi, viii, x, xiv, xv, xxx
Śhrī Singha College . . . v, vi, viii, x, xv
ultimate fruition 51
Unending Auspiciousness
 . . . . . xxviii, 4, 55, 59, 100, 125
unification luminosity 7
unification of appearance and emptiness . . . . xiii, 7
Unmoving 73
unsatisfactoriness 18, 27, 38-40, 45, 47, 55-57, 59, 92, 117, 120, 121
unsatisfactoriness of change . 18
unsatisfactoriness of the formatives 18
unsatisfactoriness of unsatisfactoriness 18
Utter Joy 72
utter knowledge 3, 4
Vaibhaśhika xv
Vairochana . . . . vi, vii, 3, 4
Vajra Vehicle . . xii, xxi, 107, 110, 111, 119, 121
valid cognition 96, 99, 121
valid cognizer 58, 121
Vasubandhu xv-17, 50, 99
Vasumitra 24
vijñāna 105
vijñāpti 10
vipaśhyanā 50, 70, 118, 121
virtuous and non-virtuous karmas
 . . . . xix, 52, 54
virtuous, non-virtuous, and indeterminate 42
visual form . . . xxiii, xxiv, xxvi, 11, 12, 22, 36, 37, 40, 42, 57, 105
visual form colours 12
visual form shapes 12
visual forms 12, 37
Who Benefits Others Infinitely
 . . . . 4, 5, 49
wholly existent 69
wisdom . . xvii, xviii, xxvi, 3, 5, 39, 61-64, 74, 76, 78-81, 94, 103-105, 108, 111, 114, 115, 117, 118, 120-122, 125
wisdom awareness . . . . xxvi, 105
without outflow 70
worldly actions of generosity . 63
yidam deity 3
Zhanphen Chokyi Nangwa . . iii,

vi, viii, ix, 4
Zhanphen Thaye . . . vi-viii, x, xi, xiii, 3-5, 49, 96
Zhan-ga . . . . 2, i, v-vii, ix-xii, xix, xxiii, 5, 19, 25
Zhechen x
Zurmang Tenga xi

www.ingramcontent.com/pod-product-compliance
Lightning Source LLC
Chambersburg PA
CBHW022007160426
43197CB00007B/314
* 9 7 8 9 9 3 7 5 7 2 1 3 2 *